How Whole Brain Thinking
Can Save the Future

How Whole Brain Thinking Can Save the Future

Why Left Hemisphere Dominance Has Brought Humanity to the Brink of Disaster and How We Can Think Our Way to Peace and Healing

James Olson

Origin Press

Origin Press

PO Box 151117
San Rafael, CA 94915
www.OriginPress.org

Jacket design by Mariah Parker (mettagraphics.com)
Interior design by Carla Green (claritydesignworks.com)

Images used under license from Shutterstock.com

Olson, James, 1943- author.
  How whole brain thinking can save the future : why left hemisphere
dominance has brought humanity to the brink of disaster and how we
can think our way to peace and healing / by James Olson.
    pages cm
    Includes bibliographical references and index.
    LCCN 2016916369
    ISBN 978-1-57983-051-9
    ISBN 978-1-57983-053-3 (eISBN)

    1. Cerebral dominance. 2. Cognitive styles.
3. Peace. 4. Dual-brain psychology. 5. United States–
Politics and government.   I. Title.

QP385.5.O468 2016   612.8'25
                                 QBI16-900005

Printed in the United States of America

First printing: December 2016

Contents

Preface

On one level, this book is about the differing perspectives of the left and right hemispheres of the brain, with a particular focus on the effects of "brain dominance" on our lives, culture, and environment. But it is also about our search for truth, who we are as human beings, and how we can achieve a peaceful world. Scientific research and observation are essential to understanding ourselves, but mere data and analysis lack the crucial dimension of those human experiences, which if cultivated properly lead to wisdom and ultimately to a life characterized by a more holistic approach to spirituality. This book attempts to marry the findings of science with such intuitive, experientially based truths—those ideas about reality that the great wisdom traditions have always attempted to convey. Only by viewing the whole picture can we gain a full understanding of all dimensions of who we are.

The increasingly important advances of brain science—which are now often subsumed under the terms *neuroscience, cognitive science,* or *cognitive psychology*—are a source of endless fascination to me personally. Nevertheless, my real motivation for writing this book is to address what I believe is the most critical issue of our time, which goes far beyond the narrow concerns of any science: *how we can create an environment of peace in ourselves and in the world—an environment that enhances and enables our best and most creative attributes—in this time of unprecedented global dangers and insanity.*

As this book will show, all of the abovementioned issues are interrelated in the most intricate way, but it is only when all or most of the pieces of the puzzle are considered that the overall picture comes into clear view. This is why I will be bringing up such a diversity of topics—from the findings of brain research to the great and timeless philosophical and spiritual insights, to cultural behavior, and to the current planetary political crisis. Like a jigsaw puzzle in which the individual pieces may seem unrelated when viewed at random, the different aspects of our discussion when fully assembled will reveal the complete picture in a way that we could not do if limited to a single perspective.

The search for truth has always been about discovering this often-elusive whole. In our information-rich society we are bombarded with facts and analysis at every waking moment, and we often believe that acquiring such knowledge is all-important; but our deeper *understanding* of ourselves—spiritually, emotionally, and relationally—has fallen far behind our ability to acquire knowledge and information. Since knowledge includes not only those things that help us to manage ourselves and our world, but also that which can destroy us—such as the capacity to build and use weapons of mass destruction—this imbalance between the utility of knowledge and the common sense of wisdom has proved to be extremely destructive on personal, societal, and even planetary levels.

Contrary to common usage, *self-understanding* does not refer to some private, isolated, internal self, apart from interpersonal, social, and environmental contexts. In my use of the term, I refer to an understanding of the whole self, which is inseparable from the encompassing reality in which the self exists. True self-understanding is necessary to establishing a viable civil society, and—of the utmost importance—in the realization of internal and external peace. We cannot achieve peace in our world without finding peace within ourselves; and it is also true that a peaceful external environment, free of distracting and soul-crushing conflicts, contributes tremendously to our ability to find inner peace.

But to achieve inner peace—and to create conditions for outer peace—requires more than that we desire it. It requires more than mere meditation or visualization or positive thoughts. It requires more than electing public officials who will work toward peaceful relations with other countries or with the diverse elements of our own society. And it even requires more than efforts to be fair and peaceful in our relations with others. All of these things are important, even essential, but they do not address a critical component. *To achieve peace, we must also understand the brain's role in informing our conscious mind.* Without awareness of how the brain works, we will not be able to make the necessary changes in our personal and collective lives to achieve inner *or* outer peace.

This book explores how we can achieve peace—with ourselves, with others, and in the world—by better understanding the functioning of the brain. In a nutshell, this book is about how to achieve peace by understanding how our divided brain processes information, why different brains function differently and perceive the world differently, and how these variances create conflict. This book attempts to convey the means for bridging the gap between our desire for peace and our ability to actually *achieve* a state of peace. We will look at how the brain influences our beliefs, the programming that governs our day-to-day existence. We will see that when our beliefs are limited to the insights of only one hemisphere, they can sabotage even our best efforts to realize our deepest longings and desires.

Everything we see, hear, and otherwise sense is filtered through the brain prior to percolating to the conscious mind. For this reason, the findings of brain science can be of immense help in assisting us to understand ourselves—and even the ways we perceive reality. But science, as valuable as its contribution is, needs the unifying influence of philosophy—which can integrate its findings with the emotional contribution of spirit—if science is to have meaning. It is in this larger, much-expanded context that we take a fresh look at the long-debated subject of brain lateralization and the contributions of the left and right brain hemispheres. Often lost in the din of controversy that has attended discussions of whether individuals are left-brained, right-brained, or none of the above are the underlying truths about the two complementary—but often apparently contradictory— forms of perceiving and thinking that I call *holistic* and *dualistic*, in which the right and left hemispheres (respectively) specialize.

Along the way we will discover that even some of the most apparently insoluble differences we have with others are the result of simple mis-understandings due to differences in perspective. This happens because the holistic and dualistic modes of thinking, taken alone, can produce astonishingly different results. In order to live in peace with others and create peace in the world, we need to reconnect with our whole brain and understand how our brain circuitry, and the brain circuitry of those around us, affects our decision-making. In other words, we need to be wise beyond the givens of our genetic and environmental inheritance. How we can do this, and connect with others more effectively, is the trick—and a subject we will be exploring.

As I mentioned above, for our task it is necessary to understand the brain's role in informing our conscious mind. But it is equally necessary to recognize that the conscious mind is not simply the brain. The picture provided by scientific materialism is only a part of the overall picture. The experiential worlds of the mind, emotions, and spirit are as obvious— actually, *more* obvious—than what we perceive with the analytic mind. At least, they would be so if only we were more attuned to what is in front of our noses. This direct perception, this immersion in the world of experience, is a given of everyone's life, but it is obvious to any perceptive observer that this input eludes the left-brained, analytic mind, which loves to escape into realms of abstraction. Cultures we call primitive know well the world of unmediated experience; so do young children, and mystics and sages, and those who enjoy a holistic perspective. During those times when a life crisis catapults us out of our ingrained assumptions and priorities, we may get a glimpse of this strictly experiential aspect of our lives. But in our left-brained culture (which includes most of the Western, "civilized" world) the holistic view is pretty much taboo. Most of us define our reality according to the "official version" of what reality is, even if we are holistic by natural tendency.

The world of spirit, as reflected in religion and spirituality in their broadest, most inclusive sense, is really about this obvious yet hidden world. Along with philosophers, mystics, shamans, and sages, as well as many ordinary people throughout history, I accept the reality conveyed by the holistic brain. I believe this reality, apprehended in its fullness, can constitute a revelation in its truest sense—not something etched in stone tablets, but something available to everyone at all times and places through direct experience and holistic observation. True revelation evokes awe, wonder, and "aha" moments. Sometimes these revelations can come through in response to reading spiritual books, much in the way that people have received and discovered truths through traditional scriptures from Eastern and Western traditions. And these books are still being written. I will quote from several of these modern sources in this book. At other times revelation can be received through philosophical or even scientific writings and insights. Einstein was open to this kind of revelation, as were many great scientists, artists, and Renaissance thinkers. But of course, in order to access the full power of revelation we must do more than study a text. We must correctly understand it, which requires that we draw on the cognitive insights of the whole brain—an approach that seems to be the exception rather than the rule, a consequence that appears to be the result of genetics and dominance, as we shall see. Ultimately, revelation depends on the recipient, for whom something very small and ordinary, such as a grain of sand, may be seen to contain the secrets of the cosmos, as it did for William Blake, who wrote:

To see a World in a Grain of Sand
And a Heaven in a Wild Flower,
Hold Infinity in the palm of your hand
And Eternity in an hour.

It is our job to manage and optimize the way we relate to each of these two worlds—the raw world of experience that is inherently peaceful, beautiful, and immediately, intuitively obvious; and the world that dissects, analyzes, discusses, verbalizes, and categorizes. These two ways of perceiving and dealing with reality can work magnificently together and enhance every part of our individual and collective life. But the world of dissection and analysis has often become a kind of obsessive insanity that tries to reduce the unity of raw, experiential reality to its component parts, and in the process, it has often led us to overlook the greater whole.

Over the last three decades, as I researched and wrote the materials that eventually became this book, I came to see just how transformative the achievement of peace through self-understanding could be. I also came to see how impoverished we have become for our inability, as a society, to embrace the holistic perspective. Ultimately, I concluded that this broad vision would be served by, rather than obstructed by, the analytic skills normally associated with the left-brain hemisphere.

The more research I did, the more I realized that the generally accepted body of scientific information, *when taken as a whole*, supports the cognitive model I propose in this book. That is not to say that most brain researchers agree with everything I propose here; in fact, it is fair to say that, with a few exceptions, little if any consideration has been given to this model by other researchers. But while a number of my conclusions in this book are original, they build upon the work of prominent brain researchers, as well as philosophers and psychologists. Also, keep in mind that my conclusions owe much to various living traditions of knowledge and observation that are far older than modern brain science and yet in many ways prefigured its findings. To cite one example, many cultures have recognized forms of sexuality or gender identity that do not fit the paradigms most of us take for granted—but would fit the paradigm I propose in this book. A similar situation applies in other areas. Consider the way that the teachings of Buddhism and Vedanta prefigure quantum theory and Einstein's theory of relativity; or the way that the revolutionary teachings of Jesus of Nazareth prefigured many of the more enlightened attitudes we have today, including some that can be derived from brain science itself.

One of my intentions—a very important one—in writing this book, has always been to help us better understand the behavior of the "opposite" sex, with the caveat that it is more appropriate to speak of a broad and rich sexual spectrum rather than simply using the traditional binary (two-sex) model. With the increasing visibility of gay, lesbian, and transgender persons, we have the opportunity of creating a new understanding of gender and sexuality in general, as well as addressing the continued ubiquity of prejudice against anyone who does not fit traditional norms. But we need not go that far afield to see the continued existence of prejudice. Men still have a huge problem understanding women, and as a result the abuse and mistreatment of women is still rampant throughout much of the world. To understand the opposite sex, or those who are a blend of the two, nothing is more important than to know how the brain "operating systems" of the sexes differ, and that is what I attempt to do here.

In the areas of sexuality and gender, as in numerous other areas, the more we know, the less we fear; and the less we fear, the more we are able to love and cooperate to create a world that will benefit us all. It is my hope that this book will inspire readers to forge a path to peace and help transform our dysfunctional world.

Introduction

Do you ever ask yourself an important question about your life and receive two very different answers? Have you ever thought, "Part of me is on board with this idea (or plan or solution), but another part isn't"? Perhaps you sense that a part of you really wants to change a particular situation in which you find yourself, and another part is totally resistant. What you are experiencing here is likely the different outlooks and different answers presented by your two brain hemispheres—which, as you will see, are governed by separate operating systems. Whenever you ask, "What is real? What is true?" each hemisphere responds from its unique perspective, producing a minimum of two possible perceptions, answers, or directions.

Those two very different voices—often one loud and one soft, with one voice appearing perhaps in the form of a thought, the other in the form of a feeling or symbolism—can leave us puzzled or confused. We are left to find a way to harmonize the two—or reject one—in order to make a clear decision. Typically we find a position somewhere between the extremes, such as choosing a position in which we feel the best—*feeling* being a typical response of the right hemisphere—or else selecting a position where we think we belong, *thinking* being the left hemisphere's preferred method of communicating. Often we end up where the pressure from our peers, family, or employer is least.

The two hemispheres of the brain work together and have overlapping functions, but their contributions are very different, and as a result they often seem to work at odds with each other. One hemisphere, usually the right, is associated with a *holistic* perspective. This perspective supplies the big picture—the *context*—thus enabling us to ask not only *how best* to get from point A to point B, but whether indeed we *should* get from point A to point B.

The left hemisphere specializes in supplying the details that help us know how to do a task. Its job is to zoom into the parts of a thing, process, or idea in an effort to find solutions—find paths through our challenges. This process of division or deconstruction gives us a *dualistic* perspective: one that perceives and shows us the parts by analyzing them. As we shall see, the left hemisphere's activities also go into more problematic areas, for this dualism results in the division of a thing or process into polarized opposites: right/wrong, good/bad (or good/evil), true/false, this/that, mine/yours, and the like.

From a dualistic perspective there is only one right answer to a given question, one correct way of looking at or doing things. The dualistic approach is one of excluding, of taking apart, and this process may assume different forms, ranging from the reductionism of scientific materialism (i.e., reducing the infinite richness of life or of the universe to certain measurable processes) to the insistence of religious fundamentalists that theirs is the "only way," which all others must follow in fulfillment of God's plan.

Our objective throughout this book is to achieve unification—that is, coherence or consistency—in our understanding of things, an act that requires the cooperation of both sides of the brain. For short, I call this *unity consciousness*—the perennial goal of philosophers and sages ever since Plato, if not before. As we shall see, to achieve true unity consciousness, the operating systems of both brain hemispheres must work cooperatively. But this unity consciousness is a complex unity. The holistic operating system and its perspective *by itself* is still just one side of the holistic-*versus*-dualistic polarity. But when our two operating systems cooperate, the holistic perspective includes and *integrates* the dualistic perspective's views and information into a unified whole.

In addition to their communication with one another, our operating systems are in communication with our outer environment. What we do, think, and feel are continually informed by cultural inputs—and herein lies a huge problem. As Iain McGilchrist, an Oxford-trained psychiatrist and author of *The Master and His Emissary: The Divided Brain and the Making of the Western World*, states it, "One particular model [has] come to dominate us so badly that we hardly notice its pervasiveness".[1] He is referring to the nearly all-pervasive dualistic culture of the left brain, which, in lacking the critical element of *context*, has resulted in the dangerous degree of polarization, fragmentation, strife, and "spin" of important issues into ineffective clichés that we see all around us today.

In this book, I have added McGilchrist's conclusions to those of Michael Gazzaniga, Joseph B. Hellige, Ned Herrmann, Paul MacLean, Robert Ornstein, Roger Sperry, and other prominent researchers and thinkers. With their help, I have arrived at my own conclusion: If we—as individuals and as a society—can find a way to achieve a more harmonious relationship between our two operating systems, and thus achieve a more unified consciousness, we can then more effectively develop *peaceful* solutions to our myriad problems. In today's culture, the default response is too often to look for the competitive, coercive, or even *warlike* solutions that seem natural to the dualistic brain.

This book is an invitation to explore how we can more consciously assist this process of cooperation between our holistic and dualistic operating systems—one of which is usually dominant, the other recessive. By understanding the purposes these systems serve, we can more consciously move toward attaining optimum internal clarity and harmony—and, ultimately, both internal and external peace. This book delivers the good news that we are not captives of the perspective of our dominant operating system; rather, we are able to access both halves of the brain and create a more integrated and all-inclusive perspective, one equipped to see the world as it truly is, or at least to view the world from the two possible perspectives that are supplied to us by the natural evolution of the brain.

The act of becoming aware of the differences in perspective as well as the different responses provided by our two operating systems will help us to better understand the strengths and the pitfalls of each. This awareness will allow us to understand how the dualistically dominated culture we live in—which operates on a partial perspective and its limited set of responses—creates distortions that seriously affect our ability to relate to one another and to understand and cope with life's challenges. We will also discover that our brain is highly flexible and that our limitations are often self-imposed. This knowledge will support us to sustain a mental environment in which we can more easily access truth, healing, and balance, and succeed in turning our best intentions into reality.

As pointed out above, the brain's perspective is really a pair of perspectives. Expressed in geometric language, these perspectives allow us to see in two different directions: we view life from the inside out (the holistic perspective) and from the outside in (the dualistic view). But, in addition to this *internal* guiding voice (or, strictly speaking, two internal voices), we are also informed by an *external* guiding voice made up of layers of cultural influences. Finally, through our own volition—combined with our brain's inherent flexibility—we are able to access both perspectives (recessive as well as dominant), thus transcending not only our genetically determined default position but also the perspectives reinforced by our social and cultural environment. These three different sources of input— genetic, environmental (cultural), and free-will-based—are discussed in more detail in chapter 1.

Scientists sometimes refer to culture's role in our mental programming as *social influence bias*. This is the voice of our environment speaking to us, suggesting its solutions to our problems. Since our cultural voice is the product of individual voices, each coming from a split brain, our cultural voice naturally has both a holistic and a dualistic component, one of which will almost always be dominant and in control. Although the dominant cultural voice among Westerners reared in industrial societies is overwhelmingly dualistic, our culture is in fact made up of multiple cultures—our family, our peers, our work associates, the culture of media, etc.—any one of which can be either holistic or dualistic in character.

An Expedition into the Brain's Operating Systems

My interest in the brain is concerned with how the split in our brain affects our mind and thinking and, consequently, with how this division influences our conscious and unconscious behavior. Since our conscious behavior is largely under our control, it is my primary focus. Depending on where we choose to place our attention and what we choose to believe, disbelieve, or ignore, we are able to exercise control over many of our behaviors. If we choose to more consciously manage our behavior, we can gain better control over our lives. The more we understand the character of the cognitive forces flowing within and around us, the more creative, loving, fulfilling, and harmonious our existence will be, as individuals and as a society.

Popular inquiry into the split brain has tended to focus on what the sides *do*, what tasks they carry out, like creativity or language. But, at a deeper level, what we do is largely a result of how we think and feel and what our brain-constructed worldview looks like. Our exploration must therefore go much further than the usual preoccupations. So, for example, we will not be considering where language is processed in the brain. A staple of most split-brain books, this subject has already been widely discussed. We are, however, going to explore the brain's two "macro processors"—the pair of operating systems that together act as directors that orchestrate things like creativity and language for us in the first place.

In order to bring the distinguishing differences of our brain's operating systems into broad relief, we will mostly look at them as though they operate in isolation—with one or the other being in control. Because of the forces of dominance and the separative nature of the corpus callosum, that sometimes is the case (the corpus callosum is often thought of as a connective organ, but many researchers think its primary function is to separate the two hemispheres). Nevertheless, in practice, both operating systems are always available to some degree. Still, when either system (especially the dualistic) heavily dominates our behavior, we will often behave in ways that strongly reflect the character of just one of them.

Because each of our perspectives has its advantages and its disadvantages, it is valuable to be aware of the differing characteristics of each. But, most of all, it is critical that we come to know, and consequently respect, our nondominant or recessive perspective. This unacknowledged contribution is our mental blind spot. Without it we are missing much of one of our two fundamental perspectives. Its insights enable us to better understand and constructively relate to the positions of those who disagree with us in such areas as culture and politics, among many others. In this way, we rid ourselves of the conflict that disrespect for other points of view breeds and in turn advance our sense of internal peace. It is a goal of this book to show how both perspectives—dominant and recessive—must work in concert if we are to achieve full understanding of ourselves and of one another.

As we begin our exploration of the brain's role in helping us to understand the complex relationship between the wholeness we seek and the divisive environment of duality in which we normally live our lives, we will start by focusing on the *individual*. Eventually, our emphasis will shift to examining the effects of dominant systems on our *collective* life. We will look at how the political, military, economic, and social spheres of our culture function, and we will observe how our perception and evaluation of them changes depending on which fundamental system—dualistic or holistic—we use in viewing them. That insight is critical because it explains the very divisive liberal-versus-conservative polarity in our politics and culture—what is sometimes referred to as the "culture wars."

We will move along an intriguing spectrum of fields of study, raising questions such as:

- What is the "ego perspective" and how does it compare with the "divine feminine perspective"?
- How does our left-brain-directed American culture shape the way we govern and legislate, determine the financial structure under which we operate, and guide the way we conduct business? How does the left brain typically handle dangerous conflicts (locally as well as globally) and deal with the people, ideas, and things we encounter in our lives?
- How do genetics and dominance relate to sexual orientation and gender identity?
- How does the concept of "war" in its fullest sense explain most of society's most intractable problems?
- What can we do, individually and collectively, to restore a balance between our brain's operating systems—and thus begin to heal ourselves, our cultural divisions, and our planet?

The scope of this book encompasses both the material and the spiritual realities of our lives. On one level, it is an exploration of what is surely one of the most important things you can know about yourself and others: how the human brain and mind function, and how to use brain and mind more effectively in their collaborative roles. On another level, it is about the same thing that the highest spiritual traditions and meditative techniques teach: the experience of internal peace, which is the prerequisite for external peace. Throughout I engage in a wide-ranging philosophic discussion intended to unify this exploration of our material and spiritual dimensions.

While our two operating systems are complementary in design, in action they are often in conflict. The "battle of the sexes" is largely the result of differences in the brains of men and women. Similarly, as we shall see in detail, the political and cultural conflict between conservatives and liberals, which figures so prominently in the daily news and in our political dialogue, is largely due to the differences in which these two groups (dualistic- and holistic-dominant, respectively) see things. Generally, the two sides are in conflict because we fail to understand how our recessive system works and how profoundly brain dominance affects the ways all of us think and feel. This conflict is so pervasive because these two systems perceive the world in two very different ways. Only when both systems (not merely one's dominant system) are understood can these two points of view be unified and the truth of each be seen. We shall explore ways to reconcile these systems for optimum understanding of ourselves, others, and the world.

The Book's Structure

Here I will briefly summarize the range of issues that will be addressed in each section and chapter of the book.

Part One: Holistic and Dualistic Systems in Action

How did a revolutionary split-brain discovery that grabbed everyone's attention a few decades ago fall out of favor and come to be largely abandoned by researchers? The reasons are rather surprising and will be explored in chapter 1, "Brain Lateralization: The Big Picture." After examining why the original discovery is valid in its larger implications (though not in all details), we will set the stage to explore the brain's two operating systems—their management systems—and their effect on consciousness. We will take our first look at what each of our hemisphere's operating systems shows us based on what we know about their perspectives and characteristic responses.

Chapters 2 and 3, titled "The Nature of Holistic Operating Systems" and "The Nature of Dualistic Operating Systems," give us our first introduction to the disposition and character that defines and differentiates the two brain operating systems, thus laying the groundwork for subsequent chapters.

In chapter 4, "Gender War," we begin by examining the tensions between men and women that result in "gender war"—a literal as well as metaphorical description—and we review both the differences and the shocking similarities between gender war and other forms of war. We then look at the reasons for this in our brains as well as in our dualistic-dominant culture—and proceed from there to review the source of gender itself (and how it differs from one's sex) and the internal conflicts that arise from sex-versus-gender issues. I conclude with a look at the many varieties of gender expression and how by understanding these issues we can take advantage of and celebrate our differences.

In chapter 5, "The Complexities of Sexual Orientation," we consider further how our sexual orientation appears to actually result from our brain-dominance patterns. We will examine several such patterns, involving not only the dominance of one system over the other but also blended dominance—and, in some cases, a more cooperative relationship such as we find in systems of relatively equal dominance. The result of these findings, and of numerous supporting studies, is that sexual orientation is *not* a choice—an important consideration for our current cultural debate. The chapter concludes with a table listing 32 variations on sexual orientation, along with their genetic connection.

Part Two: How Perspective and Brain Dominance Produce Polarization

The brain and mind that we are studying and the universe they are embedded in are parts of a unity and therefore share common patterns. For this reason, to some extent, we can learn about the brain and mind by looking at the universe of which they are a part. In chapter 6, "Parts, Wholes, and Holons: Satisfying Our Need for Wholeness," we look into wholeness at its most elemental level and uncover one of its foundations.

The greater reality we are trying to understand has a geometric framework. Perspective is no exception—as we see in chapter 7, "Sacred Geometry's Role in Perception." *Sacred geometry* refers to the ways that shapes and patterns are repeated throughout nature. Variances in our viewpoint, as reflected by changes in position—which can be plotted in terms of geometry—naturally alter the information content flowing to consciousness.

Chapter 8, "The Roles of Perspective and Perception in Cognition," explores the crucial relationship between perspective and perception. We will also look at how our choice of perspective controls which hemisphere governs our activity at any moment. The reason the subject of perspective is given so much attention in this book is because through our choice of perspective, we are often able to consciously shift from one hemisphere to another.

Chapter 9, "Polarization: The Separation of Unity into Duality," looks at the brain's underlying role in the polarization of ideas and cultures. We examine some of the factors that lead us from unity into polarization, thereby helping us to better understand how to reverse the process.

By the time we get to chapter 10, "Dualistic Operating-System Patterns Revisited," we return to and expand on the operational characteristics of the left brain—especially the typical response of left-brain-dominant individuals—based on the context gained in the last several chapters.

In chapter 11, "Further Considerations of the Holistic Feminine," we expand on our previous discussion on the experience of being holistically guided. We examine how right-brain-dominant individuals relate intuitively to spiritual energy; the nature of this energy as the most real form of energy; and how the right brain's intuitive abilities and expressions become weakened and distorted in our dualistic culture. We conclude by cautioning readers to consider some of the perceptual problems associated with right-brain dominance, as well as the fruitlessness of comparing and evaluating the dualistic and holistic perspectives in isolation.

Part Three: How Brain Dominance Shapes Culture
Beginning with chapter 12, "Understanding the Cultural Brain," we shift our perspective outward and begin to focus on the *cultural* manifestations of hemispheric dominance, and even our take on what is right and true.

In chapter 13, "How Brain Dominance Affects Our Perception of Abortion," we look at how the split in our brain affects our understanding of this culturally polarizing subject—and how, by understanding the differences in our brains, we can engage in a more fruitful dialogue leading to policies that can benefit us all, even as we continue to differ on fundamental issues.

Chapter 14, "The Brain behind the Military-Industrial-Congressional Complex," provides us with a look at selected issues involving the military-industrial complex and its congressional benefactors. We will look at these three powerful dualistically oriented subcultures, their cozy interrelationship, and the effects of this mutually reinforcing triad on the rest of us.

Chapter 15, "Making War: The Default Response of Left-Brain Dualism," is unique to this book in that it serves as an example of the depth and breath that must be explored if we are to develop a sufficiently holistic (truly comprehensive) understanding of a complex subject. In focusing on the drug war, this chapter presents a broad range of the unintended, overlooked, and suppressed consequences of using the forces of violence and coercion to deal with social problems. While we tend to view the drug war as only metaphorically a war, it actually epitomizes war in its broader and truer sense, which involves the use of force or coercion as an agent of change. The lessons to be learned from this examination are instructive not only for what they say about *all* wars, but also for what they reveal about the type of thinking that leads to such destructive behavior.

In the final chapter, "Finding Peace, Being Peace," we explore some of the barriers to peace—including religion itself—and what we can do, individually and collectively, to overcome these barriers. We look at the indispensable role of our personal choices—and we consider the role of *feeling* and contrast its role in the attainment of peace with the role of *thought*. We explore our capacity to *choose* peace at every moment, and we consider ways we can expand our capacity to live in peace and *be* peace—as individuals and as a planet.

Brain, Mind, and Spirit:
Our Multiple Interfacing Realities

In the remainder of this Introduction I will be touching on the broader implications of this book from several vantage points. In spite of its necessary scientific underpinnings, my motivation for writing this book has been to give us tools to effect a transformation of our understanding of—and our ability to positively influence—this highly polarized world, where our technological capabilities have far outrun our capacity for wise decisions. Ultimately, this book is intended as a contribution toward workable solutions that can transform our lives, our culture, and our planet.

What It Means to Be Human

From a holistic perspective, physical, mental, and spiritual energies are one complex energy that manifests in different forms. If we take a dualistic perspective, the *differences* in these energy manifestations are brought to our attention and are reported on. Both perspectives are needed in order to understand anything in its completeness; a single perspective removes dimensionality and depth and prevents us from seeing and appreciating that which is before us in its full beauty, functionality, detail, and context. When we open ourselves to both perspectives—the dualistic and the holistic—they have the opportunity to become integrated and complementary.

Many ways have been suggested for describing our essential nature, but I think the *body/mind/spirit* distinction is the most valid and useful. Working from this premise, we will look at certain broad insights common to many great religious, spiritual, and meditative traditions (ancient and modern) concerning how body, mind, and spirit interact to make us who we are.

At our core, we are spirit-based energy. We also (quite obviously) have a physical body. Mind is nonphysical energy that connects the two through its management of the brain's operation.

We view ourselves as being able to make choices, as being responsible individuals with free will and the power to change things. That much seems self-evident; but where does this choice-making—this ability to manage our lives though choices made in the mind—come from? This power resides in spirit, and spirit energy is *felt*. Spirit energy is not something hypothetical, to be "believed in"; through our feelings, our emotions, it forms the basis of our everyday experience.

Of our spirit we can say, first and foremost, that when we feel our deepest feelings, we are experiencing a genuine awareness of our inner spirit. At any time we choose, we can be in touch with these feelings.

But there is also a second aspect of our consciousness, which is *thought*. Both hemispheres of the brain think *and* feel, but they also appear to specialize in one or the other to some degree. As a general rule, the dualistic gives precedence to thinking, the holistic to feeling.

Emotional or feeling responses have their origins in spirit, as defined above; but they trigger chemical responses that affect both spiritual and physical energies, both of which have repercussions in mind. An example is someone who makes a mistake or fails at something, and suddenly feels embarrassed (their cheeks may turn red), and are—at least for the moment—mentally confused. This is an example of how the three interrelated systems can work in concert (though not always in the most positive way).

Mind is the arena into which our information comes to be managed or ignored. Although brain science teaches us a lot, it is, like science in general, largely limited to the empirical, visible world—in this case, the brain and nervous system. Obviously, mind and brain are closely integrated, and thoughts, emotions, and perceptions are affected by the brain's activities and can often even be traced to certain parts of the brain. Nevertheless, our world of experience, knowledge, and feeling is not reducible to the brain's activity. The energy of mind is nonphysical.

Humanity Is Made in the Image of God

The opinions and viewpoints that any of us hold on a given issue are inevitably grounded in who and what we take ourselves to be. As a way of expanding on the body/mind/spirit model (as described above), I offer the following a priori presumption that I believe to be experientially obvious: that spirit as I defined it above is the source of our power and free will—the ability to decide and control things beyond the limiting factors of genetics and environment. Stated most provocatively, this presumption is that *we are gods*, even if it strikes many as outrageous. Put another way, we have creative abilities and powers that we often deny or are unaware of, and that we generally attribute only to a supreme being (God with a capital G). When, for example, Judeo-Christian scriptures say, "You shall be as Gods," or that we are made in the image of God, this is what they are telling us. Certain of us—especially children, as well as mystics and meditators—are quite aware of these godly attributes, even though our dualistic consciousness does a very good job of suppressing this awareness. Nevertheless, this assertion is made in both Eastern and Western sacred texts, and it is also found in the traditions of many native peoples. I assert that it is intuitively and experientially obvious upon full consideration.

By the time we become adults, our fundamental "God nature" is mostly hidden from our own awareness, though it is always there in potential. If we resist the idea that we are gods, then we cannot live a life that fully expresses our potentials. If, on the other hand, we can nest this information inside a perspective of ourselves that is as godly as it is human, then our capacity to choose that which enhances life will be released and ripple out to create freedom, joy, creativity, and peace in all our relationships and endeavors.

The Role of Genetics in Determining Operating-System Dominance

We sit at the threshold between matter and spirit, between the material givens of our life (genes and environment) and our godlike capacities. Among the givens is our genetically determined brain dominance. Although we will be referring to "genetic dominance" throughout this book, note that the genes themselves are neither dominant nor recessive. The force of dominance that they convey is due to the effect of one of their structural components, their alleles. While this is a technical issue we will not need to refer to again, to avoid the possibility of confusion, this needed to be clarified in a general way.

A small minority of us are guided through life by the holistic and dualistic perspectives working in harmony. Others of us are given a single perspective that is a blend of dualistic and holistic perspectives. For a third group, the largest by far, one of the two operating systems—holistic or dualistic—serves as the dominant, default perspective. The factor that determines whether our mind is fed by one of the two fundamental information systems, or the two working in harmony, or a blend of them, is genetic dominance.

In other words, when genetic *complete* dominance is inherited, either a dualistic or a holistic operating system dominates the processing of information in our two hemispheres. Its complement will then be recessive. When genetic *codominance* is in effect, our two mental systems work together and manage our information input and response as a team. With genetic *incomplete* dominance, we inherit a hybrid of the two systems. The behavior of individuals worldwide is mostly a function of these three genetic systems and the four operating systems they produce.

Genetically integrated operating systems are a minority, but like the individual systems that make them up, they have their own unique characteristics—including gender types (which go beyond the culturally reinforced two-gender system) and sexual orientations (which also are not limited to the usually defined types). We will be looking at these effects on gender and sexuality in the first part of the book. In the final five chapters, we will look at the broader implications of the two main operating systems for our culture. We will mostly omit reference to combined operating systems in those later chapters due to lack of available research into this area.

Where genetic complete dominance is in effect, the brain's complementary system is recessive and its perspective is *internally* blocked. This leaves only one of our two operating systems to manage our information. However, as pointed out earlier (and elaborated in chapter 1), we are also influenced—for good or ill—by cultural inputs, and through them are able to access our recessive side at will. Nevertheless, the extent to which we actually do so, and the ease with which we do so, depends on the degree to which we exercise our free will, as well as on practice. But it ultimately depends on our full understanding of genetic dominance in the first place.

Understanding the Nuances of Neuroscience

Over the years, cognitive scientists have sought to find a word that describes the general nature of the contribution of the hemispheres to our behavior. From my perspective, since they feed us information, the brain operating systems we are about to discuss are best characterized as translators, guides, or directors. They translate reality into thought and feeling. They guide or direct our attention toward those things we need to know. But, of course, how we use this information is our responsibility.

In scientific language, looking at the split in our brain in terms of how it affects our thinking—our calculations and deliberations, for example— we enter into the realm of cognitive neuroscience. This is a branch of neuroscience that deals with thought—the acquisition of understanding and knowledge.

In the scientific community the study of the psychological effects of having a split brain is sometimes referred to as functional lateralization: *lateralization*, because our brain is *laterally* split into hemispheres; *functional*, because the sides harbor different *functions*, and have different ways of seeing and responding.

The brain's asymmetry is both physical and functional. There are differences in the shape and size of the two hemispheres as well as differences in how they perform their functions. The presence of brain asymmetry, and functional differences, is not confined to humans. The split brain with its split functionality is also a component of the design of other mammals, birds, reptiles, amphibians, and fish.[2] Furthermore, as Joseph Hellige, one of the subject's more dedicated explorers, points out, "It is clear that the direction and magnitude of hemispheric asymmetry is often different from subsystem to subsystem, precluding simple statements about hemispheric superiority for an entire task."[3]

Science has found that in most if not all cases, even if one side of the brain does most of the work, both hemispheres contribute something essential to the solution of a task. Nothing we propose will be refuting that. When we refer to one hemisphere as if it and it alone were contributing, we will be referring to its operating system or brain management system. Operating systems manage or direct the brain's task-oriented modules in order to get things done. We will be looking at *how* the brain performs its tasks rather than *what* those tasks are.

Brain operating systems are distinguished from the physical brain they operate by the fact that they are nonphysical, as evidenced by their process-based characteristics—for example, analytical and synthetic, aggressive and submissive, knowing and believing. This distinction can be useful to know, because unlike the world of the brain, in the world of mind we have a great deal of freedom of control over what is happening. We may find ourselves entirely subject to genetic dominance at first, but in truth we are ultimately free to choose where to direct our attention (our perspective), free to choose whom to listen to and what to believe, free to choose between aggressive and submissive responses or to craft a combination of them.

The integrative mental process by which we combine the two streams of information, whether it occurs at the conscious level or the subconscious level, is a continuous act of creation. Here, in the mansion of our mind, we are compelled to hammer out the differences between our two diverse perspectives, and through this process find ways to develop our personal vision and our beliefs. It is our most primal act of creation, since all of our other acts of creation derive from it.

For an overwhelming majority of people, the right brain is holistic in operation and the left brain is dualistic, so when we refer to the characteristics of a specific side, this is what we will intend. However, since it is more descriptive to refer to a system rather than a side, much of the time we will refer to our operating systems and use their functional descriptions—holistic or dualistic.

What is most important for us is to learn how to more consciously and creatively control our perspective. We access the two aspects that make up unity consciousness through our intention and attention simply by accessing their perspective. Thus, we need not be concerned with the hemisphere in which the desired system is located. What matters is that we are familiar with the functional character of the two systems, and that we make certain to consult both systems and thus give ourselves the opportunity to obtain all relevant information from all possible perspectives—at least whenever big issues and big decisions are involved.

In treating all of these topics, generalizations are unavoidable. Generalizations point to an experience that is larger than that of any individual or any group. Although it is an oversimplification, we might think of generalizations as the right brain's equivalent of the *details* that are the left brain's specialty. When we assemble a harmonious group of details (such as the parts of an engine or a theory), they reveal a greater, more detailed whole (object, process, theory, etc.).

Overcoming Polarization

Ultimately, the question we are trying to answer is, how can we make the two operating systems work in greater harmony? Or, stated another way, how can we better mentally integrate their contributions? Thus, this is a book that is more about mind than it is about brain. It is a book about the split brain's effect on our cognition and our behavior and the highly visible consequences of letting one system have too much power over ourselves and our culture.

What could be more helpful to the self than to understand the two systems that are supplying us with our information—to understand these systems well enough to distinguish their voices and reconcile their necessary but very different contributions? This is what we will attempt to do here.

Therefore, this is, among other things, a self-help book that introduces the idea that the brain can be managed to some degree—which is what is meant by "brain management." But I have not included exercises in the traditional sense. The only recommended exercise is to get to know the brain's two operating systems in terms of their temperament, attitude, character, and style, just as we might learn how to understand a friend or business partner. Only after we have gained such an understanding are we free to harmonize with them.

Polarized brains produce polarized people and polarized cultures. We live in a world that is out of balance in many ways, a world that has grown more and more polarized, splitting families and cultures and governments in the process. Polarization, like everything we see and experience, starts in the brain. The holistic and dualistic hemispheres of the brain give us two different perspectives that call for two different responses. The holistic gives us the context—the big picture—and its perception of interconnectedness results in a natural expansion of one's concerns to include other people, other cultures, and the planetary environment. The dualistic gives us a fragmented perspective that separates things for us, thus allowing us to focus in on particular problems. But this tendency to separate things is what leads to polarization. Polarization is the first step away from wholeness, as we observe in cell division, where wholeness multiplies by expanding into two cells, then four, then eight, then 16.

The good news is, there is a way back to unity. The route runs through understanding the roles our split brain plays in how we perceive the world. An excellent place to start is to observe that the two operating systems are complementary partners, but not equals. The universe has a dualistic-nested-within-holistic structure, and our brain and its operating systems share this structure in their design. In the sacred geometry of the universe, as in the systemic chaos in which we live our lives, the dualistic is an integral *part* of the holistic. It is the bedrock upon which everything is grounded.

PART ONE

Holistic and Dualistic Systems in Action

CHAPTER 1

Brain Lateralization:
The Big Picture

Imagination is more important than knowledge. Knowledge is limited. Imagination encircles the world.

—Albert Einstein[1]

In 1981 Roger Wolcott Sperry was awarded a Nobel Prize in Medicine for his pioneering work investigating the effects of the lateral split in the human brain on consciousness. Among his discoveries, he found that the two brain hemispheres could actually be viewed as separate, conscious systems. While seeming to work as one, their individual contributions were so different that they were sometimes in conflict. Nobelprize.org gives us an insider's perspective on the truly revolutionary significance of Sperry's discoveries:

> Until these patients were studied, it had been doubted whether the right hemisphere was even conscious. By devising ways of communicating with the right hemisphere, Sperry could show that this hemisphere is, to quote him: "indeed a conscious system in its own right, perceiving, thinking, remembering, reasoning, willing, and emoting, all at a characteristically human level, and . . . both the left and the right hemisphere may be conscious simultaneously

in different, even in mutually conflicting, mental experiences that run along in parallel."[2]

Many individuals have played a role in discovering that the two hemispheres provide us with independent systems of perception, but one of the earliest of many steps that led to this discovery was the surgical separation of the brain hemispheres of a cat by Sperry's graduate student Ronald Myers in the mid-1950s at the University of Chicago. Research was done "to test how information from one eye came together inside the brain with information from the other." A lateral division was made in the brain so that information coming into the cat's left eye went only to its left brain and information coming into the right eye went only to the right brain. Meyer's tests confirmed that the division "eliminated the normal information mixing at the base of the brain."[3] This discovery unleashed a barrage of research and eventually led to the conclusion that the two hemispheres were each conscious.

Prior to these findings, the right hemisphere of the brain (referring here to the way the brain is organized in most people, but not in everyone) was viewed by many scientists as decidedly inferior in function to the left hemisphere, largely because of the association of the left hemisphere with language in most people. (That is why, for example, strokes often cause impaired ability to speak and use language: most strokes affect the left hemisphere.) But, while certain linguistic abilities originate primarily in the left brain, language involves far more factors than the ability to choose or speak a word or sentence, and without the right hemisphere's contributions many linguistic abilities—the ability to understand metaphor, for example—would disappear. Perhaps the most unique contribution of the right hemisphere is the ability to comprehend the whole—to present a holistic, whole-picture view, without which the left hemisphere, with all its superb ability to analyze and dissect, would get lost in its narrow perspective. This difference between hemispheres has been shown again and again to be critical, even when taking into account all the ways that the brain's hemispheres can engage in duplicative functions.

As with other revolutionary ideas and discoveries, this split-brain research—or, rather, the ideas and beliefs that it spawned—soon took the public by storm. And with good reason. By the 1960s, psychedelics, meditation, biofeedback, mysticism, and Eastern religions were all spreading across America and Europe, and the climate was ripe for exploring holistic thinking. The idea that the right brain hemisphere—far from being the minor, secondary, or even "stupid" half of the brain—could transform our lives, enhance our experience, increase our creative abilities, and create a state of meditative equilibrium, was irresistible.

As a result, by the 1970s a whole industry of right-brain-enhancement books and products began to appear, and even educational and cultural theories—from the worthy to the ridiculous—began to sprout that would, at least in theory, add to the understanding of ourselves.

Among the most positive developments—and foreshadowing a key theme of the present book—was a recognition, at least in some quarters, that the individual cannot be separated from the larger culture, and many of the imbalances we see in everything from family life to international affairs and the way we treat Mother Earth are due to our culture's favoring of the left brain hemisphere (a subject that we will delve into in great detail in this book).

Nevertheless, the appeal of the brain-lateralization discoveries in the popular mind eventually created credibility issues and resulted in a backlash among many mainstream scientists, who ignored, dismissed, or undermined these findings. Brain-lateralization research did not come to an end, but it certainly was greatly slowed down. Indeed, this backlash was in no small part a result of the left brain's overattention to small details at the expense of the whole, which it was incapable of seeing and reporting on.

One can find precedents for scientific shifts in attitude where subjects once considered worthy were then later marginalized. For example, a little over a century ago, within parts of the scientific community there was much interest in research into the psychic realm and on the positive value of mystical and altered states. An excellent example of science's constructive role in exploring these areas is the pioneering work of America's preeminent experimental psychologist, William James.[4] But fears and other factors eventually contributed to a near-total rift between mainstream scientific studies and sympathetic explorations into the religious life and the paranormal. Although serious research into these areas is done today, these areas of inquiry are still verboten among most mainstream scientists.

The understandable desire of the public to know more about the functional differences between the hemispheres and the scarcity of available peer-reviewed information generated excessive speculation and created a gap between the interest of the public and that of the scientific community. It takes time to conduct experiments and then replicate them to the point where it can be said that something has been more or less scientifically proven. Starting out with relatively little data and dealing with a highly complex subject, it is not surprising that scientists found themselves unable to come to agreement on how to characterize the two hemispheres.

With speculation so far ahead of the hard, peer-reviewed science, the scientists tended to take a skeptical stance toward any possibilities that the peer-reviewed literature had not confirmed. Scientists tend to pride themselves on their rigor, but it can lead to the false assumption that objectivity—and therefore truth—can be discovered only through adherence to rigorous protocols. Speculation, like anecdotal evidence, seems to suggest the opposite of rigor, thus triggering an automatic reflex of condemnation—never mind that some of the greatest scientific breakthroughs have been achieved by dreamers who were not afraid of speculation.

There are also, undoubtedly, simple human elements at work here. Scientists, like nearly all of us, are subject to garden-variety peer pressure, especially where prestige (the esteem of their colleagues), promotions, and funding are involved. Thus there is great pressure to create bodies of professional, formal, peer-reviewed, and peer-approved research based on strict protocols and methodologies.

For all these reasons, functional lateralization itself has become suspect among a large percentage of the scientific community and science journalists. In today's academic climate, the study of the brain's broad hemispheric differences is still discouraged, not unlike the way that academia often rejects interdisciplinary studies—as if the truth were found only in the narrowest, most dissected view. Media writers in turn have their own pressures, which have led to many distortions over the years on both the "lay" side (speculation run rampant) and the "science" side (excessive dismissiveness) of the discussion.

As I have already suggested, one of the purposes of this book is to redress this imbalance. Another is to bring the big picture more fully into our personal, cultural, and political life—meaning, to promote a greater awareness of the context and its relationships. And, as Iain McGilchrist states, "Part of that context is the nature of the mind that does the knowing."[5] This very basic fact has been recognized by philosophers for centuries, but it has become all but ignored in many mainstream scientific circles. We cannot know reality without knowing the mind, which includes knowing the brain. It is my intention here to reassemble that which has been disassembled. We will take a fresh look at the paired structure that Sperry discovered and, through a better understanding of its dichotomy, seek its unity.

How does this book's focus differ from the usual scientific discussion? For one thing, scientists tend to focus on the *tasks* that the hemispheres perform for us, the things they *do*. I am going to focus on the *processes* they use to manage those tasks, and the *character* of those processes. Each hemisphere's system has its own unique processing characteristics governing what it/we are seeing and doing at any moment. Another way of describing this difference might be in terms of its energetics. We will be seeking to understand the character of the energies through which the hemispheres accomplish their tasks—energies such as *focused* and *diffuse*, *linear* and *nonlinear*, *polarizing* and *unifying*, *egoic* and *altruistic*, *violent* and *peaceful*.

We will also look at some of the more fascinating recent scientific studies and some potential implications in personal areas, such as sexuality, that influence—and in turn are influenced by—the collective, cultural "brain." We accept the results of recent scientific studies that suggest the brain consists of "*multiple* dynamic mental systems"—but we also recognize that aggregates of things can simultaneously be both multiple and paired, and even a unity, such as we find in a team (of more than two people) sporting event. Thus, contrary to the prevailing view, recent research does not nullify, but rather it elaborates on, the split-brain findings of the mid-20th century.

Two Versions of Reality

As mentioned earlier, perhaps the most telling significance in the brain's lateral split has to do with the very different *perspective* of each of the brain's hemispheres. The right brain (in a typical individual) provides the big picture and the overarching context—in other words, it provides a *holistic* perspective. It sees the world as a unified whole, and where apparent divisions exist it can find common ground. The left brain performs a complementary function (although it often appears contradictory instead of complementary): it identifies and explains the parts and catalogues differences, and its function is to "take things apart"—in other words, to *search for differences* and uncover details. We refer to this perspective as *dualistic* because it creates polarities. In noticing differences, it obsessively finds "reasons" for things that may in some cases prove groundless. For example, in experiments in which the hemispheres have been isolated from each other, the left hemisphere has been shown to confabulate (fabricate) reasons for choices that the right hemisphere actually made, unbeknownst to the left, but that the left hemisphere *thinks* it made.[6] Neither hemisphere alone can make us fully human, or give us a truly human culture, or discover what is true or wise. Neither hemisphere alone can set us on a course of human or spiritual progress, or give us solutions for saving our planet or creating a better future. Yet (and it bears repeating), in today's academic, political, and cultural climate, one hemisphere—the left, with its narrow, hyperfocused perspective—has taken on the role as the single arbiter of truth.

To discover the "why" of this imbalance in our personal and collective lives, we will examine how each of the hemispheres, through its operating system, acquires, processes, and conveys information from two sources, one internal (based on the forces of *genetic dominance* that give us our acquired nature) and one external, or cultural (based on *nurture*, or the messages of our culture). As each of these perspectives streams information to us, it in turn generates a response that is seen in our behaviors.

Our genetic dominance affects the relative balance or imbalance of information we receive from our two operating systems (or brain hemispheres). Ideally, the hemispheres work cooperatively. In many ways they already do, or we would be very limited in our ability to take in information, assess its importance, or communicate through the nuances of language and gesture. But most of us tend, in varying degrees, to favor one type of information processing over the other, and the consequences of this state of affairs can hardly be overstated.

In spite of the restrictions on our mental vision imposed by our genetic dominance, we have a *variable* perspective that we can exercise. Its restrictions are mostly self-imposed. There are ways to direct our attention that enhance and balance our brain function. We have all experienced "aha" moments when suddenly everything falls into place, or when we suddenly "get" what it's like to be in another's shoes, or when we are flooded with empathy for an individual we previously couldn't relate to, or when we suddenly discover the flaw in an argument or a calculation. This is holistic thinking, but it is also a unified consciousness in which both parts of the brain work seamlessly together in perfect cooperation. The problem is that these moments often seem random or dependent on outside factors beyond our control. What we need is the skill sets to be able to access this whole brain perspective at will. This requires that we learn how to direct our attention—a process that we will be discussing later, especially in the last chapter.

Our perspective informs our *perception*, or at least it does when we are paying attention. Perception is what we get when we process our perspective in light of our experience and bias. We might characterize the creation of perception as the personalization of perspective. Based on our perception, we then develop a *response*—a plan of action.

The Three Sources of Perspective

We have seen in the Introduction that our perspective (on the holistic/dualistic spectrum) derives from three sources: (1) our default (fixed) position on the spectrum, which is the result of genetic dominance and for most of us tends to be one-sided (dualistic or holistic); (2) the cultural feed that tells us what everyone else thinks and feels about the object of our attention—and a significant part of this cultural feed is also one-sided in our dualistic-dominant culture; and (3) our ability to access the full range of perspective (including the genetically recessive as well as dominant ends of the range) *at will*. Whereas the first of these sources is fixed by our genetic inheritance, the second source (involving cultural input) contains both fixed and variable elements. And the third source is entirely variable and depends on our exercising our own free will, combined with experience gained through practice.

Having this third source of perspective under our control allows us to consciously compensate for our genetic inheritance as well as for the limiting cultural inputs we have received at least since birth. We bring the freewill aspect of perspective to mind very simply through where we choose to direct our attention. It is our free will that enables us to access and incorporate both primary perspectives and achieve unity consciousness. Elsewhere in this book, especially in the final chapter, we will learn more about how to do this. But presently we will be devoting most of our attention to perspective's genetic base, since this base underlies the cultural and freewill perspectives we are trying to understand and use.

Attention and Perception

Our perception comes about as a result of the *integration* of information from these three sources of perspective into the body of information that is our belief system. Since the third, freewill source of perspective is under our control, and since we are largely able to accept or reject cultural inputs, our overall perception is a process over which we have considerable control. Perception is the result of the application of our experience, thought, and feeling to our perspective. In other words, perception takes place within familiar, personal territory, whereas perspective takes place at a level prior to personality. Perception may occur instantaneously, or over eons of evolution.

Our personal patterns of attention and perception are repeated at the cultural or collective level. Here too, consciousness is divided along the lines of the split of our brain into a team of two functionally different systems, each with its own perceptual characteristics. The broad political divide between liberals and conservatives is an example of this.

Our discussion of attention and perception will be minimal, but because they are basic concepts found in the cognitive world, we will encounter them from time to time, and they will help anchor our discussions to familiar concepts and thus help keep our mental exploration solidly grounded in known reality.

Some Problems Can Be Managed

Culture is supposed to serve as an arena where our different opinions can meet and integrate, and thus it is capable of bridging the gap between the left and right brains' systems of perception. Yet, our meeting places are often a war ground of accusations and distortions where what may appear as truth is little more than a mirage. And because we have not been able to understand the differences between the two systems well enough to find their unity, we are unable to manage information as well as we might.

If we live in a healthy culture that respects the contributions of both aspects of consciousness, having complete dominance—a single perspective rather than a pair or a blend—is not a problem, since our culture can supply the missing perspective. However—and here is the potential problem—when our internal information input is limited to dualistic consciousness, and our external input—culture—is also heavily dualistic, our access to holistic views tends to be severely limited. Even holistic-dominant individuals often take on dualistic biases in cultures such as ours where holistic thinking and the feminine are widely suppressed.

We might assume that the two sides of our brain would work together in harmony, but Sperry found that the differences between the hemispheres result in a degree of tension between them. Genetic patterns suggest that a small number of individuals are guided by both systems working in harmony, systems governed by genetic codominance, something we will look at later. In another small group, genetic *incomplete* dominance blends the two systems into a hybrid. But for most of us, one system is genetically suppressed to some degree in order to ensure that the responsibility for making decisions does not suffer the same debilitating effects that we find in polarized cultures and institutions—the U.S Congress, for example. Otherwise, the tension between the two information processors seems to serve a very beneficial purpose, as Iain McGilchrist points out:

> The great psychologist, Sir Charles Sherrington, observed a hundred years ago that one of the basic principles of sensorimotor control is what he called "opponent processors." What this means can be thought of in terms of a simple everyday experience. If you want to carry out a delicate procedure with your right hand that involves a very finely calibrated movement to the left, it is made possible by using the counterbalancing, steadying force of the left hand holding it at the same time and pushing slightly to the right. I agree with [the position] that the brain is, in one sense, a system of opponent

processors. In other words, it contains mutually opposed elements whose contrary influence made possible finely calibrated responses to complex situations.[7]

This same pattern of opponent processors functioning as a team can be found in the world of mind, in the form of opposing ideas and beliefs that push and pull us in opposite directions. The conservative–liberal dynamic in our political system is an example of the brain's operating systems functioning as opponent processors, as is the relationship between many men and women—or at least those who find themselves at stereotypical extremes.

The holistic and dualistic sides are best understood when viewed as a team, and an important aspect of their teamwork is their relationship as opponent processors. The push-pull action between opponent processors takes the form of a continuum, a linear structure whose two ends serve as poles of energy, like those of a bar magnet. A more holistic model is that of a torus, a doughnut-like energetic structure that is built around a linear core, the ends of which are the entry and exit points of energy flowing through the center of the torus. (See figure 1.) As we weigh our value choices, the opponent processor system shifts, favoring the dualistic or the holistic operating system, according to the pressure of our attention and the openness of our mind—such as the willingness to be mentally led into areas of personal behavior that bring discomfort (recognizing that fear inhibits movement).

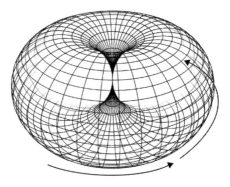

Figure 1. **Torus.**
(image courtesy of Wolfgang Däumler)

Although our genetic inheritance gives us a default operating system that, in effect, positions us on a relative fixed point somewhere on the dualistic–holistic continuum, because of free will and our freedom to choose, this position represents only a starting point. The choices we make to be able to harmonize holistic and dualistic forces are creative choices, since the decisions we make in the process of evaluating the two voices reflect our values and reflect who we truly are. Yet often, the integration of the two operating systems takes place based on what we have been taught, or else we mimic the successes of others or find some other external source of a solution.

If we choose to more consciously manage the two systems, perhaps the most obvious way to assist their integration is to get to know their character so that we might better understand what it is that we are trying to integrate. We want to understand the characteristic strengths and weaknesses of each. We want to better understand *why* they show us what they do.

As we attempt to understand the operational characteristics of the two hemispheres, we go through a process that is similar to that of trying to work or live closely with another person: we seek to get to know them in order to better work with them or, conversely, to minimize conflict with them. In getting to know them, we are trying to understand, coordinate, and accommodate their perspectives so that we might function more effectively as a team.

Unity Consciousness Characteristics

The selection of unity consciousness characteristics that follows developed organically. I had no overall objective other than to look for harmony and quality—to use pairings that, from my perspective, have a high probability that the information is accurate.

The response characteristics are categorized by function, but notice that several of the characteristics could easily fit under more than one category, *skepticism* being an example. I list it as a *spiritual* characteristic, but being skeptical might more often be considered a *mental* characteristic. Most people would probably put *love* under *spiritual disposition*, and *analytic* under *cognitive disposition*. In fact, because of the oneness of spirit and mind, ultimately, all of the spiritual characteristics are related somehow, and so you are welcome to make other pairings if that feels right to you. The reasons for my choices? Unusual pairings can bring new insights to mind.

Unity Consciousness

Perspectives:
Operating-system inputs—shaping our perception

Dualistic Consciousness	Holistic Consciousness
Viewpoint: Structurally inward, attending to the parts	*Viewpoint: Structurally outward, attending to the whole*
Linear, directional	Nonlinear, omnidirectional
Gives us a polarized picture	Shows us unity
Focuses on smaller elements	Focuses on larger elements
Limited by focus on parts	Unlimited in scope
Focuses on elements	Sees relationships of elements
Reveals text—the details	Reveals context—the big picture
Focuses on what we know	Shows us the new
Nonliving things	Living things
Interiors of holons	Holon exteriors
Individual aspects of holons	Collective aspects of holons
Individual self	Collective self, culture
Scarcity	Abundance
Material values	Spiritual values, felt values
Personal needs, security	Service to others
Egoic	Godlike outlook

Responses:
Operating-system outputs—shaping our reactions

Dualistic Consciousness	**Holistic Consciousness**
Viewpoint: Structurally inward, attending to the self	*Viewpoint: Structurally outward, attending to the world around us*

Geometric Disposition

Linear, directional	Nonlinear, omnidirectional
Polarizing	Unifying

Energetic Disposition

Energized by fear	Energized by love
Electric, which is disruptive	Magnetic, which is integrative

Spiritual Disposition

Materialistic values	Spiritual/emotional values
Primacy of individual rights	Primacy of collective rights
Secures the individual	Serves the collective
Impersonal	Personal
Egoic concerns	Altruistic concerns
Freedom-taking (for self)	Freedom-giving
Skeptical	Trusting
Exclusive	Inclusive
Protective	Vulnerable
Rejective, intolerant	Receptive, tolerant
Violent, warlike when provoked	Peaceful when provoked
Aggressive	Submissive
Controlling	Caring
Competitive	Cooperative

Acquisition Disposition

Responds to what we know	Gathers the new; becomes known
Acquires by force/coercion	Acquires by attraction
Disintregral, analytic	Intregral, synthetic
Separative, reductionist	Cohesive, connective

Cognitive Disposition

Thinking/feeling is secondary	Feeling/incorporates thinking
Sensing	Intuitive
Rational (Greek logos)	Reasonable (Greek nous)
Judging	Nonjudging
"Knowing"	Believing
Sequential processing	Simultaneous processing
Serial processing	Parallel processing

Social Disposition

Masculine	Feminine
Conserving	Progressive or liberal

CHAPTER 2

The Nature of Holistic Operating Systems

If your head tells you one thing, and your heart tells you another, before you do anything, you should first decide whether you have a better head or a better heart.

—Marilyn vos Savant

The right brain hemisphere has sometimes been called the feminine brain, as it is characterized by the more intuitively contextual and inclusive approach that is generally more common among women. It has also been referred to as the God brain, because our God-nature (as discussed in the Introduction) is revealed in the workings of our holistic operating system.

Brain researcher Jill Bolte Taylor has given one of the most graphic descriptions of how the holistic operating system functions, based not only on her impressive credentials as a neuroanatomist but on her personal experience. In the late 1990s she suffered a massive left-hemisphere cerebral hemorrhage — chronicled in her book *My Stroke of Insight*[1] as well as in a famous video on the Internet (excerpted below) — that temporarily left her with only one normally functioning brain hemisphere (the right) and resulted in a spiritual epiphany in which she seemed very much at one with God, or a cosmic, universal mind. In this video, using computer terminology, she explains that

> our right hemisphere functions like a parallel processor, while our left hemisphere functions like a serial processor. . . . Because they process information differently, each of our hemispheres thinks about different things, they care about different things, and, dare I say, they have very different personalities. . . . Our right human hemisphere is all about this present moment. It's all about "right here, right now." Our right hemisphere . . . thinks in pictures and it learns kinesthetically through the movement of our bodies. Information, in the form of energy, streams in simultaneously through all of our sensory systems, and then it explodes into this enormous collage of what this present moment looks like, what this present moment smells like and tastes like, what it feels like and what it sounds like. I am an energy being connected to the energy all around me through the consciousness of my right hemisphere. We are energy beings connected to one another through the consciousness of our right hemispheres as one human family.[2]

In most people, one operating system (or hemisphere)—the holistic or the dualistic—becomes the default system. In this chapter we look at some of the characteristics associated with holistic dominance. We refer to the operating system typically associated with the right hemisphere as being *holistic*, because it is associated with the whole of things—the big, inclusive picture—rather than the fine details whose discovery involves the process of exclusion.

Although the qualities represented by the holistic right hemisphere tend to be associated with women, technically there is nothing sexual about the characteristics we will be looking at. They are simply different ways of functioning and interacting (as, for example, *cooperative* or *competitive*, and *submissive* or *aggressive*). However, within these opposite pairings (see the list of unity consciousness characteristics at the end of chapter 1), the dualistic side is most often associated with the typical behavior of men, whereas the holistic side is more likely to be associated with women. Even when the terms *masculine* and *feminine* are spoken of in the abstract—such as in the behavior of nations or natural forces—

holistic (contextual, unifying) qualities have, at most times and places, been viewed as more feminine, and dualistic (detailed, differentiating) qualities as more masculine. It is in this sense only that we will be associating certain functional characteristics with gender in this book.

Over the centuries, certain aspects of the feminine have been seriously suppressed or treated as mysterious and unreliable, intuition being an example. The often-discussed reemergence of the feminine at this time in the evolution of our planet is sometimes associated with "the Divine Feminine," a concept that can be seen as either countering or completing and balancing out the patriarchal God-image that has prevailed for so many centuries.

What is meant by the Divine Feminine? What are the forces that shape the character of the feminine vision and response? How can the feminine assist in the transformation of our war-torn, male-led culture? I believe that the answers to these questions are best found by understanding the character of the holistic right hemisphere and studying its effect on consciousness—it being our purest window into the world of the forces that we consider characteristic of the *feminine*.

Whatever the characteristics of the feminine might be, the Divine Feminine might be looked upon as the feminine in its most natural or primal state, prior to the cultural distortions imposed by our unbalanced, patriarchal society. Imagine the feminine with all of her imperfections removed.

The Holistic Perspective—
Our Brain's Information *Input*

Whereas the *dualistic* viewpoint (discussed in detail in the next chapter) gives us a perspective that analyzes, criticizes, and differentiates (or reveals differences)—and thus can be compared to a magnifying glass or microscope—the *holistic* viewpoint takes in the broadest perspective. It provides context as well as a perspective of unity, since the "big picture" can be seen as a single thing, event, or process rather than just as many related parts. If we were to use a geometric analogy, we could think of a sphere, with an omnidirectional viewing point (capable of viewing in any direction) located at its center.

In giving us different views of our world, the two hemispheres supply us with somewhat different types of information. One way of looking at the difference is that our holistic operating system has its attention on the larger elements,[3] thus relegating the smaller components of reality—the bits and pieces (literally or metaphorically)—to the dualistic system.

From what we have said, the "God-brain" analogy referred to above begins to make sense. Shamans and mystics—and, for that matter, young children—seem capable of tapping into an unlimited, boundless universe and vision, in which the spiritual or perhaps magical nature of reality is taken for granted. Having its attention directed toward the larger components of reality and being omnidirectional and, in principle, unlimited, holistic consciousness perceives the unity of everything we know and experience. This unity is the larger context of our lives—a truth that becomes obvious to many of us when life presents us with unusual experiences or challenges. Having the big-picture view makes us less inclined to shut off new information and new sources of knowledge and truth. In fact, whenever new information comes into view of mind, it is the holistic right hemisphere that directs our attention to it.[4] Of course, there are also more immediate and intimate contexts that the holistic system is attentive to. The right hemisphere is more interested in the personal[5] and in living things in general. The left hemisphere, in contrast, has a strong tendency to *objectify*—in the literal sense of making what is seen and observed into objects, rather than living things or beings. In a sense, we associate objectification with objectivity, perhaps because the left hemisphere specializes in abstract thinking—the kind of thinking that is divorced from concrete situations or immediate contexts. Our American criminal justice system (which we'll discuss in Part Three) is an example of this. "Justice" tends to be viewed by the system as requiring a kind of strict adherence to legal protocols that makes human considerations all too often "inadmissible." Unlike more community-based systems of justice, this creates a kind of standardized, one-size-fits-all approach that the holistic mind often finds flagrantly unjust. Just one such example is the "three-strikes-you're-out" system, in which very small or merely technical offenses could put a person in prison for life if he or she had a previous history of more serious offenses.

Several studies—beginning with one by the neurologist Francois Lhermitte in 1973[6]—have even shown that the perception and recognition of nonliving entities is almost exclusively the province of the left hemisphere itself, while the right hemisphere connects us with the world of living things. Some research shows that living things are the province of both hemispheres of the brain, but that doesn't mean both hemispheres perceive living things in the same way. In the case of the left hemisphere, living entities may be abstracted to the point of not seeming to be alive and not evoking empathy.[7] The same can be said of the left hemisphere's perception of the world (or the field of experience) as a whole.

The role of informing us of the *living component* of the situation at hand is one of the right brain's most important functions. Being aware of this living component is a critical part of our humanity. For so much of human history, and even in so many cultures today (including our own), we see countless examples of the inability of the dualistic-minded to empathize with individuals and life-forms different from themselves. In fact, over much of history and in many cultures today where the dualistic "male" mind holds sway, women, slaves, foreigners, and individuals of different racial/ethnic makeup or religions are not considered human. A similar situation applies to animals and nonsentient living things. The sacredness and intelligence of animals are only beginning to be understood in "advanced" Western culture; and until recently, most Westerners have viewed the natural world only as a collection of resources to be exploited. Thus, I believe there is a strong connection between the above-mentioned experimental findings and the dysfunctionality we see all around us today—a subject that we will discuss much more in later chapters.

With the holistic right hemisphere focused on *living things* and *relationships*, it naturally attends to our collective life, our cultural life. In general, the collective focus of the holistic operating system allows us to develop closer personal connections, since holistically directed people more readily *feel* the connections between themselves and others than is the case with dualistically oriented people. When the holistic system, with its broad, unconstructed focus, is informing us, we see and feel the abundance of life, in which our "cup runs over," to use the biblical metaphor.

Being all-encompassing, the brain's holistic operating system includes spiritual values. What we are all trying to achieve can be described in multiple ways, but for most of us, most of the time, we are trying to achieve a specific *feeling*, usually a good one. What we call physical feelings are more accurately described as *sensations*; true feelings, experienced as emotions (which include sensations), are spiritual in nature (for example, joyful). We are attracted to certain feelings, and so we seek to maximize them however possible.

Perhaps because people who are more closely in touch with their feelings are more sensitive and better able to sense the feelings and needs of others, a prominent characteristic of the holistic system and those who are guided by it is to be of service to others. This is love expressed in the world. When our holistic system is dominant, we see oneness; therefore we see ourselves in others and are sympathetically drawn to respond to their needs. The second of two commandments Jesus gave that expressed the underlying *essence* of Mosaic law was to love one's neighbor as oneself. This perfectly expresses the relationship between love and service as recognized by the holistic mind.

The list of right-hemispheric attributes or characteristics that we have been discussing suggests a godlike perspective: all-inclusive, characterized by abundance and unity, and instant apprehension (making it the first operating system to know). These are qualities associated with the Divine in general, and the Divine Feminine in particular; and *love*—and the attractiveness of its energy—permeates them all. Love is a part of everything the holistic system does. We now turn our attention to holistic *responses*.

The Right Hemisphere's *Response* to Its Perspective—Its *Output*

To better distinguish the following characteristics, the responses of holistic operating systems are divided into six broad categories, which are also reflected in the list of unity consciousness characteristics: *geometric disposition* (wholeness), *energetic disposition* (loving), *spiritual disposition* (personal), *acquisition disposition* (attraction), *mental disposition* (intuitive), and *social disposition* (feminine, liberal).

Geometric Disposition
We have a geometric disposition as a consequence of differences in viewpoint; the brain's two operating systems literally look in opposite,

back-to-back directions. In contrast to the linear disposition of the dualistic OS (think of a straight line bookended by polar opposites such as good/evil, right/wrong, true/false), the disposition of the holistic OS is omnidirectional (again, think of the center of a sphere in which awareness and personal interest or empathy radiate outward in all directions).

Another aspect of the geometry of holistic consciousness is the directional characteristic associated with unification. Using a space-time analogy, unification involves a drawing together or gathering to a common point—such as agreement, which can be represented as a single point.

Energetic Disposition

The force that powers attraction and builds the cohesion of unity and wholeness is love. Love is an energy that is obviously very attractive and cohesive, and thus magnetic. Whenever the holistic hemisphere is dominating our responses, love's magnetic effect on our overall disposition is more powerful than when the dualistic hemisphere is in charge, all else being equal.

Spiritual Disposition

A system that is energized by love and cooperation naturally exhibits and supports spiritual values, including service to others. Spiritual energies are *felt* energies. They are reflected through our emotions. In the processing of our emotions, the right hemisphere is dominant.[8]

Because the brain's holistic system is focused on the collective aspects of life, it naturally focuses on the primacy of collective rights (which are rights we have in common), rather than individual rights (which tend to be focused in the individual as an isolated unit and therefore are championed by those who view themselves in an adversarial relationship with society or government). Of course, collective and individual rights are far from mutually exclusive; but for the holistic mind, the focus on the collective is broader and more inclusive, emphasizing common interests more than the interests of one individual against perceived outside threats. Naturally then, people who are guided by holistic vision tend to work and advocate for social justice, the environment, and other large-scale issues outside of one's immediate individual sphere.

Given that holistic-dominant individuals attend to living things and service to others, we might expect that they respond in a personal manner in dealing with the universe—and this, as we've already seen, is what research shows. The close relationship between the right hemisphere's attention to the personal aspect of things and its attention to *living* things suggests its source energy, which is love. Love is personal. Service is loving.

The holistic-minded are interested in helping others even if there is a steep personal cost, *because they view others as parts of themselves*. Since both hemispheres contribute to our behavior, all mentally healthy individuals experience these responses to some degree, but when the altruistic hemisphere is the dominant hemisphere, we can expect the altruistic quest to be more pronounced. When our dominant hemisphere is dualistic, the energy of altruism may still prompt us to act—perhaps on the external authority of our religion or ethical upbringing or societal pressures—but such acts do not come as naturally. Our capacity for empathy is diminished by the dualistic system that is informing us.

Being trusting and tolerant, and seeing others as extensions of themselves, those with a strong holistic side tend to be freedom-giving.[9] In real life, this holistic response can be altered by cultural factors. But the holistic-minded person understands that in order to have freedom we must give freedom, and this incentivizes us. When dominated by our holistic hemisphere, we are energetically assisted in being able to do this because, in large part, we are being guided by a system that is personal (has an attitude that is understanding of the need for personal freedom), nonjudgmental (what you do is your business), and peaceful and cooperative (has no desire to fight the natural inclination of peaceful others to seek their ideas of freedom).

In harmony with the character of love, holistic consciousness is naturally inclusive, trusting, receptive, and tolerant of others. (In a healthy individual, the holistic system has the dualistic system watching out for its interests and informing it of danger, so the holistic system need not be directly concerned with threats.) To be loving, trusting, and tolerant is to be whole and in harmony with the world; and to be in harmony is to be at peace—even peaceful when provoked. We see quite clearly that losing our peace is neither loving to self nor loving to others. When holistic systems dominate, and our culture has not altered them by reprogramming us to accept fearful beliefs and responses, our attitude when provoked becomes, "What can we do to help you find your inner peace and love?" With such energies in play, the holistic individual is free to be submissive, not in the "rolling over and playing dead" sense or in the self-deluding sense, but in the sense of being truly available and enabling to others—even while drawing upon the dualistic system for sober analysis and protection.

Submission in the sense stated here implies a *caring* disposition, in contrast to a controlling (or using or exploiting) one.[10] There is a passionate quality to caring, which tends to override the strictures of control that predominate in the dualistic system; thus, the caring disposition, like many things in life, involves a degree of risk. On the other hand, controlling behaviors are extremely risky; ultimately, they involve the risks inherent in all forms of warfare.

When guided by a management system that is in harmony with the natural flow of the universe, where love and a sense of abundance predominate, cooperation becomes the natural state of affairs. And even the dualistic-oriented individual might be convinced by the obvious truth that cooperation is by far the more efficient way to run things.

Acquisition Disposition

To acquire the things we want and need, our holistic right hemisphere relies on the power of attraction. The holistic offers us something we want—beauty, wealth, information, power, sex, or some other aspect of unity—and pulls us in with it.

Holistic systems attend to or seek unification. Another word for unification is *synthesis*. We can contrast this with the left hemisphere's response of *analysis*, which involves differentiation. Whether processing our thoughts, our emotions, or the things we see in our world, the right hemisphere is looking at them in their wholeness or working to bring them into a state of wholeness and integration.

The integral (or integrative) approach of our holistic system is to bring the mind's diverse concepts together and connect them (the complement of the dualistic response to separate).

Cognitive Disposition

How does the brain's holistic operating system go about trying to understand the world for us? The brain has two primary approaches to learning: feeling and thought. Brain studies show that both hemispheres feel and think; nevertheless, our holistic hemisphere seems to take the lead in processing information that involves feeling (the spiritual aspect of life), whereas the dualistic hemisphere is believed to focus more on thought, which in its narrow sense is a linear, analytic process and is tied in to language. Perhaps we might describe the holistic hemisphere as a *thinking feeler*.

Thought in the broader sense is the mental approach to understanding things. Holistic thought is *intuitive*. And since the two systems are a team, with the dualistic feeding the holistic, it is not surprising to find that intuitive insights have been shown to have their origin in the sensing characteristics of the left brain's dualistic system—although intuition is not limited by what the senses have to tell us. Intuitive information is the product of an internal personal or cosmic source, and, contrary to the beliefs of those who dismiss intuition, it is grounded in reality and in universal processes.

Brain scientists have found that the right hemisphere *gathers what is new or novel to our experiential world*; only then can it come into the left hemisphere's focus.[11] The holistic system is aware of the whole of things, which means that it sees everything in its field of view. Naturally, when something new comes into its field of view, it is the first to see it. If we wish to make a closer inspection, the dualistic system will do so for us; it will judge its merits as a way of deciding what to believe.

Holistic consciousness conveys to us a mental attitude that is characteristically *believing* (in the sense of believing something to be true), in contrast with the *knowing* response of dualistic consciousness. The holistic's intuitive awareness that something is right or true does not necessarily equate with certainty, in the sense that the dualist's *knowing* does. Acting from dualistic consciousness, we are confident that we know the answer; acting from holistic consciousness, we understand that the certainty with which the dualistic left hemisphere views the world may well be an illusion. In a world as highly complex as the one in which we live, accurate answers are difficult to come by. As a result, the right hemisphere's holistic information system recognizes that the flexibility inherent in a sense of belief is usually a more accurate way to express our relationship with understanding and truth than is a sense of knowing.

Our holistic hemisphere can multitask. The speed with which intuition unfolds in the mind is a reflection of the simultaneous processing capabilities of holistic systems working in harmony, among other things. One of the reasons why the holistic right hemisphere is able to process information more rapidly than the left hemisphere is that it relies on parallel processing.

Social Disposition

Consider the qualities of the holistic hemisphere. It acquires by *attraction* (rather than dualistic aggression). It is *intuitive*, it *multitasks*, and it possesses a heightened *spiritual* sensitivity. It is *inclusive*, intent on *service*. It is oriented to the *personal*. Among the general population, these characteristics certainly appear more often in women than in men.

With the emphasis of holistic systems on the collective and on the needs of others, holistic systems tend to convey progressive social, cultural, and political attitudes and positions. This trait, however, can be greatly modified by the strong predominance of the dualistic mind-set in Western culture and, in particular, in American culture. A progressive attitude means that we are moving in new directions, taking chances, and eventually making progress in advancing the human condition. We have mentioned research that shows that information appears to the holistic hemisphere first. Those who see things first are naturally the first to notice when a useful new idea comes along, and consequently, they tend to be the first to use it in their response.

The reader might conclude from a too-casual reading of this chapter that the holistic mind-set is so superior that it can go it alone. Nothing can be further from the truth. Its ability to integrate the dualistic viewpoint is critical to our insights—and we are all dependent on the intercommunication between our two brain hemispheres, even though for most of us this process may be greatly compromised through our genetic dominance or flawed cultural programming that sets up limits or barriers.

In the next chapter we will look at the functions, capabilities, and shortcomings of dualistic operating systems.

CHAPTER 3

The Nature of Dualistic Operating Systems

The first principle is that you must not fool yourself and you are the easiest person to fool.

—Richard Feynman

Knowledge and the ability to control one's environment are typically associated with our capacity for language, and language has long been associated with the functions of the left brain hemisphere in most people. However, research over the last several decades has shown that both brain hemispheres have their unique linguistic functions—for example, the left brain by itself takes language too literally and does not understand the subtleties of metaphor as well as nonverbal cues that are a part of the larger picture of language. It is also, of course, true that when there are two functioning brain hemispheres, they are constantly intercommunicative and overlapping. Nevertheless, as we have already seen in the last chapter, there are real differences between the brain's two operating systems, and these differences are critical to how we—and our culture—process information. In this chapter we look at how the dualistic system (typically associated with the left brain) operates.

The Left Hemisphere's Analytic,
Detail-Oriented View

The viewpoint given us by our left hemisphere specializes in details, or parts. Details or parts are what appear if we take something apart, and that "something" may be a physical apparatus, an idea, an argument, or another human being. (In the last case "taking apart" might mean surgery, killing, analyzing, or simply describing, among other things!) We equate this process with discovery, and we equate new discoveries with expanded knowledge. This is largely how we conceive of technological and scientific progress. Actually, it's not quite as simple as that. Scientific breakthroughs are often made through intuitive leaps based on whole-picture views. But that is for another discussion.

Children and adolescents (especially boys) are well-known for taking things apart and then (one hopes) putting them back together; this can initiate a marvelous process of discovery and learning. The inside of a clock includes the mechanism that makes it tick; the hardware "under the skin" of a computer or electronic device includes the same thing, metaphorically. Closer to home, getting inside the brain and performing surgical procedures (a physical "taking apart") can tell us a lot about how our brain functions; without these procedures, our knowledge of the brain would be primitive indeed, and this book would not have been written.

Just as physical things have "insides," so do ideas. We can think of these insides as being hidden until they are "uncovered." If we are given a general "picture" of what is going on in some area, and we want to know more, we engage a process of uncovering the details. We see this in the news all the time; analysis uncovers the exteriors and shows us what is "behind" the headlines.

Analysis—a form of dualistic thought—tells us much of what we need to know. However, as we shall see, it also has a destructive side and is not always useful for finding the truth. And the bigger the "truth," the less useful the dualistic habit tends to be.

We previously discussed how the dualistic operating system tends to deal with smaller pieces of the whole—an observation that has been confirmed experimentally. However one looks at the dualistic method as it operates in the physical and mental worlds—as analysis, deconstruction, destruction, uncovering details—the "insides" that are revealed are, or can be viewed as, smaller pieces. Thus, there is the tendency to *look into things* and uncover what is ordinarily hidden. The advantages gained by such activity might include such areas as uncovering fraud and lies (something consumer watchdogs and news media often do), discovering false assumptions in an argument or scientific premise, breaking down statistics and variables to reveal public opinion (such as in polling), and finding and correcting omitted details of various and sundry sorts—and the list can go on and on.

The Dualistic Perspective— Our Left Brain's Information *Input*

In seeking to understand the nature of our dualistic perspective, we must always keep in mind that it is one half of a complementary system; the other half takes in the big picture, the context, and relationships. Together, the two viewpoints combine to see the whole of things. When the holistic system sees something that interests us, the dualistic then responds by focusing on it. By looking at the details, the left hemisphere attempts to give us a better understanding of hidden forces at work and the potential for threats, among other things.

A critical distinction to keep in mind is that the holistic takes in and includes all—*including the dualistic.* One may think of the holistic as horizontally expansive, in contrast to the dualistic, which plumbs the depths of something in an abstracted mode but fails to see the items around this "something" (the contexts and relationships) with which it interacts. If expressed diagrammatically, the two operating systems, rather than being expressed as two circles side by side, are one circle (the dualistic) *inside* the other (holistic). Ultimately, even the depth of the dualistic is subsumed by the holistic to create unity consciousness.

Expressed another way, the left hemisphere cannot see or understand that which the right hemisphere sees and understands; on the other hand, the right hemisphere, being holistic, *is* aware of what the dualistic is seeing and doing. (This is likely why women typically understand men better than men understand women.) And even though the left hemisphere "cannot see and does not understand what the right hemisphere understands," research shows that "it is expert at pretending that it does, at finding quite plausible, but bogus, explanations for the evidence that does not fit its version of events."[1]

Our dualistic hemisphere's focus, its perspective, can be expressed geometrically: it is *linear*. Focus, one of the most prominent characteristics of the brain's dualistic operating system, is linear in form. The nature of focusing on something is such that focus *directs* our attention toward a particular point or area within the viewing area. We can also get a sense of the linear structure of focus by drawing an imaginary line from our eyes to the object of our attention. And linearity can be expressed by the vertical metaphor of a plumb line—something that plumbs the surface and views what is beneath.

As previously discussed, dualistic consciousness is focused on and therefore shows us the *smaller* elements in our view.[2] Put another way, individual elements make up the focused view of the dualistic hemisphere. Size is, of course, like wholes and parts, a relative measure that shifts as our focus shifts. If we are looking at our solar system, its smaller elements are the sun and surrounding planets, and they are thought of as parts. If our consciousness is limited to the sun or a planet, the sun or the planet then becomes our whole and our focus will fall on some element of it.

In keeping with the size distinctions that characterize the attention of the two systems—larger and smaller components—dualistic systems can be said to see and show us the *text* of the holistic hemisphere's *context*. Another way of describing this behavior is to say that the dualistic operating system provides the details that we use to fill out the big picture.

The following characteristics of the dualistic operating system limit its field of view—a problem that is exacerbated by the fact that, by itself, it is unaware of its limitations:

- Its cognitive arena is confined to *that which is already known*.
- As previously pointed out, its focus is on *nonliving things*, rather than living things; and even where it might be interested in living things, it tends to regard them as nonliving (such as when we say that a person treats someone else as an object).
- It focuses on the use of *thoughts* to determine a response, largely at the expense of feelings and intuition.
- Its pattern of bringing things into focus is exclusionary—a focus on a particular thing implies lack of focus, or lack of attention, on other things. (One might say, in this connection, that the dualistic OS doesn't know what it doesn't know, so it falsely believes it knows everything relevant to the subject at hand.)

Dualistic consciousness tends to direct us to think and act in polarized terms. The nature of the brain's dualistic operating system is to separate things out, and this often gives us a polarized and polarizing view of our world. A corollary to this polarization is the dualistic system's strong competitive aspect; this competitiveness both reflects and encourages an oppositional, us-versus-them attitude, which is the attitude we see in war and conflict of all kinds. This attitude also seems to naturally follow from the dualistic system's narrow-focusing specialty, which results in hyper-concentration on one part of the picture at the expense of other parts.

Brain processing differences perhaps account for the tendency of the dualistic mind to engage in laborious procedures—such as conducting elaborate scientific studies—to discover things that the holistic, intuitive mind knew all along (such as, overeating causes sleepiness, or listening to certain types of music can stimulate or relax the mind, or Grandma's—or some "primitive" tribe's—strange cure for some ailment actually works). Why is the dualistic mind so clueless and inflexible in certain areas? When we are being guided or directed by our dualistic hemisphere, we are making our decisions based *not* on the *current* information of the holistic brain, but on historical information—in other words, *what we "know"* (or, really, what we *think* we know).[3]

Recognizing that this is how our dualistic hemisphere makes its decisions can be valuable. Once we become aware of this limitation, we can be aware of how our dualistic culture influences us, and—if the holistic system is our dominant one—we can proactively manage the system by seeking complementary perspectives.

The aforementioned tendency of dualistic consciousness to attend to nonliving aspects of life[4] goes a long way in explaining the highly materialistic nature of the world's dualistically managed cultures. When ideas are discussed and analyzed in the abstract, apart from feelings (the living component), life and spirit can be overlooked or even denied. As with other limitations of the dualistic mind-set, we can compensate for this deficiency—in ourselves or in our culture—in the manner described above.

To achieve a desired result often requires a devil's advocate approach. Wholeness is always the case, and the holistic brain sees this. But for this wholeness to shine through the various areas of our individual and collective life, real work is often required, and some trial and error is inevitable. The dualistic system is good at discovering flaws in the system—something we do when we find holes in someone's argument and tear it apart. One of the many jobs of the left brain is to determine if anything is missing from something that otherwise appears to be complete. Discovering a lack of wholeness helps to protect us from the deceptions of dishonest people or tricky situations that can be hidden behind a false façade of wholeness or truth. In this way the skeptical left brain is able to assist the trusting right brain in its pursuit of wholeness. It does this by finding problems before they become greater problems, and by helping to avoid costly detours.

Since dualistic consciousness is focused on the nonliving component of reality—and (as we have seen) on even looking at the living components through the same lens as nonliving components—there is a preoccupation with the material, with the sensory, with objects (or with objectification). Dualistic values, therefore, tend to be material, because that is the domain of the sensory and analytic mind. When this attitude is combined with what Iain McGilchrist describes as a hemisphere that is primarily motivated by power, we can better understand the source of the potent force that is responsible for so much of the world's chaos.[5] In contrast, holistic consciousness, as we have seen, provides us with a connection to nonmaterial—*felt* or *spiritual*—values. Of course, material security and enjoyment can enhance our emotional and spiritual life—and vice versa—so there is real need to integrate these values and functions in our consciousness.

Research has found that the right hemisphere (specifically the right frontal lobe) is the principal repository of all types of emotional energy and expression, except anger, which is mainly connected to the left hemisphere.[6] Nevertheless, certain behavioral dispositions stand out for each hemisphere. For the right, we can say that *love* is the energizing force (although I am not aware that this point has been made in any studies), because it sums up the holistic system's caring, inclusive, altruistic, and cooperative energies. Similarly, we can say that the left hemisphere is driven by *fear*. Even though fear is part of the emotional energy complex of the right hemisphere, it is the left hemisphere's dualistic system that generates the fear-driven and fear-causing qualities of violence, aggression, control, skepticism, and doubt.

The Left Hemisphere's *Response* to Its Perspective—Its *Output*

As was done with holistic operating systems in the last chapter, here I have divided the responses of dualistic operating systems into the same six broad categories—but in this case, of course, opposite or complementary characteristics define each category. Hence, for the dualistic operating system, the *geometric disposition* is one of linearity (rather than wholeness); the *energetic disposition* is energized by fear (rather than love); the *spiritual disposition* is impersonal and material (rather than personal and spiritual/emotional); the *acquisition disposition* is one of force and coercion (rather than attraction), the *cognitive disposition* is sensory-based (rather than intuitive), and the *social disposition* tends to be "masculine" and conservative (rather than "feminine" and liberal).

In those of us with left-hemispheric dominance, our default response—our mindless automatic response—will tend to be dualistic, just as those with right-hemispheric dominance will have a holistic default response. Again, however, there are two big caveats: First, as previously discussed, we are also influenced in a very big way by cultural factors. And, second, as we are spiritual beings, our responses to life's encounters are ours to choose of our own free will. The following detailed descriptions, then, refer to default dispositions, not inevitable points of view or behaviors.

Geometric Disposition

Dualistic systems respond in a manner that reflects their linear structure. Sequential thought (in which ideas are processed in sequence rather than all at once) is an example of this. Another example is the tendency to focus on particulars, resulting in the loss of context (or environment) and, consequently, built-in limitations to the information being processed.

In the process of breaking wholes down into parts for a more detailed inspection, dualistic systems must separate them, and the most basic division is into two parts based on their broad differences. When an idea, for example, is divided up into its two most fundamental characteristics, we refer to the action as *polarizing*. Using a geometric analogy, we may think of polarization as two energetic poles separated by a gap within which lies the continuum between the poles.

Energetic Disposition

Fear is universal among human beings. Without it, we would not survive. But, more often than not in our Western industrial civilization, it can be unhealthy and toxic to both the individual and society (the collective). What we fear, and how much we fear things, often bears little or no relationship to actual threats.

It may not be too much to say that fear—that is, the fear-inducing mind-set and the perpetuation of fear—is the energizing force of our dualistic operating system. The dualistic system looks out for our safety, and all safety concerns are accompanied by some level and version of fear. When implemented with intelligence and care, these concerns can be highly beneficial. On the other hand, fear is a strong controlling mechanism; it drives us to be exclusive, intolerant, and rejective of that which we judge (often mistakenly) to be harmful. Fear of losing our freedom (whatever that freedom may actually consist of) engages our aggressive nature and, rightly or wrongly, feeds our willingness to use violence to help us solve problems.

Dualistic systems are *electric* and therefore disruptive, in contrast to the attractive and integrative *magnetic* quality of holistic systems. Consider the effects of lightning. Like a bolt of lightning, the disruptive quality of the left brain's electrical system enables aggressive, violent, and warlike behavior. But because most of us have some contact with our holistic impulses, our holistic system tones down our dualistic impulses and holds them in restraint—at least most of the time—though they may still remain close to the surface.

Spiritual Disposition

Because dualistic consciousness dissociates from the personal, the emotional, and the empathetic, and tends to view things in an abstract, detached, and impersonal or "objective" way (that is, as objects and parts), it lacks the means to engage the subtler, more spiritual dimensions of life. Its focus therefore tends to be more materialistic. Materialism by its nature fails to fully notice, appreciate, or perhaps even acknowledge the existence of the energetic and spiritual dimensions of life—which include such nonmaterial qualities as love and joy, grief and sadness, awe and a profound sense of oneness. Thus, even though the dualistic mind-set may perceive itself as religious or as upholding strong values, it tends to be at the service of things we can see, touch, taste, smell, and hear.

Because it is impersonal, our dualistic system is more adept at avoiding sympathy with those people or things that might be threatening to us. This ability to detach from feelings can be an advantage when it comes to security—provided its judgments are grounded in reality.

Along with an emphasis on personal security comes a passion for individual rights and personal freedom. But this concern tends to be self-centered and is often blind to the rights of those who may be disadvantaged or simply "different" in some way that is interpreted unfavorably. The emphasis is on freedom *from* outside influences and the right to be left alone—a stance that tends *not* to be proactive in helping others. In addition, since those who are disadvantaged often fit into "collective" categories such as ethnicity, sex, or sexual orientation, helping such individuals tends to involve government agencies and the like, which are viewed as threatening to freedom.

Because the left hemisphere focuses on safeguarding and protecting the individual—particularly oneself and those in one's immediate personal sphere, as well as those with whom one identifies in a strong way—it exhibits an overall response that is *egoic*, or existentially selfish. *The left brain is the ego brain.* The responses we associate with the ego are quite simply a product of a self-centered, dualistic perception.

It should therefore come as no surprise that brain research suggests that the left hemisphere is *freedom-taking*,[7] in spite of its advocacy of freedom. In taking away the freedoms of other people, we are trying to control our environment and ensure our peace of mind. In other words, the dualistic brain sees one's own freedoms and the freedoms of others as antithetical, at least at times—so we limit people's options to do things that are seen as threatening our security. Dualistic operating systems are thus always on the lookout for people who might take advantage of us, and this leads to a default attitude of distrust and skepticism.

To secure our peace and our property, and to make good use of our opportunities, it is sometimes helpful to be distrustful, even intolerant and rejective. Although these qualities can indeed be harmful, they can also be helpful and necessary at times. For example, certain forms of self-destructive and other-destructive behavior—violence against others and certain addictive and criminal behaviors, for example—should not be tolerated under any circumstances. And sometimes it takes a dualistic mindset to see this.

The left hemisphere uses processes that are *excluding* or *exclusive*. Just as some kinds of intolerance have their place, the process of excluding does as well. To be secure in a dangerous world, certain things need to be excluded. The popular movement toward simple living and living in smaller spaces, for example, involves a lot of clearing of "dead wood." Sometimes exclusion gets more personal — it may be necessary to exclude friends and associates who may be seen to have a toxic influence on one's life. Likewise, exclusion of the unnecessary, expensive, unworkable, or dysfunctional is sometimes necessary in government and in industry. Exclusion is even an underlying principle of meditation, in which we take time off from obsessive activities and thought patterns in order to move closer to our true center.

The brain's dualistic operating system is *aggressive* in its response. This energy can be subtle and virtually unnoticed in action, or it can be annoying or even dangerous. It is the perfect complement to the holistic system, which, as we have seen, is submissive — in the sense of being open and accepting, and yielding when appropriate. When we integrate our aggressive and submissive tendencies, the combination allows us movement in the arena of life. The complementary nature of these two qualities can perhaps best be observed in traditional partner dance, where the male leads and the female follows. In the interest of providing us with security and fostering our freedom in a world where our cultures often try to dominate us, we need to have an aggressive side. Aggression allows us to reach outward to engage the world. It is a tool of acquisition. Energetically the continuum of aggression begins — at its "low" end — with a gentle nudge that we would usually find quite acceptable. At the opposite end, it can be elevated to an extreme — even a ballistic state. Of course, most aggression takes place somewhere on the continuum between the two extremes.

At its most negative extreme, the left brain's aggressive focus on security, combined with being impersonal and energized by fear, sets up conditions that can be favorable to violence and war or warlike activities — actions it justifies based on a need for security and "freedom."

Another characteristic contributing to the tendency toward war is the dualistic hemisphere's strong competitive streak. Competition, like other characteristics of the dualistic brain, has both a helpful side (it can contribute to great achievements) and a dark side. War and other forms of conflict involve winning and losing, and war and killing activate a kind of exuberant intoxication in many people[8] that is enhanced by the dualistic system's objectification and depersonalization of others—especially those viewed as the enemy.

Being in control of our environment is an essential requirement for security, and this may also require a degree of control over others. In other words, to maintain our own freedom, it may be necessary (or perceived as necessary) for others to lose some of their freedom. This trade-off is not particularly bothersome to the impersonal and egoic left brain; self-protection is its priority.

Acquisition Disposition

Whereas the holistic attracts things to itself, the dualistic reaches out for what it wants. Although we may view *aggression* as a spiritual choice, as discussed in the preceding section, it also underlies the acquisition disposition of the dualistic.

In moderation, aggression can be a force for good. However, it hangs out in the same operating system with other rowdy forces, and when they get together, they have a tendency to cause trouble. In keeping with the selfish left brain's acceptance of aggressive responses, its natural response in acquiring things is the use of force or coercion. Because of the sense of separation that the dualistic brain experiences, when it is our only guide, we do not feel the discomfort of the unwilling who bear the brunt of our aggression—unless we exert conscious control and/or there is sufficient holistic input.

Cognitive Disposition

Perhaps the most commonly used description of the left brain's dualistic approach to cognition is that it is *analytic*. The process of analyzing is a reductionist, separative, and disintegrative process that takes us deeper into our subject in a quest to acquire new details. In keeping with its viewpoint, analysis is a focused, abstracted process. The brain's analytical systems break down wholeness into more comprehensible, more mentally manageable sizes for us to wrap our minds around. When we analyze something, we inquire into the nature of things through an exploration of its parts. If one expresses an interest in having more specific information about something than we have seen from our big-picture perspective, our dualistic operating system springs its analytical function into action to search for answers.

There are several facets to being analytical, as mentioned above. One of these—the *reductionist* approach—explains things by breaking them down into smaller parts to see what is driving them. In addition, as elements of a whole are divided up, they are separated, so we characterize the dualistic as *separative* in function. A process that works to separate and reduce reality can also be described as *disintegrative*. From his extensive research into functional lateralization in humans, McGilchrist has commented, "If one had to characterize the left hemisphere by reference to one governing principle it would be that of division."[9] Whereas holistic systems are always open to new information and experiences, dualistic systems are closed systems, dealing only with what they already know.[10] Dualistic systems are characterized by a sense of certainty, but this certainty is based on a limited focus. Thus, the left brain believes that the answers it needs are contained in its closed system—which leads, ironically, to certitude that it knows everything relevant to the issue being focused on. In contrast, holistic systems—which are able to take in and be awestruck by the magnificent scope of the universe and the significance of the new—respond with a strong, intuitive affirmation that shows up as belief but not certitude. The left hemisphere's disposition can be expressed as "This is the way it is"; the right hemisphere takes in new data and says, "Wow, this seems to change things."

Under the influence of dualistic consciousness, we respond to the information already available to it. When our dualistic system is in charge, unless we step in and choose otherwise, our response will almost certainly be based on stored information, meaning we will tend to respond based on the response patterns that have proved most successful in the past.

The bulk of the internally sourced information sent to mind comes from two main sources, *sensing* and *intuition*. The processing of data given to us by the physical senses—seeing, hearing, smelling, tasting, touching—is led by the left hemisphere. Intuition and immediate apprehension are specialties of the right hemisphere.

Information coming to us needs to be evaluated in order to be correctly sorted. Evaluation is a judging process in which we discern between options, estimate, and assess. Judging is a part of the dualistic system because it is a separative process. Being separative, the process of judgment has the capability to lead to destructive consequences. On the other hand, from the fullest holistic perspective we accept what we see as an expression of the universe and have no judgment. Seeing from both perspectives as we do, we naturally position ourselves somewhere in between. But judging does not take place without input from both hemispheres. Both play an important role in judging; for example, the right hemisphere sees the overall relationship of the elements, a perspective that is essential to making good judgments.

Social Disposition

Although not all of the characteristics that we have associated with the two systems suggest gender, those that do seem consistent with a pattern based on the usual ways masculine and feminine behavior are perceived. For example, when we consider that the natural response of dualistic operating systems is to be *analytic, aggressive, controlling, egoic, thinking,* and *impersonal,* with a tendency toward the use of *force* and *violence* to obtain whatever is wanted, we are faced with a group of compatible characteristics that are strongly suggestive of a masculine temperament; and the opposite qualities suggest a feminine temperament.

Another prominent social characteristic of the brain's dualistic operating system is to encourage and support the conserving and protecting of what we have—whether it is our lives, our things, our comfort, or something else we identify with or value. The conserving and the controlling aspects of the dualistic system work closely together, because to be in a position to conserve something it helps to have control over it. Another example of a conserving response is the dualistic operating system's primal focus on *individual* security and survival—specifically, one's own security and survival; and this includes all the things we identify as parts of us, such as our lifestyle and our relationship to the material world.

The dualistic left hemisphere analyzes, ranks, reduces, and deconstructs whatever it finds in its mental view—and in a cultural context especially, it destroys, devalues, and takes reductionist stances. The dualistic hemisphere is a superb tool for arriving at what is true by separating the wheat from the chaff, and for making fine and necessary distinctions of all kinds. However, its tendency toward abstraction can result in such total separation from the whole that whatever lies outside of its focus is either completely devalued or not even acknowledged. Therefore, effective and humane decision-making requires the cooperative efforts of both brain hemispheres.

With such cooperation, every characteristic of the dualistic system can be put to constructive use. Indeed, its point of view is necessary for the attainment of a full perspective in the context of unity consciousness. But this can happen only if the dualistic and holistic perspectives are integrated in the culture and in ourselves. The good news is, this is possible even if the dualistic hemisphere is the dominant one for us.

CHAPTER 4

Gender War

Justice cannot be for one side alone, but must be for both.

—Eleanor Roosevelt

Differences in behavior that arise from differences in gender account for much of the conflict that we experience in life. Gender-based variations in how we respond to events create such a powerful tension between men and women that the situation has often been described as "the war between the sexes." All too often, this gender war goes well beyond the metaphorical.

The extensive physical abuse of women by many of the men of this planet is an act of war in all but one respect—its one-sidedness. It is really a war waged against women *by* men, and even by women who adopt the male viewpoint. We could use the same war analogy—with the same qualification—to describe the widespread abuse inflicted on individuals whose sexual identity differs from the culturally accepted norm.

Like all wars, gender wars are weaponized. The weapons used in gender war are physical, mental, and spiritual in their energy, and include discrimination, condemnation, intimidation, ostracism, beatings, and other fear-based aggressions—any response that might cause pain and thus perhaps serve as punishment and a deterrent to resistance.

The damage caused in gender warfare is most often emotional and thus hidden from outside view. However, we can get a good sense of the power and emotional damage inflicted by this war from the many suicides it generates.

Like so many conflicts, gender war is the product of a lack of understanding coupled with an unwillingness to tolerate things that we have not learned how to accommodate. Gender issues tend to cause trouble because they trigger confusion and aggravation as we try to accommodate the problems that they generate. Am I now required to refer to him as a she? Do we have to add transgender restrooms to our schools and our workplaces? Won't we need one for transitioning males and one for transitioning females?

What do we need to do to end wars based on gender differences? To start with, we need people to understand the nature of the forces driving the behaviors that trouble them. Only then can they hope to begin to learn to accept the strange but real other world in its wholeness as normal and deal with it knowledgeably.

Gender and *sex* are often used interchangeably, but they are not the same. The key to understanding their difference is simple. Sex is a physical attribute; gender is a nonphysical attribute. You can usually tell someone's sex by looking at their body. Gender, on the other hand, has more to do with a person's mental and spiritual demeanor.

The intensity of gender can vary greatly from one individual to another. At the low end of the range we may have great difficulty recognizing a person's gender at all. But in most cases there are clues to one's gender—such as physical responses that may be reflective of the individual's gender identification, or taking on an outer appearance that matches one's gender.

In most people, gender and sex match. If you have a female body, you also have a feminine gender. But that is just the dominant pattern. In another pattern, gender is reversed, thereby fitting a female body with a masculine gender or a male body with a feminine gender. As one might imagine, coping with this alternative pattern can create profound internal conflict. And sometimes the conflict is so powerful that individuals can be mentally and emotionally driven to do anything to achieve a state of harmony, including surgery.

Cognitive Dissonance

As with those who are transgender, those who are troubled by the idea that someone else might be transgender inevitably experience *cognitive dissonance*, mental disharmony arising from an internal mental conflict. Most of us have been taught that if someone has a male body, he should possess a masculine gender. As this is our customary education and experience, other combinations are considered abnormal and create a conflict in our mind between what we expect and what we find.

When contradictory situations such as this occur in our lives, a sense of dissonance arises, signaling that something is wrong. It is often the beliefs we bring to the situation that create the discordant experience we may have when confronted with transgender individuals—or when confronted with any other situation perceived as ambiguous or contrary to our sense of order and propriety. Thus the required adjustment is not in the perceived situation but in our own system of beliefs and assumptions.

When we are faced with the conflict of dissonance, a typical dualistic response is to seek to *control* the dissonant elements of the situation—usually the person or persons seen as being responsible for the discomfort created by the dissonance. But controlling the situation often means that we need to control others' behavior—in other words, force them to change their behavior or beliefs to support our goals. Of course, forcing people to do something they don't want to do is an act that often leads to conflict and war. This force need not be direct; it often occurs by proxy, such as when we make a mark on a ballot to support a politician or initiative that places restrictions on the rights and freedoms of others. Remember that when we are operating under the influence of dualistic consciousness, our responses tend to rely on control methods such as abdication and suppression, both of which often require violence to enforce.

The Challenges of Determining What Is Normal

Having established the link between masculine behavior and the consciousness typical of the left hemisphere's dualistic operating system, and being aware of the link between feminine behavior and holistic consciousness, we are now ready to look at how gender and sex combine in novel ways to create a diversity of sexual orientations. Our exploration of gender and sexuality will rest solidly on neuroscience as well as dominance and genetics, but with an exploratory reach that will undoubtedly lead to controversial conclusions. With that in mind, I suggest you keep the following in mind. First, our understanding of gender and sexuality is undergoing a revolution, as suggested by *Time* magazine's June 9, 2014, cover story titled "The Transgender Tipping Point." Second, this revolution has a basis in neuroscience and genetics, but it also is energized by powerful forces of a spiritual and energetic nature that involve a great expansion of the boundaries of self-exploration. A deeper understanding of these issues must have scientific underpinnings, but it also must explore beyond the strict observational protocols of the laboratory. A broad understanding of the issue must encompass all of these things.

Another thing that has come to the attention of researchers is that this "revolution" is not entirely new, and some other cultures are well ahead of us. Just as the left and right brain hemispheres were studied and theorized about for centuries before the work of Sperry and his colleagues, sexuality and gender likewise have been defined and expressed in many ways in both modern and traditional societies. Many cultures have a long history of recognizing a nuanced complexity of sexual orientations based on gender expressions that go beyond the exclusive male/female duality.

Finally, I view the "conclusions" presented here as part of an ongoing process of understanding gender and sexuality that will continue to evolve and be debated. Research in these areas is still in its infancy, and there is a lot that we don't understand; but responsible speculation, based on but not limited by the current science, cannot wait for final understanding. (For the sake of brevity and precision, I will generally *not* be taking on the speculative voice; so, as you read on, please keep the present discussion in mind.) At this time in our history, when ancient hatreds threaten to overwhelm timeless insights, we must feed the insights through a speculative conversation. The issues are too crucial for us to ignore. It is imperative that we understand each other, through all our variety, rather than fearing "difference." If we can reach this point, then wars against each other—and wars within ourselves—will begin to dissipate.

Normal means many different things to different people. In determining what is normal, by necessity we draw heavily on our education and upbringing, our experience, and the prevailing scientific and religious understanding.

In truth, *normal* is a reflection of reality rather than of belief. So, for example, if evidence were to show that bisexuals make up 1 to 2 percent of the population as a result of genetic factors (I have not found a number that I feel is reliable), bisexuality would be considered normal. That the number might be small does not make bisexuality abnormal.

One of the roles of science is to find out what is normal, but the study of sexuality even among scientists has been rife with dogma, phobias, and cultural biases—as demonstrated, for example, by the fact that, before 1973, the psychiatric profession in its official diagnostic manual (DSM) regarded homosexuality as a disorder. Even now, in spite of a more open attitude toward sexuality, gender studies that might shed a favorable light on "nonconventional" gender identities and sexual orientations still receive limited acceptance.

If we are to accurately understand the fundamental forces that are driving human sexuality, it is critical that we comprehend the simple foundation on which gender and gender relationships are built. Because gender is a multifaceted subject, we can only begin to explore it here. In this chapter and the following one on sexual orientation, we will look at how genetic mechanisms and the forces of dominance combine in various ways to produce gender variations and sexual orientations that are truly normal yet lie outside the bounds of our current definition of the word.

The Fundamental Nature of Gender

In *Gay, Straight, and the Reason Why: The Science of Sexual Orientation*, Simon LeVay explains, "Sexual orientation is an aspect of gender that emerges from the prenatal sexual differentiation of the brain. Whether a person ends up gay or straight depends in large part on how this process of biological differentiation goes forward, with the lead actors being genes, sex hormones, and the brain systems that are influenced by them."[1] In the remainder of this chapter, as well as in the next chapter, we look at the relationship of these three elements and their contribution to gender and sexual orientation.

To start our brief exploration into the nature of gender, we want to recognize that gender is perhaps most profoundly experienced through the energy of feeling—specifically, the feelings associated with the functioning (perspective and response) of our dominant hemisphere. In addition, our concept of gender reflects a sense of being, and so gender is closely tied to our identity. So, for example, because the right hemisphere's holistic system embodies the functional characteristics we identify with a feminine viewpoint and response, the holistic operating system can be said to function in a way that has a feminine feel, or *gender*.

Gender as we have come to know it is a two-part reality, a complementary division of wholeness into masculine and feminine parts. Divided in this way, gender allows us to more easily and accurately experience the range of differences that exist within the boundaries of wholeness.

The separation of wholeness into the two established genders is accomplished through a genetic mechanism that institutes dominance. By suppressing the contribution of the nondominant system and its gender, dominance sets up the dominant side to have full managerial control. Under this system of dominance we are given conscious access to just one of our two hemispheres, and thus we learn to identify with its characteristics; nevertheless, both hemispheres continue to function as information gatherers and processors. Under this system, one side manages both sides, meaning that unity of command is maintained, which ensures that someone or some process is in control rather than the two fighting over control.

Our Four Operating-System Options

In discussing brain operating systems, we have considered only two, but we can inherit any one of four. In addition to holistic or dualistic operating systems acting alone, genetic dominance mechanisms can configure to operate as either a unified team or a hybrid integration.

Each of the four operating systems has its own unique perspective. Each has its own characteristic approach to processing and responding to its information inputs, and so eachsees and shows us a somewhat different view of our world and has different methods for responding to what it detects—the ideas, people, and events that populate our lives. Therefore, each system type possesses its own characteristic differences in function and feeling. As we have suggested, function and feeling produce the bulk of our experience and awareness of gender.

Although the mainstream scientific community recognizes the existence of only two genders at this time, we might (and, I would argue, ought to) classify various integrations of gender as gender, in the same way that spice combinations in a recipe have their own unique characteristics and are often given unique names.

If you feel it is presumptuous to refer to integrations of gender as third and fourth types of gender, you may wish to think of a different descriptive term as you read through this chapter. However, there is precedent for this in traditional cultural settings, and this kind of terminology is increasingly used by individuals who do not fit the gender norms.

I am proposing that there are at least three genetic systems governing hemispheric dominance. They produce at least four expressions of gender.

In *genetic complete dominance*, one of two hemispheric operating systems completely dominates the other, imbuing us with its functional characteristics, those we associate with masculine or feminine attitudes. Since genetic complete dominance produces two expressions of gender, it is a dualistic system. The next two operating systems that we will look at are holistic systems; each system is all-encompassing and produces just one expression of gender.

When our genetic assignment is *codominance*, our two operating systems work together cooperatively to give us a harmonious *unity* of masculine and feminine perspectives and responses. A codominant operating system gives us *unity consciousness* and *unity gender*. In this team-oriented operating system, the masculine component of one's operating system is attracted to women and the feminine component to men. Genetic codominance produces bisexuals.

The third type of brain operating system is produced by *genetic incomplete dominance*. Incomplete dominance produces a *hybrid version of unity consciousness*. A *hybrid version of unity gender* is made up of a *blend* of masculine and feminine gender. I refer to members of this group as polysexuals, though this might or might not be the best term to describe them. A lack of research focused on hybrid behavior greatly restricts our ability to understand, and consequently to describe, the sexual behavior of hybrids.

To illustrate the difference between the two genetically integrated systems, we can turn to our knowledge of nature. Consider a red and a white flower and their offspring. *Codominance* will produce flowers that display both red and white, whereas *incomplete dominance* will give us a different color, a mixture—some shade of pink. Similarly, incomplete dominance transforms our two hemispheric operating systems (OS) into a hybrid OS, and as a hybrid, our gender reflects some mixture of masculine and feminine characteristics. While the composition of the mixture might or might not be fixed in an individual, our knowledge of mixtures suggests that we might expect the mixture to range from extremely masculine with just a touch of the feminine to extremely feminine with a hint of the masculine.

It is important to remember that the lines we draw in order to categorize a gender are artificial and arbitrary efforts used in an attempt to distinguish among a vast array of differences in characteristics along a dynamic continuum. In our discussions it is useful to totally separate the contributions of the two hemispheres, but in real life these clear-cut divisions do not exist in this way.

The strength or presence of gender—the degree of intensity of masculine or feminine responses—is highly variable from individual to individual. It also depends to an extent on the beholder: what constitutes masculine or feminine characteristics varies depending on which individual or culture is making the determination. Nevertheless, there is a consensus on the core characteristics of masculinity and femininity—and the variability of these qualities from individual to individual (animals as well as humans) is indisputable. In addition to the genetic systems discussed above, there appear to be hormonal determinants of this variability as well. Both animal and human studies have shown that the sex hormone responsible for this variation appears to be testosterone.[2]

Thus, variability in both brain operating-system dominance and hormonal levels (supplemented by cultural factors) accounts for our sense of gender. The dominance of one brain operating system over the other may be overwhelming (totally dominating), high (strong), low (weak), barely perceptible (extremely weak), imperceptible, or somewhere in between. Consequently, there may be equally high, low, or imperceptible levels of gender awareness and expression.

When someone is positioned near the center of the masculine/feminine continuum, for example—as might be the case for someone with a hybrid OS—it might not be apparent to others, or even to that individual, what their gender is. In that case, cultural forces might dominate. For this and other reasons, there will be many apparent exceptions to the patterns that we are discussing. Some of these are not *really* exceptions, but rather are secondary patterns that are not yet widely recognized.

The Continuum of *Response* and Its Role in Determining Gender

In addition to giving us a default *perspective* of our world to serve as a base viewpoint from which to guide our journey through life, our brain provides us with a default *response*, an innate reaction, selected examples of which can be found in the list of unity consciousness characteristics in chapter 1. *Problem solving* and *self-protection* are examples of two critical responses carried out by the brain. The brain also suggests responses to us that we can implement or ignore.

We have been focusing on information inputs—what we see from our perspective, given our genetically determined viewpoint. We are now going to shift our attention to the brain's information output, its response. *Response*, as used here, is intended as an exceptionally broad term that encapsulates the brain's attempt to serve us physically, mentally, and emotionally, and to understand and deal with issues brought to its attention by our various inputs. Our response begins by producing a perception, a cognitive response developed from an information input as we think about what we have seen, heard, smelled, tasted, or felt. Choosing to do nothing is a response.

Like our default *perspective*, our default *response* is partly inherited (and therefore fundamentally fixed) and partly a freewill choice (and therefore fundamentally variable). And of course, in addition to our personal response, we can and do look to our culture for an appropriate response—how do our friends, our neighbors, and our parents respond to similar events? If a certain response worked well for them, perhaps it will work for us. Our brief observations will focus on the inherited or default aspect of our personal response—as that will be of most value to most individuals in coming to understand themselves.

The brain's responses, like the perspectives that initiate them, appear divided into complementary pairs that seem to be opposites. Thus, *peace*—the harmonious, cooperative, "we"-serving response of the holistic perspective—comes paired with *war* (in the broadest usage of the term), the forceful, "me"-serving, "us-versus-them" response associated with the dualistic perspective. Challenged by others as they constantly seek to impose their choices on us and get us to stand with and support them, we need to decide where on the continuum of ideas (such as war and peace) to place ourselves and express who it is that we truly are.

Because our responses are formed and executed in gender-specific operating systems, *our responses convey characteristics of gender*. When responses originating in our dualistic operating system predominate, regardless of our sex, our responses tend to be forged primarily from characteristics such as those we find on the dualistic side of the unity consciousness list, several of which are viewed as masculine. When responses originating in our holistic operating system predominate, then our responses tend to be feminine or integrated in character.

Whereas our brain's *perspectives* are relatively private—after all, they are just inputs of information—our brain's *responses* often make an appearance through our behavior. As a result, they can be very public—even if they are subtle, as body language often is. And although a response can come from a different OS than the one that triggered it, quite often perspective and response are matched. If we view life through dualistic consciousness as a result of dualistic dominance, our tendency is to respond dualistically.

In spite of the hidden quality of our perspective, because perspective and response tend to operate as a team, we can often identify someone's perspective from observing their responses, perhaps the most obvious of which is how they move their body. Determination is easiest when dominance is strong and unrestrained. Of course, the purity of natural bodily movement can always be consciously altered, but in the absence of purposeful changes, by observing someone's body language, we can often identify the perspective that generated it.

How the Brain's Input and Output Functions Affect Gender

We have seen that the operating system that gives us our *perspective* has a gender associated with it based on its operational characteristics. Our *response* too is the product of an operating system that has a gender associated with it. We see this reflected in the fundamental differences in behavior between men and women. And since information input and information output are separate actions, and thus separate variables, we are given *two* opportunities to experience one of four operating systems and their gender characteristics. We can, for example, inherit a holistic input and a dualistic output (handedness studies suggest that this might include a majority of women). That our information input may express one gender and our information output may express another is most easily recognized in masculine-acting straight women and feminine-acting straight men.

Each of us has an *input* gender and an *output* gender. Of course, if the input and output gender are the same, we will identify as simply masculine or feminine. But even if the input and output genders are different, one may be strong and the other weak. In such a case, our experience might still be of possessing only the stronger (input *or* output) gender expression. Because our *input* gender can be either feminine, masculine, hybrid, or a team effort, and our *output* gender can also be any one of the four, the scene is set for us to inherit any one of 16 gender combinations. With each sex having 16 possible variations in gender, there are 32 total variations. We will explore the consequences of having 32 combinations in the next chapter.

The Complexities of Gender

Each of the four genetically determined operating system types—*holistic, dualistic, hybrid,* and *unity*—has its own way of seeing and understanding the world, its own functional characteristics and feel, and thus its own identity—and these four systems, along with the sexual hormones that vary the intensity of gender and otherwise help characterize it, are the main components that underlie our sense of gender.

Brain operating systems have two primal functions. They inform us (input information through a perspective), and they give us a response (output information through action, including thought). Both our consciousness of perspective and the character of our response embody characteristics of gender, and sometimes the gender of our dominant perspective is different than the gender provided by our dominant response.

Combining the four types of perspective and the four types of response gives us sixteen possible operating-system combinations and sixteen possible gender variations for each sex. For many people, both operating systems are the same, so they experience having only one gender. Others might find that they have a feminine input of information and yet typically employ a masculine response—or vice versa. Or, instead of two of the traditional genders, we may experience one or both of the integrated genders.

Handedness studies suggest that most women are right-handed, which means that their left hemisphere is dominant for output. This combination gives these women a feminine view of the world, which allows them to see the wholeness of things, to see the context without having to look for it, to have special insight into the world of feeling and thus see where we are going spiritually. And in addition, by having a masculine output, these women also have an innate ability to respond in kind to our masculine-dominated world and thus compete well in dualistically organized cultures. As compared with women possessing a feminine input *and* output, these women enjoy an enhanced ability to share their feminine insights with the masculine world. *Feminine input/ masculine output* women have the inherent ability to communicate with the separative consciousness of a masculine culture on its dualistic terms. In doing so, they help prepare the way for the resurgence of the Divine Feminine.

CHAPTER 5

○○

The Complexities of
Sexual Orientation

Well, actually, I'm a bisexual lesbian in a man's body . . . but it's more complicated than that.

—Tony Parker, professional basketball player

Although sexual-orientation research is still heavily focused on genetics, social conditioning, and hormones, the role of the brain is increasingly being taken into account. A body of scientific research has now established that the brains of gay men show strong similarities to the brains of heterosexual women in many respects; and the brains of lesbian women show areas of similarity to those of heterosexual men.

The hypothesis I present in this chapter takes these findings a step further. I am proposing that the brains of homosexual men and heterosexual women are similar in that they involve *shared mental perspectives, the result of shared brain operating systems*; and the same holds true with the brains of homosexual women and heterosexual men. Furthermore, as we saw in the last chapter, from the integration of masculine and feminine characteristics we gain two additional gender types; and, as we shall see, each of these has its own effect on sexual orientation.

The characteristics that we associate with gender and sexual orientation are born out of the functional characteristics of the brain's operating systems. Each system has its own characteristic viewpoint (or, in the case of codominance, viewpoints), and each has its own specialized approach when it comes to responding to the information that we encounter. As a result, each system sees and shows us a somewhat different view of our world and offers us different methods for responding to people, ideas, and events. If we are to truly understand sexual orientation, a part of that job is to understand how our operating systems interface with each other and with the rest of who and what we are.

Is our sexual orientation a choice? Recent research—both brain-based and non-brain-based—lends strong support to the position that it is *not* a choice. I believe my findings are consistent with and complementary to most of this research. I've found no credible evidence that we can permanently change inherited dominance patterns or the natural behaviors that result, sexual orientations included. Nevertheless, it is possible to *temporarily* switch out of our dominant perspective or response by inquiring into areas that demand insights in which our recessive hemisphere specializes, and we will occasionally refer to that possibility. We initiate the temporary switch when, based on an understanding of our own dominance, we consciously seek (or allow) a nondominant perspective or response.

Perspective and Gender

Perspective is a relatively simple concept, yet because it feeds the all-important perception that we rely on for guidance, how we manage our perspective determines how we ultimately behave, and it contributes to our personal and social identity as well. Those of us who view life from a dualistic perspective develop a substantially different perception than those who view life from its holistic complement. Because our attention is literally engaged with different parts and aspects of the whole most of the time, it is as if we inhabit two different universes.

If your dominant brain perspective were to suddenly switch, you would see things very differently—in fact, everything about your life would change. One of many areas that would change would be your sexual orientation. To generalize: most men respond or behave as they do because their dominant view of life comes to mind through the separative lens of their dualistic hemisphere, which is masculine in character. Most women behave as they do because they perceive life from the feminine orientation of the holistic perspective, which gives us an integrated, big-picture perspective that is inclusive of the dualistic operating system's more specialized functions (thus, as we've said, women generally understand men better than men understand women).

Although *most* males are guided by dualistic consciousness as a result of a dominant left hemisphere, and *most* females are guided by the holistic consciousness of the right hemisphere, there are many exceptions. The most notable of these include lesbians and gay men. In those groups, my research suggests, perspective (and thus perception) is the *reverse* of what it is among heterosexuals of their sex. In other words, gay men respond in ways that show holistic system dominance, and lesbians respond in ways that show dualistic system dominance. Another exception to the standard orientation of masculine and feminine is found in dualistic and holistic operating systems working together as equals. When masculine and feminine systems are *both* dominant (genetically codominant), we are drawn to both genders and sexes, making us bisexual. If, instead, masculine and feminine perspectives are integrated, as in the case of incomplete dominance, we experience a blending of gender, producing a mixed orientation such as we might find in polysexuality.

Research mentioned later in this chapter suggests that women enjoy a broader range of sexuality than do men. If so, we might logically expect a hybrid perspective that includes a strong feminine component to widen the sexual range of such individuals.

Dominance and Sexuality

My insights into the connection between brain-dominance reversal and sexuality came about while developing a list of characteristics to explain the typical behaviors of left-brain-dominants (or those who are on the dualistic end of the spectrum)—the majority of whom are males. What effect, I wondered, would right-brain (or holistic) dominance in males have on their behavior? Similarly, what would be the effect of left-brain dominance in females?

I quickly remembered something we all know at some level: mind is dominant over matter. Our sexual organs are activated by signals coming from our mind and brain. When the holistic operating system informs a man, his experience of life will be based on the perspective typical of holistic heterosexual women and he will tend to respond accordingly. (Remember that we are discussing perspective here, not perception, which is far more complex due to its diverse contributions.) *That he has a male body does not alter the fact that the screen of his mind is constantly dominated by holistic observations, but having a holistic perspective does alter his sexual response.*

When a male is fed, and thus effectively led, by a holistic operating system, the complex of factors that make up his sexual identity and orientation are profoundly affected. Guided by the OS that typically guides women, such individuals see and want more or less what the typical female sees and wants—and, as we might expect given this scenario, that often includes a male partner. Likewise, a female, informed and thus directed by the OS typical of men, will be turned on by the same experiences as men with a dualistic OS, and that includes a strong interest in other women.

Sexual attraction has its roots in the brain/mind complex. Specifically, sexual attraction is the product of two complementary operating systems seeking completion or wholeness and working through the brain. By way of example, I'll illustrate how this works through our visual sense.

In sacred geometry—which involves the study and contemplation of pure form and reveals the underlying structure of reality—straight lines are considered male lines and curved lines are thought of as female lines. The holistic system, being feminine in perspective and seeking completion (wholeness), is visually attracted to her complement, as expressed through male lines—to the geometry of the male body—including, but not limited to, the sexual organs. (See chapter 7, "Sacred Geometry's Role in Perception.")

A recent Harvard University study[1] involving attraction to various types of faces lends support to the concept of structural relationships implied by sacred geometry. It showed that gay men—which my research suggests are men guided by their holistic, feminine OS—were most attracted to the more masculine-faced men (those with generally more angular, less rounded features). Heterosexual men were attracted to the most feminine-faced women—and when choosing the *men* whose faces they preferred (in a nonsexual sense), their choices were more feminine than those of gay men. Straight women, like gay men, were most attracted to the more masculine-faced men (although women's preferences were more complex because they were influenced to a greater degree by other factors, such as ovulation, contraceptive use, self-perceived attractiveness, and sex drive). Lesbian women in that study preferred more masculine female faces than did straight women or men.

Of course, many factors contribute to sexual attraction and behavior, ranging from genetic and hormonal factors to cultural influences. Cultural factors can weigh heavily on our decisions and even dominate. Nevertheless, in important and decisive ways, our mind—which is the arbiter of our *creative* energy—is in the driver's seat. The creative energies of the mind are in charge of and direct the body, not the other way around—although when I suggest that the mind directs the body, I do *not* mean to imply that sexuality is subject to being changed by mental intention.

Our sexual response is the result of a dominant perspective acquired through genetic forces, and then reinforced through years of experience. The evidence suggests it is fixed. We see evidence of the mind's influence over the body in observable, mind-directed behaviors such as gestures, body language, speech patterns, and the like. Obviously the way one speaks or moves his or her body can be either suppressed or exaggerated, but there is still a strong connection between mental energy and the *natural* bodily expressions of any individual—gay, straight, bi, or hybrid.

A gay man can try to respond like a straight male and can suppress outward behaviors, thus bringing him a bit more in line with cultural expectations, but it is not going to change his primal holistic orientation—his dominant perspective. At a deeper level he is still going to respond to life in the same way that we all respond—based on what his brain is showing him rather than on what others see and suggest. The experiences of gays and lesbians who have desperately tried to go straight in order to avoid negative social stigmas and potentially life-threatening bullying attest to the futility of trying to be someone we are not.

In numerous studies covering a wide range of subjects, neuroscientists have found that gay men and heterosexual women tend to exhibit similar responses to stimuli, and even that they demonstrate similar abilities and behavioral tendencies. This is also often true of lesbians and heterosexual men.

In areas ranging from verbal fluency and/or verbal association (often strongest in straight women and gay men) to childhood activities and sports participation (with gays and lesbians participating less in gender-typical activities and more in activities associated with the opposite gender), numerous studies have shown these associations.

Thirty-Two Variations on Sexual Orientation

We tend to think of both gender and sexual orientation in binary terms. You are either male or female, straight or gay (or bi, which is both straight *and* gay). But, just as gender has been recognized by many as much more complex than we thought—thanks in large part to the increased visibility of the transgender community—sexual orientation too is more complex than it appears on the surface, as we shall see.

Since males and females can inherit one of four operating-system types, the effect is to produce eight primal sexual orientations. Females may be informed by a holistic OS (straight), a dualistic OS (lesbian), a unity OS (bisexual), or a hybrid OS (polysexual). Males likewise may be informed by a dualistic OS (straight), a holistic OS (gay), a unity OS (bisexual), or a hybrid OS (polysexual).

The eight types just mentioned are the result of the brain's responses to information *inputs*. As we saw in looking at gender in the last chapter, the four input genders can be further subdivided according to which of the four operating systems dominates their *output* response. This combination results in 32 distinct sexual orientations—16 male and 16 female. (See table at the end of this chapter.)

But the reality of sexual orientation is even more complex. Remember what we have said about the variable effects of a continuum. Whether our gender identity is feminine, masculine, both, or a mixture, expect the depth or intensity of our experience to vary. So, for example, on one end of the continuum we find extremely masculine males, sometimes referred to as "macho," who tend to respond hyperaggressively and are strongly identified with this aspect of themselves; and on the other end are those men who appear to have few if any obvious masculine characteristics. In between we find a wide range of responses, and *a single individual may embody a wide range of behaviors, some more masculine than others.* Females, too, range from the hyperemotional, ultra-feminine stereotypes to those women who, although biologically female, appear androgynous in their energies.

Consider the fate of a female whose dominant response is strongly masculine. Likely to be characterized as a tomboy when young, when older and in a relationship we might find her characterized as a woman who "wears the pants in the family," especially if paired with a male whose responses tend to be feminine or androgynous. On the other hand, if her masculine traits are sufficiently weak or subtle, she might not even be aware that she has a dominant masculine response and assume it to be feminine.

As we can see, this range of diversity applies as much *within* the gay and lesbian communities as it does outside it. And among gays and lesbians, as with straight individuals, opposites attract.

Whereas lesbians with a *strong* masculine output response might be identified as "butch," a subtle masculine response might go unrecognized. The same patterns of variation are found in lesbians whose output response is holistic and feminine. Default responses can range from highly feminine in style and attitude to androgynous.

Of course, these same patterns of input and output responses ranging from strong to weak in degree also apply to males—straight, gay, bisexual, and polysexual.

Input and Output Affect Sexuality Differently

Input and output perspectives affect sexual orientation in different ways. Our input perspective gives us our most primal sense of gender identity and sexual orientation. It determines the sex to which we are attracted. Our *output* perspective and response are revealed in the sexuality we present to the world, something that can often be seen in our physical presentation. We see evidence of this in straight women who are inherently (as opposed to culturally) predisposed to elements of a masculine appearance, and in straight males who are inherently drawn to express their feminine side.

If our *input* OS is dualistic and thus *masculine* in character, causing us to be sexually attracted to females, having a dominant *output* OS that is holistic and *feminine* apparently does not cause an attraction to men (contrary to what one might assume). More research is needed before we can determine with any degree of specificity how our output perspective and response affects our input perspective and response, and thus how it affects our overall sexual orientation, but certainly a second source of activity adds depth and diversity to sexuality.

The Normality of Diversity

When a strong dominant feminine perspective combines with a male body or a strong masculine perspective indwells a female body, the disconnect and resulting conflict between mind and body can be so powerful that individuals having such experiences feel that they are inhabiting the wrong body. I see nothing to suggest this is not a natural outcome—another of the challenges or opportunities that life offers us as vehicles for spiritual growth—but cultural beliefs and pressures are strong, and as a result, some individuals choose gender-reassignment surgery in an attempt to bring mind and body into a higher degree of harmony (Chaz Bono and Caitlyn Jenner are well-known examples of this). But in most such individuals the dichotomy between mind (or operating system) and body is not so extreme as to cause them to choose to change their body.

Reason suggests that those who are most likely to change their body would be those whose perspective *and* response are the opposite of their biological sex and are also strong, giving them a gender identity that is in stark contrast to their sex. If that were the case, such individuals would have either a strongly dominant masculine perspective and response in a female body, or a strongly dominant feminine perspective and response in a male body.

For a variety of reasons, the terms used to describe variations in sexual and gender identity and experience have been changing and evolving. Because of some disagreement in the "trans" community regarding proper word choice, for clarity I'll explain my usage. Those who choose to change their body to match their mind (how they see themselves—their perspective) are generally known as *transsexual* individuals. Lori B. Girshick (in *Transgender Voices: Beyond Women and Men*) describes the experience as that of "an individual who feels his/her gender identity does not align with his/her physical body, as traditionally defined."[2] Those who also experience this dichotomy strongly, but choose to live with their body more or less as it is, sometimes refer to themselves as *transgenderist*. "Transgenderist," according to Girshick, refers to those who "live full-time as another gender without undergoing any surgery."[3] Those whose experience of a perspective reversal is moderate or subtle may not recognize that their gender is reversed until they reach puberty and discover that their sexual orientation is reversed.

The accompanying chart (figure 2) shows the spectrum of sexual orientation and sexual/gender identity. Transsexuals start out on one continuum and through the gender reassignment process move to the other.

Figure 2. **Brain dominance and gender orientation.**

The "Feminine" Brain and Full-Spectrum Sexuality

A number of researchers and observers have commented that bisexuality seems more natural—and less threatening—to women than to men. The surveys of Kinsey and others have shown that, over a lifetime, a significant minority of males have also had experiences with both sexes. But in most males, the tendency *in adulthood* is to be exclusively involved with one or the other sex, with comparatively little overlap. Women, on the other hand, may seem more naturally inclined to the whole spectrum of sexuality.

Some recent studies have concluded that between 20 and 60 percent of all women have reported being sexually attracted to other women,[4] even though only a small fraction of those identify with the "bisexual" label. Instead, according to a recent 10-year study conducted by University of Utah psychologist Lisa M. Diamond,[5] many women with attraction to both sexes did not label themselves at all, and this tendency toward being "unlabeled" or "bisexual" (rather than gay or straight) actually became stronger as these women grew older in the course of the study. (Interestingly, this group was even more likely to maintain stable monogamous relationships than self-identified lesbians or straight women. This finding strongly indicates that, for women, being "unlabeled" or "bisexual" is not a transitional state and does not translate into noncommitment or promiscuity.) Thus, the Diamond study shows that women's sexuality, over time, becomes less defined and moves toward the center of the spectrum (bisexuality or unlabeled).

Another very interesting finding of these studies concludes that sexuality for many women seems to be part of a continuum that includes other kinds of physical affection and emotional bonding—thus, "several experts mention that women's friendships are hardly different from romantic friendships."[6] For men, in contrast, sexuality is more often in an exclusive compartment, in keeping with the separative nature of the dualistic operating system. Traditionally, males tend to have fewer intimate friends, and friends and sexual partners often seem to be nonoverlapping categories.

Brain research offers some clues as to these differences. As we have seen, the holistic (usually right) hemisphere—the one that typically provides the vision that most women rely on for guidance—is inclusionary, meaning it encompasses the dualistic perspective as well as its own. It tends to integrate rather than separate or compartmentalize experiences and relationships (such as "friends" and "sexual relationships"). In contrast, heterosexual males not only tend to be dualistic and rely on a focused perspective; they also tend to exclude their nondominant or recessive (in this case, holistic) perspective much more than do females.

Brain Connectivity and Sexual Orientation

There is some intriguing anatomical evidence that gay men share with most women a more interconnected brain than is the case with lesbians and heterosexual men—and also that areas of their brain are connected very differently. Research findings suggest that most gay men and most women hear equally well in both ears (whereas straight men tend to hear better in the right ear), which "supports earlier findings that homosexual men [like most women] have larger connections between the hemispheres" than heterosexual men.[7] In a landmark 2008 Swedish study involving 90 individuals almost evenly split by gender and sexual orientation,[8] brain scans showed that "in gay people [both lesbians and gay men], key structures of the brain governing emotion mood, anxiety and aggressiveness resemble those in straight people of the opposite sex," and that these differences are likely to be present in infancy or earlier. In addition to finding that some physical attributes of the brains of gays and lesbians resemble those typical of the opposite sex, the researchers "used PET scans to measure blood flow to the amygdala, part of the brain that governs fear and aggression," and "revealed how the amygdala connected with other parts of the brain. . . . In straight women and gay men, the connections were mainly into regions of the brain that manifest fear as intense anxiety. . . . In straight men and lesbians, the amygdala fed its signals mainly into. . . regions of the brain that trigger the 'fight or flight' [action-related] response."[9] The authors of this study note that these results show a basis for previous findings that heterosexual women and gay men tend to be more depressive, and heterosexual men and lesbians tend to be more active and aggressive ("fight or flight"). The study noted that "homosexual men and straight women showed significantly more neural connections across the two brain hemispheres than heterosexual men did."[10]

A 2007 study led by Sandra Witelson of McMaster University in Ontario (Canada) "found that the posterior part of the corpus callosum [by far the largest interconnecting structure between the brain hemispheres] is larger in homosexual men than heterosexual men." Most amazing was a "correlational analysis" undertaken by the researchers, which included "size of the corpus callosum, and test scores on language, visual spatial and finger dexterity tests." Witelson noted that "by using all these variables, *we were able to predict sexual orientation in 95 percent of the cases.*"[11] A 2010 York University study found that "gay men can recall familiar faces faster and more accurately than their heterosexual counterparts because, like women, they use both sides of their brains."[12]

The more easily each of us can access and integrate our nondominant perspective, the better off we will be, and the better off our world will be. There is no evidence that the attainment of a more integrated mind-set creates a shift in our sexual orientation, nor is there reason to suspect such. The quest for mental and spiritual unity transcends sexual orientation.

Sexual orientation is born of fixed, inherited factors that our moment-to-moment choice of perspective or response cannot change. A straight man cannot "go gay" by momentarily adopting the perspective of women and gay men; nor, quite obviously, can gay men and straight women change their sexual orientation by focusing heavily on the dualistic attributes so prevalent in modern Western cultures. A more integrated perspective only makes us more mentally whole and capable.

Sexual Orientation Can Take Any One of 32 Forms

Sex is deeply rooted in the brain. In the specialized systems of the brain, the perception of wholeness is divided into two highly specialized operating systems, each bearing characteristic behaviors that we associate with gender.

Together, the brain's two operating systems—the dualistic and the holistic—give us complementary ways of perceiving and complementary ways of responding. For most of us, the left hemisphere is dualistic and masculine and the right hemisphere is holistic and feminine. Although we have free will and can see or do what we want, for most of us, one system will dominate our deliberations and bias our view of our world and the way we respond to it. But this way of stating the situation in itself reflects the traditional dualistic model. It supposes a binary system in which there are two opposite ways of perceiving and responding. Holistic systems seek to unify the masculine and feminine and present us with a unified viewpoint. From the seemingly limitless expanses of a holistic perspective there are *many* ways of perceiving and responding.

In addition to the pure masculine and feminine experience—the products of genetic complete dominance—a third group of people will experience genetic codominance and its double (masculine/feminine) perspective functioning as a harmonious team. With their masculine side attracted to women and their feminine side drawn to men, these individuals are naturally attracted to both sexes.

A fourth group of individuals possess a blended integration of holistic and dualistic operating systems, and will experience a mixture of masculine and feminine characteristics—what we are calling a hybrid perspective. Rather than seeing life from a dualistic or a holistic perspective, or both, the hybrid perspective positions us, metaphorically speaking, somewhere on the continuum between the poles of masculine and feminine. At least, that's how dualistic consciousness sees it. From the perspective of holistic consciousness, sexuality is nonlinear. (Remember the red and white flower analogy when distinguishing between hybrid and unity consciousness.)

The result of having one of four operating systems creates eight primal sexual identifications: females with a feminine perspective (heterosexual women); females with a masculine perspective (lesbians); females with a unity perspective (female bisexuals); females with a hybrid perspective (female polysexuals); males with a masculine perspective (heterosexual men); males with a feminine perspective (gay men); males with a unity perspective (male bisexuals); and males with a hybrid perspective (male polysexuals).

Our experience of life is one based on information inflows and outflows—both ours and those of others—any of which can be governed by either a holistic, dualistic, unity, or hybrid system. As a result, the eight primal types can be further subdivided according to which system—dualistic, holistic, unity, or hybrid—manages their output response. This produces 32 varieties of sexual orientation—16 male and 16 female—as the following table shows.

I trust that a greater understanding of our sexuality will produce a greater peace.

32 Variations on Sexual Orientation

	Brain Input		Brain Output		Input and Output
	Perspective	Response	Perspective	Response	Sexual Orientation
FEMALE	Holistic (Genetic complete dominance)	Holistic Consciousness/ Straight	Holistic	Feminine	Straight w/ feminine traits
			Dualistic	Masculine	Straight w/ masculine traits
			Unity	Bisexual	Straight w/ bisexual traits
			Hybrid	Polysexual	Straight w/ polysexual traits
	Dualistic (Genetic complete dominance)	Dualistic Consciousness/ Lesbian	Holistic	Feminine	Lesbian w/ feminine traits
			Dualistic	Masculine	Lesbian w/ masculine traits
			Unity	Bisexual	Lesbian w/ bisexual traits
			Hybrid	Polysexual	Lesbian w/ polysexual traits
	Unity (Genetic codominance)	Unity Consciousness/ Bisexual	Holistic	Feminine	Bisexual w/ feminine traits
			Dualistic	Masculine	Bisexual w/ masculine traits
			Unity	Bisexual	Bisexual w/ bisexual traits
			Hybrid	Polysexual	Bisexual w/ polysexual traits
	Hybrid (Genetic incomplete dominance)	Hybrid Consciousness/ Polysexual	Holistic	Feminine	Polysexual w/ feminine traits
			Dualistic	Masculine	Polysexual w/ masculine traits
			Unity	Bisexual	Polysexual w/ bisexual traits
			Hybrid	Polysexual	Polysexual w/ polysexual traits
MALE	Dualistic (Genetic complete dominance)	Dualistic Consciousness/ Straight	Holistic	Feminine	Straight w/ feminine traits
			Dualistic	Masculine	Straight w/ masculine traits
			Unity	Bisexual	Straight w/ bisexual traits
			Hybrid	Polysexual	Straight w/ polysexual traits
	Holistic (Genetic complete dominance)	Holistic Consciousness/ Gay	Holistic	Feminine	Gay w/ feminine traits
			Dualistic	Masculine	Gay w/ masculine traits
			Unity	Bisexual	Gay w/ bisexual traits
			Hybrid	Polysexual	Gay w/ polysexual traits
	Unity (Genetic codominance)	Unity Consciousness/ Bisexual	Holistic	Feminine	Bisexual w/ feminine traits
			Dualistic	Masculine	Bisexual w/ masculine traits
			Unity	Bisexual	Bisexual w/ bisexual traits
			Hybrid	Polysexual	Bisexual w/ polysexual traits
	Hybrid (Genetic incomplete dominance)	Hybrid Consciousness/ Polysexual	Holistic	Feminine	Polysexual w/ feminine traits
			Dualistic	Masculine	Polysexual w/ masculine traits
			Unity	Bisexual	Polysexual w/ bisexual traits
			Hybrid	Polysexual	Polysexual w/ polysexual traits

PART TWO

How Perspective
and Brain Dominance
Produce Polarization

CHAPTER 6

Parts, Wholes, and Holons:
Satisfying Our Need for Wholeness

Everything you do counts forever. You are an expression of the whole
process of creation; you are a cocreator.

—Barbara Marx Hubbard, *Conscious Evolution:*
Awakening the Power of Our Social Potential

To better appreciate the differences in character of the brain's two
operating systems, it is essential that we understand them in their
context, and that we understand something of the universe of which they
are an integral part. After all, it is the universe around us and in us—our
physical, mental, and spiritual environment—that the hemispheres are
describing to us.

Like the brain's operating system, which—though a unity—is split
into two parts, our universe can be conceptually divided starting with two
parts: a linear element and a holistic element. Just as two reporters might
divide up the work of investigating a complex story, the two hemispheres
divide up the immensity of the task of explaining our universe. By better
understanding the territory that the hemispheres cover for us, we are aided
in our efforts to understand what they are trying to tell us. In clarifying
the relationship between the brain and its context, we help ground our
mental adventures in physical reality.

In this chapter we address some of the universe's underlying structural characteristics. Of particular interest are the organizational relationships, which consist of a series of nested structures such as we find in electrons nested within atoms that are nested within molecules. This is a relationship that we refer to in general terms as one of *parts* and *wholes*. But, upon closer examination, it soon becomes apparent that the definition of what it means to be a part or a whole changes as our perspective shifts.

Planet Earth, for example, can be viewed as a whole, which of course it is, but it can also be viewed as a part, since it is a part of its solar system. As we begin to explore this issue, we soon notice that the concept of part and whole describes a *relative* relationship. Our view of wholeness shifts as our viewpoint shifts and introduces or removes elements from our consciousness. All of life is caught up in this nesting pattern, and naturally, the brain is intimately involved in observing and reporting this pattern.

The confusion between parts and wholes is widespread (even if we don't recognize the part these concepts play in our thinking) and can give rise to major conceptual errors. And so, in recent time, a new word, *holon* (coined by Arthur Koestler in his book *The Ghost in the Machine* in 1967), has come into circulation to properly indicate the relative nature of wholes and parts.

Parts, Wholes, and Holons

Subatomic particles, cells, symbols, images, concepts: all of these words reflect a common design element. All are wholes in and of themselves, and they are also parts of something greater. Philosopher Ken Wilber has in recent years become one of the most influential explicators of holons,[1] and this chapter owes a debt to his work.

Whether we shift our perspective inward or outward, toward individuals or collectives, we find a structure in which wholes become parts, or vice versa, depending on our focus. But we can also go beyond space-time references, in which case the whole becomes an all-encompassing singularity (which we might capitalize as the "Whole"). A *Course in Miracles* describes the relationship this way: "The whole does define the part, but the part does not define the whole. . . . The idea of part-whole relationships has meaning only at the level of perception, where change is possible. Otherwise, there is no difference between the part and whole."[2]

In a universe of relationships, all wholes are parts, and all parts are wholes; that is, everything can be described as a holon. Although we will sometimes use the contrasting (or dualistic) terms *part* and *whole* rather than the holistic term *holon*, we will be using *part* and *whole* in full knowledge that every whole is also a part, and every part is also a whole.

Whether something is seen as a part or a whole depends on the relationship being viewed, as well as the viewpoint of the viewer. From the viewpoint of dualistic consciousness, we tend to equate the object/holon of our focus with wholeness. Objects nested within the holon on which we are focused, or scattered around it, tend to be seen as parts. Our right hemisphere experiences a viewpoint that sees the wholeness, whereas our left hemisphere tends to focus on the parts (sequentially)—but in truth, everything functions as a whole made up of parts, and as a part of another whole (and ultimately, a series of wholes).

The same kind of relativistic principle applies to the individual and collective realms. For example, we think of ourselves as individuals, but Bruce Lipton points to the fact that each of us can also be viewed as a collective. "As a cell biologist I can tell you that you are in truth a cooperative community of approximately 50 trillion single-celled citizens. . . . As a nation reflects the traits of its citizens, our human-ness must reflect the basic nature of our cellular communities."[3]

As we have seen, whether we perceive a particular thing as a part or a whole (or as an individual or a collective) depends on our perspective. As our focus shifts, our perspective shifts, and along with it our perception of wholeness. When we are focusing on something, the object of our focus tends to become our whole, and the rest of reality becomes a part or context. When this happens, if the focus is sufficiently strong, context can be completely overlooked, a good example being religious leaders and followers who, although they seek to understand and serve the same God—and thus share the same goal—nevertheless irrationally divide themselves by arguing whose leader or doctrine is correct—as if the truth can only be stated in one way, and any alternative formulations are not only wrong but blasphemous and evil. A corollary to this twisted logic is that God, or the organizing principle of the universe, will only recognize and bless one formulation or interpretation and will punish—perhaps for eternity—the holders of alternative interpretations!

The Building Blocks of Wholeness

Quantum physicists tell us that we live in a universe of multiple possibilities. They have discovered that some very small particles of matter are able to completely disappear and then reappear in another place. They have found that some particles can even be in many places at once![4] Quantum physicists have also found that the observer has an effect on the reality he or she observes. Our creative minds activate the creative energies of our world and cause matter to shift. In other words, in the process of simply *observing* our physical world, we alter reality at the particle physics level—*we literally change physical reality as we interact with it*. What we perceive depends largely on where we look and what we expect to perceive. Quantum physics is revealing the mechanics of how we create.

When we observe the properties of what we call physical matter, we find waves where we expect to find particles, and we find process where we expect to find structure. That has led some to conclude that there is no such thing as a smallest particle (or a fundamental building block, as we would ordinarily think of it). More and more, it is looking as though energy manifests in the form of a wave. What we have long thought to be particles now appear to be waves of energy that reflect light.[5]

Could the waves be made up of particles of energy such we see in a torus? Perhaps the basis of a particle is the axis it spins around. (See the torus illustration in chapter 1, figure 1.) However we might best describe a smallest particle, it would appear to start out dualistic, reflecting the structure of the universe: dual into nondual, linear into multidimensional.

Whatever the smallest particle might eventually prove to be—assuming there is one—in a dualistic design every structure has a companion, since a dualistic structure has two parts. Thus, the wholeness that we refer to as "reality" is traditionally thought to be composed of two fundamental parts: *elements* (waves, particles, molecules, plants, people, planets, etc.) and *relationships* ("seen" in connections and spacing—and felt).

From the dualistic perspective we see elements and relationships as separate; nevertheless, as two parts of a whole, we know that they are integrated, even if we don't know how. In other words, elements do not merely exist side by side, in isolation; at the very least, elements relate to other elements, but on closer examination we find that the identity of elements cannot be conceived apart from relationships. What is it to be a human being without any reference to our environment—or without reference to the way the "parts" of our body, brain, and mind work together?

When we look closely, we see that elements such as waves or particles *embody* (contain) a relationship component—suggesting that elements and relationships are not as different as they seem. Depending on one's perspective, relationship may be seen as a characteristic of elements (as evidenced by the fact that relationships can be found internally in elements), or elements can be seen as a part of relationships (since elements exist in a complex field of relationship to other elements). Both elements and relationships are holons—both are parts of greater wholes as well as wholes consisting of parts.

Since relationship is based on spiritual energy (we know this because relationship is felt and possesses neither physical nor mental characteristics), and since spiritual energy is characterized by oneness or wholeness, it follows that relationship points to—or, stated differently, is an aspect of—wholeness. Relationships may change in their qualities, and they may grow closer or more distant. We might say that relationship is the oneness in which the parts assemble to form the whole.

Every Holon Has Four Essential Parts

We could describe each holon as containing at least two parts, and each of those parts as in turn containing at least two parts. In other words, a holon is a pair of pairs.

First, every holon is expressed both individually and collectively; that is, every holon (including ourselves) can be viewed either as a single part of a greater whole or as a whole comprising parts. In keeping with the split in our brain, the management systems operated by the hemispheres are split into two parts. The holistic right monitors the larger, collective aspect, and the dualistic left monitors the smaller, individual aspects.

The second pair of characteristics that are required of a holon is to always have an interior and an exterior aspect. The *interior* aspect is more or less "hidden" in the sense of being only experientially (subjectively) accessible, or in the sense of needing to be "discovered" through analytical rigor or dissection. The *exterior* aspect presents itself outwardly—as part of the objective, empirical, publicly observable world, or as a part of the big picture in which every whole is in relationship to other wholes.

At the conscious level we are mostly unaware of this four-part (individual/collective and inner/outer) structure. At the subconscious level, however, we are highly aware—as can be seen in our efforts to find a mate. In looking for a mate, we clearly recognize that people have an *inner* and an *outer* persona, a private and a public face. We know that their inner persona—their subjectivity, or what they are like "inside"— lies hidden and is discovered only gradually and often indirectly, as a result of how it affects other areas of their life and relationships. We often have to probe to find it out, though at some point in this discovery process there may be an "aha" moment.

We also recognize that when we connect with someone, we are connecting to more than an *individual*—we are also connecting to a *collective* of people and events—to family, friends, and our colleagues at work. When we enter into personal relationships, we know we are entering a complex set of relationships that include family habits, attitudes, responses, genetics, and a more or less complicated past that affects the present in countless ways.

A whole *always* consists of these four fundamental parts, but almost without exception, those parts have parts—and they too can have parts (and so on). Furthermore, beyond the fundamental four, some of the parts can be absent, leaving the whole incomplete, as when we have forgotten facts to support our argument or lost the keys to the house. Missing parts can make the whole nonfunctional, as when an automobile is missing its engine, or be of little consequence, as when it loses an identification medallion. The same pattern applies to the body of beliefs we have acquired, beliefs that serve as our programming. Missing parts can deceive us and lead to problems.

The Problem of Incompletion

In trying to be more holistic in managing our information, we must do more than seek wholeness. The complexity of reality ensures that critical parts are sometimes missing from wholes. Therefore, when dealing with important issues, we need to be aware of the possibility of incompletion, of missing parts—an awareness that is instinctive in some circumstances, such as when we have been cheated out of something. The detection of missing or flawed parts is managed by our detail-oriented dualistic operating system.

We care about incompletion because an incomplete or fragmentary holon can mislead us and prevent us from discovering the truth we seek. We care because through our own initiative (our choice of perspective, for example), we have the power to move toward or away from greater wholeness and its insights and power.

The workbook for *A Course in Miracles*, referring to the effect that incompletion has on our ability to find truth, explains: "The aim of all defenses is to keep the truth from being whole. The parts are seen as if each one were a whole within itself. . . . Defenses must make facts unrecognizable. . . . Every defense takes fragments of the whole, assembles them without regard to all their true relationships, and thus constructs illusions of a whole that is not there."[6]

Wholes Connect Horizontally and Vertically

Any time we make important decisions involving two or more components, we need to consider their *relationships*. This is common sense, and we usually do this, but it bears reminding. We cannot manage holons in isolation without a significant risk of inducing error into our deliberations, since holons are interconnected (physically, mentally, and spiritually) in a complex energy system. For that reason, we must consider their various relationships in the context of their greater whole. Most women seem to understand this, but most men, acting under the influence of dualistic consciousness with its narrow focus, too often fail to notice or comprehend the extenuating consequences of their actions.

Holons no doubt connect with one another in many ways, but the term *nesting* perhaps describes the nature of connectivity as well as anything. Wholes can be said to nest in two fundamental ways—*horizontally* and *vertically*. A clearer way of explaining this structure might be to say that wholes nest both *with* and *within* other wholes. *With* describes horizontal nesting; *within* describes vertical nesting. But rather than envisioning a dualistic structure, it might be more useful to envision a holistic structure such as we find in a series of concentric spheres (see figure 3). Notice that, starting from the center, each sphere includes and envelops (nests) the preceding one.

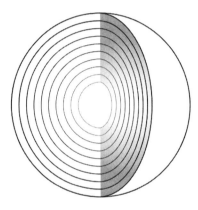

Figure 3. **Collective wholeness.**

Vertical nesting is the structure we are familiar with in Russian nesting dolls, where we find a hollowed-out doll that contains, or nests, a series of progressively smaller dolls *within* it. We see this vertical one-within-another nesting pattern in nature where the nucleus of an atom is vertically nested within an atom that is vertically nested within a molecule. We see this pattern expressed in cultural nesting where individuals nest within families, teams, schools, and businesses. These holons, in turn, are vertically nested within rural or urban communities that vertically nest within states or provinces. Vertically nesting all of these nests is a nation nested within a planet that is in turn nested in a solar system, and so on. This structure is sometimes called a *holarchy* (a hierarchy of holons).

Horizontal nesting refers to the relationship in which we find elements connected *with* others having a (more or less) similar purpose, such as the individual members of a team (sports or business) working to support a common greater whole or goal—or sometimes working to interfere with it, as is the case with defective parts, or selfish players, for example. When nesting dolls are placed individually in a box, they are horizontally nested. In terms of a single doll, the horizontal elements include the wood, the paints of different colors, and the artistry—the beauty that manifests as a result of the creative relationships.

Horizontally nested collectives such as teams also take part in a vertical nesting structure. For example, a football team might enlist its supporters (which it nests) and the university (*in* which it nests) for a fundraising drive. In this horizontal and vertical connection, the "seams" of connectivity in our universe can be seen.

The nesting activity of holons takes place in an environment of *interdependent* relationships. Being connected, the various parts depend on one another. From the viewpoint of holistic consciousness, we see that what hurts one hurts all to some degree, and what benefits one benefits all to some degree. This contrasts sharply with the view we are given by dualistic consciousness. From its perspective of separation and winner-take-all competition, what hurts one individual often helps another. Although we sometimes hear mention of win–win situations, the more common point of view tends to be that if you win, I lose, and vice versa.

In *horizontal* nesting, the elements of wholeness are relatively *competitive*. Members of a family compete with one another for family resources. Business and governmental departments compete with one another for funding, material resources, or personnel. Animals tend to compete with one another, as do students. Competition usually implies a certain similarity of function between competitors.

Contrast that with *vertical* nesting. There, competition is usually absent. Students do not compete with their schools. Nor do schools compete with the cities in which they nest, except in unusual circumstances, such as cases where a school and a city may both apply for the same grant for funding. In general, students compete with students; cities compete with cities.

In vertical nesting, the focus is inherently encompassing and, at least in ideal circumstances, supportive—although in interpersonal, cultural, and institutional contexts there can also be acrimony (such as when a state usurps money intended for a local government).

We find an environment of *domination* in vertical nesting. Whether or not the domination creates problems in interpersonal or institutional situations depends on how it is managed. If the relationship is managed by individuals coming from a harmony-seeking, holistic perspective, the relationship can be very cooperative and mutually beneficial. On the other hand, if management takes on separative characteristics, then the relationship can be bullying and coercive from the dominant side, and rebellious or nonfunctional from the weaker side. Size, we all know, tends to dominate. So, for example, a city, because of its size, has more power and control than the individual families that are nesting within it. Likewise, states dominate their schools, and schools dominate their students (or at least try).

Because every whole is both horizontally and vertically nested, we face, for example, horizontal pressures to cooperate with our friends and associates, and vertical pressures to succumb to more powerful cultural forces such as parents, schools, businesses, and governments. And we must deal with another pressure as well. Sometimes a horizontal element (a sibling, coworker, or partner, for example) will try to dominate us. We deal with a complex mix of entangled nesting structures, and what we predict doesn't always happen.

Due to the egoic clashes inherent in competition, horizontal nesting within a culture or country (not to mention between countries) can present a variety of problems. Vertical nesting, on the other hand, involves hierarchy and domination, so the element of competition is greatly reduced. Still, because of people's natural resistance to being dominated, acceptance of vertical nesting is often heavily resisted. As Ken Wilber explains, "When any holon in a natural holarchy [a *vertical* nesting of holons] usurps its position and attempts to dominate the whole, then you get a pathological or dominator hierarchy—a cancerous cell dominates the body, or a fascist dictator dominates the social system, or a repressive ego dominates the organism, and so on. But the cure for these pathological holarchies is not getting rid of the holarchy per se—which isn't possible anyway—but rather in arresting the arrogant holon and integrating it back into the natural holarchy, or putting it in its rightful place, so to speak. The critics of hierarchy—their names are legion—simply confuse these pathological holarchies with holarchies in general, and so they toss the baby with the bathwater. . . . Without holarchy, you simply have heaps, not wholes."[7] In other words, you become heapistic, rather than holistic.

In summary, whether a given holon is physical, mental, or spiritual in energy; whether it be a book, house, cat, tree, idea, hero, or villain; whether it be boundlessly large or infinitesimally small—it is always connected into the unified matrix of holons that makes up the universe. At minimum, *individual* holons have an *interior* and an *exterior*, and are part of a *collective* existence that also has an interior and an exterior. Interior, exterior, individual, and collective: these are the four essential parts that constitute the basis of wholeness.

In this chapter we have seen that every holon, as an individual and as a collective, nests (connects) horizontally *with* a number of other holons—holons sharing a generally similar goal such as we find in a sports team, a company, or a country. In addition, every holon—individual and collective; physical, mental, and spiritual—is also connected vertically by virtue of being nested *within* a series of holons that are in turn nested within other holons, ad infinitum.

From the dualistic perspective, we are made up of parts. From the holistic perspective, we are parts of a greater whole.

CHAPTER 7

Sacred Geometry's Role in Perception

If the doors of perception were cleansed, everything would appear as it is—infinite.

—**William Blake,** *The Marriage of Heaven and Hell*

Helpful to the discussion of the process of cognition is an understanding of sacred geometry. Euclidian geometry and systems of mathematics are a part of our public knowledge, and we all are exposed to these in our educational systems. But *sacred* geometry is much less well known. Because this discipline views forms and ratios as having sacred significance, it is perhaps not surprising that most mathematicians, scientists, and academics are unfamiliar with it; or, if they are familiar, they likely dismiss it as arcane, superstitious, or unscientific. Yet, in spite of this, the principles of sacred geometry have been consciously utilized by nearly every culture through most of recorded history.

Sacred geometry refers to the ways that shapes and patterns are repeated throughout nature, including the mental and spiritual worlds. Although we can scarcely scratch the surface of this subject in this short chapter, full study of these patterns reveals the myriad ways that we are connected at (and to) all levels of life.[1] Every discipline, every way of knowing (such as chemistry, physics, architecture, music, even one's emotional states), can be shown to have a correlation in sacred geometry. Even mathematics would not be possible without sacred geometry, for numbers and their laws arise out of (and could not exist without) shape, form, proportion, and the relationships these reveal.

"Geometry deals with pure form," Robert Lawlor reminds us in *Sacred Geometry: Philosophy and Practice*.[2] Geometry can be said to be sacred because it reveals the underlying structure of reality, what we might call the framework of God's body, of All That Is—the Whole. Our own bodies are also geometrical in form. We see an illustration of the connection between sacred geometry and the body in Leonardo da Vinci's famous drawing of Vitruvian Man, a man with outstretched arms surrounded by a circle.

Everything embodies an element of geometry. Our perspective, which feeds information to consciousness, is no exception. As we have seen, each of the four operating systems—which I have called holistic, dualistic, hybrid, and unified—has its own viewpoint (a hybrid system would seem to convey a variety of potential viewpoints). Having different viewing points with respect to a given object or issue means that the four OSs possess *different viewing angles* and thus have different geometry with respect to a given object.

Because holistic and dualistic operating systems see the world from different angles, each sees something different. Differences in viewpoint then result in differences in the content being sent to consciousness, and this results in differences in perception.

Energy appears to disperse along geometric lines. Geometry starts with straight lines, which in sacred geometry are thought of as "male" lines. They then transition into curved, "female" lines such as we find in circles and spheres. When we integrate the two geometries, we find a structure that combines elements of both, a structure that is rounded but embodies a linear characteristic, as seen in a *vesica piscis* (see figure 4). Although this form contains no visible straight lines, having been created out of the shared space of two circles of the same diameter, nevertheless, it has a vertical linear dimension (depicted in figure 4 by a dotted line).

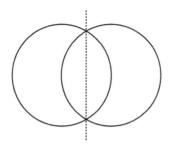

Figure 4. **Vesica piscis.**

Masculine and feminine geometries, like the two brain operating systems that detect and communicate them, are complementary. Feminine geometry is inclusionary, meaning that the feminine nests the masculine. We can see this relationship expressed with precision in our physical bodies by considering how female sexual organs nest male organs.

Whereas from a dualistic perspective our view of reality sees a *linear* foundation of individual forms, when our perspective is holistic, reality appears to us as *spherical* and *ovoid*, as can be observed in the geometry of a vesica piscis. The brain's integration of lines and circles can be seen in the progression of platonic solids from the simplest to the most complex, evolving from tetrahedrons to hexahedrons (cubes) to octahedrons to dodecahedrons to icosahedrons. If we take this process further, we come to recognize that perfectly round spheres can be constructed by using straight lines short enough that their linear dimension cannot be seen.

Circles, too, possess a linear component, something we can see by evenly bending a line back on itself so that the two ends connect. As the two ends come together and their polar separation is terminated, the line becomes a circle and inclusion is created.

Linear and Holistic Patterns in Sexuality

The male sexual organ, being *primarily* linear in structure and *secondarily* round, reflects the typical, dualistic-dominant male perspective, which is primarily linear and secondarily holistic.

Likewise, in most women, the geometry of the physical (sexual) and the geometry of the mental (perspective) are in harmony. Both physical and mental aspects are inclusive, holistic behind a linear façade, supplemented with one obvious detail shared with males: the mouth, which is vesica piscis in form and serves as common ground in terms of human geometry and sexuality.

We are all innately led to seek that which we lack as a way to achieve completion. A complete view or understanding of something is obviously desirable whether the holon on which we are focused is physical, mental, or spiritual; that is, whether our brain is trying to understand physical realities such as sex, mental realities such as ideas, or spiritual relationships.

To achieve completion in a dualistic world, we must acquire our nondominant viewpoint and integrate it into our dominant viewpoint. We see this drive to achieve completion in the choice of a mate, for example, in which the principle that opposites attract is often clearly apparent. Of course, the diversity of life ensures that there are exceptions to the rule as well as complications. For example, *a mate can complement us in one energy form and not in another*—as when our mate complements us physically (sexually) but not mentally—or vice versa. To more clearly understand the effects of this situation, we need to know more about the relationship between dominant perspectives and human sexual drives, so let us look at this relationship.

The dualistic perspective that is typical of males streams us information that is dualistic, linear-based, focused, and analytical. It is a view that is probing, designed to penetrate into the hidden nature of holons. Typically, this perspective comes paired with a linear sexual organ that, when focused (erect), is also linear-based, probing, and designed to penetrate.

The holistic perspective, which guides most females, looks outward, and is seeking unification with the surrounding universe. The holistic, feminine side of us achieves greater mental completion through inclusion, by nesting masculine linear elements. We find the same pattern in the sexual tendencies of females, as embodied in the ancient Hermetic saying "As above, so below." In most females the object of desire is an *exterior* organ, and completion is achieved through the *inclusion* of a linear element.

The Power of Geometry to Change Lives

"Fundamentally, sacred geometry is simply the ratio of numbers to each other," explains acclaimed photographer and anthropologist Martin Gray. To late medieval and Renaissance painters, "The positioning of elements within the frame of a painting was considered as important as the subject matter itself." This concern for positioning reflected their belief that a composition needed to be laid out "according to the mathematical principles of the golden ratio, or phi—a geometric ratio occurring throughout the natural world that the ancients believed to be a divine proportion." The golden ratio is reflected in many buildings and in the orientation of the buildings to one another—and it can be seen in examples that span the globe. In trying to explain the drawing power of sacred spaces, Gray quotes an ancient Hindu architectural sutra: "'The universe is present in the temple in the form of proportion.' Therefore, when you are within a structure fashioned with sacred geometry, you are within a model of the universe. The vibrational quality of sacred space thus brings your body, your mind, and, at a deeper level, your soul into harmony with the universe."[3]

My introduction to the power of sacred geometry came in Egypt. After having visited numerous temples and, with one exception, having felt nothing special, I stepped onto the grounds of the ancient temple complex at Abydos and was suddenly flooded with a powerful and wonderful feeling that I can only describe in terms of waves of love. It was like falling in love, true love, in the space of a couple of seconds. An hour later, on the back side of the complex, I had my first encounter with the ancient Flower of Life (figure 5), a symbol found at spiritual sites around the world that depicts a sphere filled with interconnected spheres, as two-dimensionally represented—a form said by Drunvalo Melchizedek to incorporate in one drawing "all knowledge of the universe, both male and female, no exceptions."[4]

In chapter 6 we spoke of the vertical and horizontal nesting structure of the universe and how, through this structure, all of life connects into a singularity, into wholeness. In the Flower of Life symbol we see a representation of that structure made out of spheres. As such, it symbolizes the universe.

Figure 5. **Flower of Life.**

Most of us think of geometric shapes as interesting but not particularly useful unless one is, say, a mathematician, architect, or engineer. But the evidence is otherwise, and this evidence has been known for thousands of years and in nearly every religious and cultural tradition. Even in our culture, where sacred geometry is ignored or devalued, these geometrical structures are fundamental to our understanding of ourselves and all aspects of manifestation—physical, mental, and spiritual. Their significance lies in their immense creative power. These structures describe—in the abstract symbolism of geometry—the places where the "universes" of the left and right brain hemispheres meet. The process of transforming the linear into the holistic, even on the physical level, is an immensely creative one, producing transformative spiritual consequences.

An example of the spiritual shift that can occur when we transform a linear structure into a holistic structure is contained in the story of how the legendary Knights of the Round Table came together. According to the story, an ongoing quarrel among a group of knights over who would sit at which position at the table was blocking an effort to unify them and bring peace. Tables were long and narrow, and those who sat at the ends had an advantage. Seated at an end, a knight had a more visible presence and a linear perspective that allowed him to clearly see everyone's face. In case of a fight, a knight could more easily draw his sword and protect himself. Because the ends clearly offered the best seats, they were reserved for those of the highest rank. Given the natural competitive spirit of left-brain-dominant males, some of the knights were unwilling to come to a negotiation if it required them to accept an inferior position.

Eventually a solution was found when someone recognized that by creating a round table, they could eliminate the superior position, and then no one would have a physical or spiritual advantage. The act of getting away from a linear structure and adopting a circular structure—a change of physical dimensional relationships—created sufficient spiritual and ideological harmony to allow the individuals to come to the table and assume the power of their collective self.

The Directional Nature of Perspective

In the physical world, once we find a place where we would rather be, we can develop methods to try to get there. Movement is initiated by intent. Movement to or away from a *mental* position is initiated in a similar manner—by our intention to seek new perspectives.

Mentally, we achieve outward movement within the whole of knowledge by building onto what we already know, by acquiring accurate information and placing it in context. We discover the insides of things—what makes things "tick"—through analytical examination. We discover larger contexts by moving outward into the universe—and thus becoming more whole, or "holy." We expand the size of our wholeness through adding experiences to our lives, which influence and are influenced by our accumulated knowledge and past experience.

Although the holistic hemisphere provides us with a big-picture view and is conscious of everything in our sphere of reality, there is a fundamentally important aspect of wholeness that it is not equipped to see, at least not directly: it doesn't see *into* wholes. For that information it draws on the dualistic hemisphere.

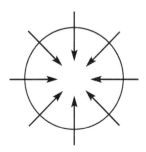

Figure 6. **Dualistic perspective.**

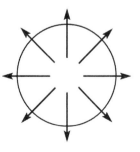

Figure 7. **Holistic perspective.**

As we have seen, dualistic consciousness gives us a perspective that delves into the insides of holons and wholeness. With its zoom-in capabilities, it probes and dissects, one part after another, to find out what might be hidden beneath the surface—to look into the details, to check the authenticity, *to search for Trojan horses.* And all this happens, on demand, automatically, based on our intent, plus the focus of our attention.

Dualistic brain operating systems employ analysis, meaning that they probe into the relatively "hidden" parts of the interiors of objects, ideas, motivations, causal chains, and the like with a view to achieving simplicity, and through simplicity, an enhanced understanding. The deeper we go, the simpler things appear to get. Holistic operating systems, because they give us the opposite or complementary view, look *outward* into an ever-expanding unity (see figure 7).

The cautious (self-protective) dualistic left brain reacts to mental energies such as ideas in the same way that it reacts to physical energies. It zooms in and examines the insides of things to find details such as faulty data or a revelatory piece of data, flaws or clinchers in an argument, subtexts, proofs or contradictions, and bad motivations—the list is endless. Ideas can be born of deception and sometimes need to be taken apart or analyzed.

In contrast, the holistic right brain, which is fearless and inclusive (open to the consideration of all ideas), focuses on our ideas as a whole (our ideological context, the big picture). Just keep in mind that the quality of holistic consciousness is heavily dependent on the skeptical abilities of dualistic consciousness to identify flawed ideas. A poor performance by dualistic consciousness can leave us harboring ideological errors that severely limit the ability of holistic consciousness to successfully guide us through a minefield of ideas and convey to us a complete view from the perspective of unity consciousness and truth.

When holistic and dualistic operating systems explore *spiritual* realities for us, we find similar patterns of response. The identity that people present to us—the appearance of peacefulness and honesty, for example—is not always a true representation of their spirit, and so we sometimes need to look deeper and get behind the spiritual facade. Note that although the limitations of being linear largely disqualify the dualistic operating system from helping us to *understand* the multidimensional reality of spirit, it can still be effective in helping us to sharpen our comprehension of what is going on in the spiritual realm of feeling.

By being paired and separated, our eyes perceive physical depth. The split in our brain's perspective appears to produce a similar stereoscopic effect on our perception. There is an important difference, however: whereas the perspectives obtained with our eyes are almost identical, differing in that they are slightly offset, the two brain perspectives see totally different views.

Although we've often described the two hemispheres as embodying opposite perspectives (in conventional terms), another way of looking at the difference is to say that they give us back-to-back perspectives (which we see illustrated in figure 8), which are complementary. We need to embrace the world in its fullness (the broad perspective) while always remaining attuned to the details (the zoomed-in perspective).

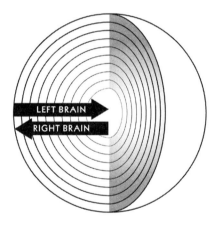

Figure 8. **Perspective directionality.**

In order to more consciously manage our attention and its perspective and thereby produce a more accurate and effective perception, it is essential that we establish an internal environment of honesty and stability.

By *honesty*, first and foremost, I am referring to *input* honesty. By input honesty, I mean being honest in our treatment of the information we *receive*. (Normally we think of honesty only in terms of the information we give out.) Input honesty requires that we embrace honesty internally in our deliberations. Input operating-system honesty results in internal honesty, whereas output system honesty reflects our honesty with the world around us. When our input OS is characterized by honesty, we tell ourselves the truth about things even if we lie about them to others. However, when our input OS is dishonest, it is almost inevitable that we lie to ourselves about things. And when this happens, we automatically and unconsciously lie about them to others, even though that might not be our intent! From what I have observed, self-dishonesty is very common, even pervasive.

Stability requires that we have a clear, focused internal mental center—one in which we are a conscious observer of our world and don't feel pushed or pulled to act in any way other than in harmony with our beliefs. Stability is facilitated by harmonizing our masculine and feminine sides and their attendant perceptions to the degree that they are no longer at war with one another. Maintaining mental stability in a dynamic world is a bit like dancing: if the rhythm of one side of the pair is out of sync, both feel the absence of harmony as conflict. As we come to understand how the two operating systems relate to one another, and learn to eliminate barriers to their integration by disabling disharmonious beliefs and faulty practices, they start to dance rather than fight.

CHAPTER 8

The Roles of Perspective and Perception in Cognition

Perspective is what shuts out the universe—everyone with their little perspective. It keeps the love out.

—From *Taking Woodstock*, directed by Ang Lee

Because perspective supplies the information that leads to the development of perception, in this chapter we will be looking deeper into the relationship between the holistic and dualistic perspectives, and reflecting on their relationship with perception. These perspectives, and their contribution to perception, when better understood, can give rise to a new level of holistic integration as well as cultivate a culture that honors growth and integration.

The creative choices that we make as we manage our lives spring from a complex brain system that is a whole of many parts rooted in a reptilian brain and brain stem. On top of the reptilian brain we find a more highly evolved, mammalian brain (also referred to as the limbic system), which in turn is capped by the most recent evolutionary development in the human brain system, the neocortex. Just as our brain as a whole is divided laterally, each part of the triune brain complex is likewise laterally divided to form a complementary pair.

The two halves of each brain system are functionally nested both horizontally and vertically. They are nested *horizontally* in that the dualistic system of the left and the holistic system of the right work together as a team to the degree allowed by genetic dominance, the effects of cultural programming, and the creative choices we make. They are also *vertically* nested since the right's holistic system encompasses (nests within it) the dualistic operating system of the left hemisphere.

Since the triune complex appears in both the left and right hemispheres, we are in effect talking about six "brains" here; but on each side of the hemispheric divide, the reptilian, mammalian, and human brains function as a whole. As wholes comprising three parts, the two wholes nest *horizontally*, functioning as two three-member teams. In addition, the three "brains" on each side are also *vertically* nested, the lower serving the higher. The reptilian on each side is vertically nested within the mammalian on its side, and the reptilian/mammalian nest is vertically nested within the neocortex.

The reptilian brain controls involuntary, automatic life functions such as breathing and heart rate and does not think (as far as we know), whereas the mammalian brain and the neocortex do think. So whenever we mention the cognitive functions of the left or the right side of the brain, we are largely referring to the contributions of the two *thinking* brains, a distinction that is reflected in brain researcher Ned Herrmann's four-part Whole Brain Model.[1] Herrmann's research also found that the brain uses a three-dimensional process that functions from side to side, front to back, and top down.[2] To simplify our exploration of a complex subject, we are focusing on the most heavily researched and functionally controllable of these divisions — the split into two sides.

"Most of the time the marriage of our two brain hemispheres is completely harmonious," Rita Carter observes in *Mapping the Mind*. "Conscious decisions, although they may seem to be made by the dominant partner [brain hemisphere] alone, are in fact fully informed by the findings of both hemispheres. Sometimes, though, the conversation between them falters. The dominant hemisphere may ignore the information supplied by its partner and make a decision based purely on what it thinks. The result may be an emotional disquiet that is difficult to explain. Conversely, the nondominant partner sometimes bypasses the executive control of the other side and triggers an action based purely on instinct."[3]

The harmony of the hemispheres can also be lost as a result of cultural interference such as comes from peer pressure. An example of this is a belief in war as a solution to our problems, a belief that often incites polarization through "patriotic" appeals, organized propaganda, and the stifling of dissent by government, the media, and powerful individuals and organizations generally. We see our individual and collective polarization acted out and mirrored back to us by our polarized political representatives and the polarized governments that they form.

Surely the best way to contribute to the collective and individual self is to be authentic, which involves acting from a position of hemispheric harmony. But being authentic is often challenging. To one degree or another, we are programmed by cultural influences to act against our best interests—programmed to see a perspective that others want us to see so that we can respond to it in a way that supports their vision and their response to things. And often we choose to take in these influences without understanding *what* we are taking in, just as we have chosen to eat junk food without understanding what it might do to our body. But cultural influences, however strong, can usually be reversed; and the more we understand how and in what ways we can be influenced by them, and how and why they disrupt our mental harmony, the easier we can be in control of these influences.

Although perception is generally thought of as a process that happens *to* us, perception is very much a creative choice that we make. Yes, brain dominance plays a substantial role in setting us up with a default viewpoint and thus heavily influences the underlying frame of our perception; nevertheless, the default can be manually overridden, at least in the moment. We have free will. The freedom to change our situation and our perspective—whether we use it to make a personal choice or bow to outside pressure or to a habit—is part of what it means to be human.

Our choice of perspective determines what we *see*. What we see then affects what we *do*—which starts with *perceiving* and *believing*. What we perceive and believe then influences how we respond to the outside world. Consequently, what we perceive, believe, and do then reverberate in what we *create* and *feel*, and this in turn affects what we see, believe, and do—which in turn affects where we look and what we believe, create, and feel. As we see, these processes are cyclic. Brain perspective—whether that of the dualistic left, the holistic right, or an integration of the two—resonates in everything we encounter.

The Nature of Perception

Scientifically, the process of thought is known as *cognition*. How the process might best be explained is still being debated, but the popular Myers-Briggs model, which is based on the work of Carl Jung, generally views *perception* as a stage in which we become aware of information, and *judgment* as the process of arriving at an understanding of it. In this model, cognition is a sequential process in which we do at least two things: we *grasp* the information coming to us from our perspective as it unfolds in front of us, a process known as *perception*; we then *judge* the validity of the information.

The process through which we arrive at our perception, and are thus "informed," involves the development of an image in our mind of something we have seen, heard, tasted, smelled, or felt. Viewed from *dualistic* consciousness, the cognitive process is seen as unfolding in a zigzagging linear flow that takes the form of a wave as the process of perception and the process of judgment share their findings back and forth with one another—and as we evaluate and reevaluate what is before us.

From a three-dimensional *holistic* perspective, this same flow that appeared linear and zigzagging from the dualistic view can be seen to spiral as perception and judgment alternate back and forth, checking and rechecking, processing and reprocessing the information or experience that has our attention until our comprehension is advanced to the point of being satisfied.

When we stretch out the spiral, as shown in figure 9, its underlying waveform is most readily apparent, as seen in figure 10.

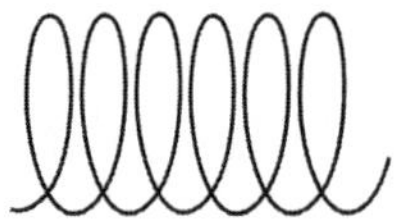

Figure 9. **Spiral.**    *Figure 10.* **Stretched spiral.**

In the study of cognition, perspective is widely viewed as a component of perception. However, as is often the case with foundational elements, the focus tends to fall later in the development. In this case the focus is the role of *attention*, which selects and captures the information provided by our perspective. We might say that attention grabs and nests perspective, and as such, it starts the process of perception and cognition.

Perspective can be described as a stream of objective energy that comes from outside of us and is brought into the mind. There it is subjectively explored by our judgment and otherwise processed to form a mental perception. Perspective is the element that feeds and sets perception in motion. As such, it is not a part of the developmental process through which perception comes into being. Rather, perspective precedes and feeds perception. For this reason, my model of cognition separates perspective from the traditional scientific definition of perception. Whereas perspective is objective, perception is subjective; and whereas perspective reflects information from the universe outside of us, perception reflects our interpretation of it. Therefore, I believe that if we are going to limit cognition to only two primary elements, the logical place for a division is between perspective and perception.

Fortunately, the common view of perception is of a process that includes all of the steps involved in developing our perception, including judgment. Thus, we will continue using the common definition of perception—inclusive of judgment—rather than the more scientifically accepted definition.

If perspective is the foundation around which perception is built, the forces that build perception include personality traits, experience, genetic brain functions, intent, self-honesty, and the like. Given that there are so many variables at work in the development of perception, even if two individuals view reality from nearly identical perspectives (as a result of having nearly identical brain dominance patterns and educational experiences, for example), we can expect them to develop different perceptions due to the unique way they processes their perspectives.

The Nature of Perspective

Perspective conveys raw information to the brain. Perspective comes to us instantaneously. Perception, on the other hand, develops over time. The process of perception is one that can take anywhere between a nanosecond and years to complete, but typically it takes place in a matter of seconds or days. For example, whereas it might take only a millisecond to perceive that the man in the bank with a gun is a thief, it might take years to perceive that the bank's manager is a thief.

Although both brain hemispheres contribute to our perspective and perception to some degree, in most people one side or the other will dominate because of genetic complete dominance. Nevertheless, as we have noted, in spite of the effect of complete dominance, we are capable of shifting our perspective through our intention. Such shifts can be so small as to be imperceptible or inconsequential, but they can also be very meaningful and enrich our lives in countless ways.

The Energetics of Perspective

Since the life that the brain is trying to help us understand is composed of three energies, our perspective likewise may take any of three different energy forms, depending on which form happens to be the object of our attention. Our *physical perspective* is fed by the physical senses as they reveal what is going on around us in our physical world. Through the energy of feeling, our *spiritual perspective* informs us of our feelings and the feelings of others. Using our *mental perspective*, we take in our physical and spiritual perspectives and look at them from the perspective of mind, where they take the form of ideas and other experiences that are known rather than sensed (physical) and felt (spiritual). Although from a dualistic perspective we perceive them as three energies, remember that holistically they are considered to be one energy with different aspects working closely together and sharing functional patterns with each other. For example, what we feel triggers thoughts in the mental realm and sensations in the physical.

Because each of the four brain operating-system types possesses its own unique viewpoint and perspective, each sees and reports something different in its encounters with the three energies. Each of the three energies can be seen from a dualistic view, a holistic view, a hybrid view, or a unity view, resulting in twelve different perspectives. Even as individuals under the guidance of a single dominant system, to the degree that we incorporate the information of our nondominant hemisphere and hybridize or unify holistic and dualistic influences, we can experience all 12 perspectives. And keep in mind that we are only taking into account information *input*.

As we have seen, information *output* is a separate operation and has its own set of four genetic options. Since each of the four inputs can have any one of four output options, there are 16 possible brain-operating-system combinations (discussed in chapter 5). Given that each of the 16 operating systems gives us a physical, a mental, and a spiritual perspective, that means that there are 48 different operating-system/energy-system perspectives based on our genetic inheritance. This perhaps suggests another reason why individuals can have such varied perceptions of things.

Of course, since our perception is also subject to the influences of our cultures, the 48 combinations are further differentiated as a result of the added influence wielded by the effects of our culture's perspectives and responses.

The Management of Perspective

What does all this complexity mean to us as managers? It means that the left-brain-dominant male or female that we are trying to work or live with might have a *spiritual*-perspective *input* like that of most women (and thus be highly sensitive to feelings), but have a spiritual-perspective *output* characteristic of most men (and thus be reluctant to expose their feelings). At the same time, they might have a *physical-* and *mental*-perspective *input* typical of men (aggressive and analytical) and a physical- and mental-perspective *output* typical of women (acquiring via attraction and seeking to integrate things).

It is one thing to talk about the existence of mental and spiritual perspectives, but how do we gain and apply this knowledge? How do we work with something that we are unable to see, touch, or even feel? Fortunately, the three energetic systems and the perspectives that they give us reflect one another in fundamental structural ways. As a consequence, mental and spiritual perspectives are perhaps best understood by drawing on our knowledge of physical perspectives.

As we move through a physical environment and our position changes, we experience a change in our perspective. This brings about a change in the view we have of the world around us. For example, when we turn our torso and look in a new direction, the expansion of information is generally more contextual than if we only move straight ahead. We can further increase the scope of our perspective by turning our head. Once our torso and head are turned, we can expand our perspective even more by also turning our eyes.

Another thing we know about physical perspective is that physical limitations can somewhat restrict it. If our neck or eye movement is limited, for example, our visible perspective is narrowed. And at the extreme—such as sitting paralyzed in a chair with no neck movement and loss of eye muscles—unless we can move the chair, we lose all but one perspective.

Much the same can be said of our mental situation: Our mental positioning gives us a viewpoint within the world of mind and establishes a perspective. The information it conveys is restricted by where we direct our attention—that is, where we choose to go in the realm of mind (in other words, what ideas we are willing to consider). As in the physical world, in the world of mind we can become fixated in one direction—as is typically the case with zealots—with the result that we greatly restrict the inflow of information except from one area. And as with our physical perspective, the viewpoint of our mental perspective determines which parts of a holon get seen by consciousness. Our perspective is also limited by the amount of attention we give it (in other words, the degree to which we are attentive). In one case, we are working with physical objects in a physical environment; in the other, we are working with ideas in a mental environment. In both cases we see the same patterns being expressed.

When rigid beliefs restrict our ability to exercise our perspective, we call the result tunnel vision or narrow-mindedness. A similar limiting condition occurs when for some reason we become fixated on something (because we like it, or fear it, or feel traumatized by it, for example). Eventually, stealthily, a fixed position can become habitual, with the consequence that we lose flexibility of vision, we lose part of our mental perspective, and in doing so we restrict our ability to make needed additions and refinements to our perception. Being rigid, we unknowingly limit our ability to think, feel, and explore. As with our physical body, when we keep our mental body healthy and flexible, we aid its efforts to show us what we need to acquire from the world of ideas in order to advance our goals.

The brain serves as a tool of communication. It processes the information that creates our belief systems. It runs our body and can even heal it. When we are able to understand the functional relationship of the two perspectives, we create a mental environment in which we can more easily find our bearings, enhance the acquisition of truth and healing, and thus achieve greater success in our efforts to create.

Perspective is easy to operate. Ask right-brain questions—holistic questions that deal with the larger components of life, with higher issues, with feeling, with constructive processes, and questions that seek context—and the right brain will answer (but not necessarily via thought). Ask left-brain questions—detail-oriented questions that require the special insights of a dualistic system—and the left brain will answer.

To enhance your perspective and perception, seek to harness the power of each operating system to do what it was designed to do. Learn the character of the two fundamental perspectives and their associated responses well enough that you can start to see their influences on your, and other people's, perceptions and responses. Seek out internal conflict and find ways to resolve it and bring the extremes into harmony. Developing a relationship that respects the contribution of both operating systems establishes a unified matrix and opens the field of opportunity.

Our perception of people and things largely determines our *under-standing* of people and things, and our understanding of people and things affects the way we *treat* people and things. How we treat others then affects the way they *feel*. When we stir people's feelings, we stir energies that can influence the way we are treated and the way we subsequently feel. When we understand this cycle, we empower ourselves to more intelligently manage the energies swirling about us in our environment.

CHAPTER 9

Polarization: The Separation
of Unity into Duality

Until the left brain is able to see the unity running through everything, to know that there is truly one spirit, one force, one consciousness moving through absolutely everything in existence—until it knows that unity beyond any doubt—then the mind is going to stay separated from itself, from its wholeness and from the fullness of its potential.

—Drunvalo Melchizedek,
The Ancient Secret of the Flower of Life, Volume 1

We have been exploring the relationship between the brain's two operating systems in order to better understand how they inform us and influence our behavior. The rewards of this quest for self-understanding are a more unified consciousness and the gifts that accompany cognitive unity, such as greater clarity, accuracy, and success. In this chapter we will continue to apply our knowledge of physical structures to help us better understand the managerial structures (systems) of the brain.

The cognitive consequences of the separation of unity into duality are dualistic and holistic brain operating systems. In discussing dualistic and holistic brain operating systems, we are referring to the behavior of *polar* and *nonpolar* systems.

When the oneness of the right brain's universe is viewed through the lens of the left brain's dualistic operating system, the unity of the universe appears to be split along polar and nonpolar lines. The polarization we experience in life, whether we are considering its effect on politics, religion, gender, or something else, is a product of the left brain's polar operating system.

Polar systems are sometimes referred to as *dual* systems, and nonpolar systems as *nondual*. These terms are most often used in a spiritual context, For example, in the Indian system of Advaita Vedanta ("Advaita" is Sanskrit for "nondualism"), nondualism—the singleness of reality—is the primary philosophical tenet. While the terms *dual* and *nondual* are most often used in a spiritual context, *polar* and *nonpolar* are more often used in a scientific or physical context, but they can also be used in general discussion, as we do in this chapter.

Eastern cultures refer to these two systems in terms of the knowledge they produce. In *The Tao of Physics*, Fritjof Capra describes the ways different Eastern traditions view these systems.

> The *Upanishads* . . . speak about a higher and a lower knowledge and associate the lower knowledge with various sciences, the higher with religious awareness. Buddhists talk about "relative" and "absolute" knowledge, or about "conditional truth" and "transcendental truth." Chinese philosophy, on the other hand, has always emphasized the complementary nature of the intuitive and the rational and has represented them by the archetypal pair *yin* and *yang* which form the basis of Chinese thought. Accordingly, two complementary philosophical traditions—Taoism and Confucianism—have developed in ancient China to deal with the two kinds of knowledge.[1]

The Power of Unity

Why is unity valuable? A unified body of beliefs creates cognitive clarity and a singleness of purpose and intention (the opposite of duplicity). The word *integrity* is often used to describe this state. Ultimately, an interest in unity is valuable to us because of the powerful positive feelings of harmony that unity generates.

To the degree that we are able to unify our hemispheric viewpoints— our inner liberal and inner conservative, our inner male and female—we unify our consciousness. *This is not a balancing of the hemispheres.* If one hemisphere is dominant, don't expect that to change. What we seek is an acknowledgment that the cognitive contribution of the nondominant system can be extraordinarily valuable. In doing this, we open ourselves to its specialized insights rather than viewing its ideas as being in competition or opposition, as so often happens when our dominant operating system is dualistic. We are looking for an internal ideological unity, an internal honesty, an absence of conflict.

Truth is unified. Truth is revealed through the unification of fact. When the ideas that program our behavior are unified and in harmony, they are more likely to be truthful and successful. We see cultural respect for unity demonstrated in our law courts where we demand agreement or coherence of witnesses' testimony with known facts.

Our other interest in unity is due to its effect on consciousness. Since the right brain draws information from the left by virtue of being holistic, the resulting unity of the two cognitive systems gives those with right-brain dominance a degree of unity consciousness that those with left-brain dominance are inherently missing. As we have seen, the left brain does not have access to the right brain's viewpoint. Left-brain-dominants must try to understand holistic or unity consciousness based on what they know from experience.

With genetic codominance in effect, our two operating systems work in harmony, giving us a version of nondual or nonpolar consciousness. As we saw in chapters 4 and 5, one result of this is bisexuality, with each operating system attracted to its complement.

Unity of consciousness can be achieved intentionally. Of course, to achieve mental unity through intention, we must work at it. In that case, the acquisition of unity is a developmental process that takes place over time. Note that this process affects only the organization and management of ideas, and therefore has no effect on our genetically determined sexual orientation.

When we attempt to unify two of *anything*, there are not just two discrete elements to deal with—there are two elements *in relationship*. The relationship between two holons is an energized space that the two elements combine to create, and that energized space *results in a third element*—a new holon based on the other two and felt through the energy of love (resulting in attraction) or fear (causing us to move away). The manner in which we go about the integration of holons—things, ideas, feelings—reflects our spiritual/mental artistry.

Conscious integration begins with *intention*. If we are to consciously unify our inner liberal and conservative and our inner male and female, we start by establishing a clear intention to do so. The next step is to set our intention in motion, which we do by applying the energy of *attention* to the task, an act that involves a focusing of consciousness. So, for example, when a decision is important, we might focus our attention to include both perspectives. And since our dominant system informs us automatically—it is literally dominating the arena of thought—it is our *nondominant* system to which we must attend in order to advance the process of integration. We must seek out our nondominant perspective, consider its response, and then integrate this into our normal thought processes.

We can achieve cognitive unity by coming to understand the parts of things well enough to see how they fit together. We achieve unity as a natural byproduct of the experience of living. But, as we have seen here, we can also enhance this process by cultivating unifying experiences through the application of intention.

Regaining Flexibility in Our Perspectives

What does it mean to be guided by holistic or dualistic forces?

As we have seen, from a purely holistic perspective we perceive our world in a unified state; we perceive the wholeness of things, the big picture. Our dualistic perspective breaks this enormous complexity into two—still enormous, but less enormous—parts. And those parts get divided, and they have parts that have parts, all of which get divided down to create our world.

The dualistic character of the left hemisphere's viewpoint can be seen in our reliance on spatial concepts such as *left and right*, or *ahead and behind*. And yet, *left and right*, as we know, can also be viewed from a central and somewhat more inclusive perspective, and yield a somewhat more inclusive or holistic perception. The same is true of *ahead and behind*, which have *here* as a central perspective, and *past and future*, which have *now* as a central perspective.

The idea that a fundamental aspect of our world is dualistic is an ancient one. The Fourth of the Seven Hermetic Principles included in the *Hermetica*, a set of primarily Greek mystical tracts believed to have originated in the first to third century CE, sums up the dualistic nature of our world by saying that "everything is dual; everything has poles; everything has its pair of opposites; like and unlike are the same; opposites are identical in nature, but different in degree; extremes meet; all truths are [partial]; all paradoxes may be reconciled."[2]

When we view reality from a holistic perspective, we perceive others as one with us, and so our attitude is a cooperative and supportive one. When we view the same reality from our polarized perspective, we perceive others as separate and in competition with us for resources, and this often leads us to view them as being in opposition to us—in opposition to our goals, to our ideals, to our values.

To begin to approximate the view of life from a holistic perspective, imagine having a clear view of an environment containing an immense and rich landscape, such as a great city. To be in position to see the whole of it, we must have a distant perspective. However, being that far away, we can clearly perceive only the larger elements and relationships; the details cannot be accurately perceived. We can use binoculars and focus in on the details, and in that way obtain more information, *but then we lose the big picture*. Given time, we can have both, and through their integration we are able to develop a relatively unified vision.

Mentally, our situation is similar. By switching back and forth between the dualistic and holistic perspectives, we are able to build a mental image of our universe, one that incorporates both depth and breadth. However, for most of us, the flow of information to consciousness is largely dominated by just one of these systems, and thus the process of perception is heavily skewed toward either depth or breadth.

Keep in mind that "holistic" is a comparative measure that is highly variable in meaning, since the degree to which something can be complete is highly variable. When dealing with highly complex holons such as governments, ideas, and human emotions, as we are doing here, we are dealing with holons that are incomplete, and therefore only relatively whole.

Those individuals who rely heavily on dualistic consciousness for guidance actually value wholeness. Consider that their destructive (or deconstructive) tendencies and their desire to "take things apart" are based on their need to find what is missing from the whole and correct it in order to make us, or the situation, safer and more complete. In order to achieve this safety, the dualistic system is defensive, a job that sometimes requires offense. Probing for weaknesses, the ever-skeptical dualist wants to find out if there are missing parts, possible dangers, or deception. On the other hand, when we are acting under the harmonizing influence of holistic consciousness, we are more likely to be trusting and accept things as they are, without judgment.

To many people, the description of holistic consciousness as harmonizing might seem rather fantastical, unbelievable, and in direct conflict with what we see around us—a multitude of right-brain-dominants who seem no more capable of getting their act together than left-brain-dominants. But keep in mind that right-brain-dominants are getting much of their information about what is happening in the world from an often deceptive, polarized culture at war with holistic values. And their problem is compounded because their all-important, detail-discerning ability (a feature of their nondominant left brain) is compromised, which places them at a disadvantage in our detail-oriented culture.

We have considerable control over the energies that form our mental attitude and the perspectives this gives us. Therefore, the limitations of living in a dualistic culture are mostly those we unwittingly impose on ourselves. The skeptical response of our dualistic operating system places false limits on our potential. Our truly unlimited nature is often revealed to us in our dreams, which the dualistic brain dismisses as unreal. As children, we did not assume limitations, but as we became socialized, we learned to live within the constricting framework of group consensus and to rein in our naturally expansive nature. And so we withdrew our instinctive belief in the value of extraordinary, transcendental events and have lived in this suppressed state ever since. But by simply accepting that the potential is there, we free our mind to let it show us greater visions, meaning more highly unified ones.

Nonpolar and Polar Systems

The polar hemisphere's dualistic division of the universe into complementary parts separated by a continuum leaves us with a series of polar opposites—such as we have in up/down, black/white, yes/no, and past/future. In the functioning of polar operating systems we find a dynamic operation (a system involving movement and change) driven by the tension between the energetic charges of the two extremes. An example of this division into nonpolar and polar is found in love, which is nonpolar, and fear, which is polar. Another is peace, which is nonpolar, since it is in harmony with love and attractive, as contrasted with war, which, with its separative, aggressive qualities, is polar.

Moving from the spiritual to the physical, another example of dualistic structure can be found in the molecules from which our world is constructed. "All the molecules in our Universe can be divided into nonpolar and polar categories based on the type of chemical bonds that hold their atoms together," says cell biologist Bruce Lipton. "The bonds among polar molecules have positive and/or negative charges, hence their polarity. These molecules' positive and negative charges cause them to behave like magnets, attracting or repelling other charged molecules. Polar molecules include water and things that dissolve in water. Nonpolar molecules include oil and substances that dissolve in oil; there are no positive or negative charges among their atoms."[3]

"All things turn," Robert Ornstein explains in *The Right Mind: Making Sense of the Hemispheres*. "All things also turn in a preferred direction." Perhaps this helps explain why molecules come in two shapes that are mirror images of one another. Thanks to Louis Pasteur, we have known of this mirroring for over a century and a half. Ornstein continues, "Many organic molecules can form in two different shapes, isomers, that are mirror images of one another, just as a right-handed glove is a mirror image of the left. While they are chemically identical, such molecules are physiologically different. . . . Consider the orange and the lemon, each with its distinctive fragrance. The smells come from the same chemical, limonene. But the limonene of oranges is the mirror image, the 'left-handed' one, of lemons. A reversal in the molecule leads to a distinct smell. The same elements, in the same structure, simply reversed, give off different properties. Lemons turn left into oranges."[4]

Our body is lateralized by the two systems. In *The Whole Brain Business Book*, Ned Herrmann explains that "the human body is seemingly symmetrical but actually significantly asymmetrical. That is, there are differences between paired structures throughout the body system."[5] We can see this in people's faces. In almost every case the two sides are slightly different—and often significantly different—reflecting the differences in the brain operating systems controlling them.

We see this dualistic pattern emerge in brain dominance, where we again find that (quoting Ornstein from above) "the same elements, in the same structure, simply reversed, give off different properties." We have seen this dramatically in the areas of gender and sexual orientation, as spelled out in chapters 4 and 5.

Scientists don't necessarily agree on handedness or hemispheric dominance numbers, but evidence, we have said, suggests that up to 90 percent of the world's population might be right-handed. Since each hemisphere controls the opposite half of the body, whatever their numbers, it is generally accepted that right-handed individuals tend to be left-brain-dominant. (This reflects an output dominance, not to be confused with input dominance.) The same mirroring structure that Ornstein discusses is also found in the world of ideas, where the two hemispheres can produce apparently opposite takes on a single idea. Consider the contrasting solutions offered by a polar versus a nonpolar approach to problem solving. The belief that fear and force create the best results in dealing with individual, societal, and cultural issues reflects a mental response derived from polar thinking; the belief that love and harmony create the best results reflects a mental response derived from nonpolar thinking.

Polarization in Our Culture and Within Ourselves

The sense of otherness and conflict that we commonly experience in life comes from the left brain's division of reality into apparent opposites. When refraction separates white light into its constituent wavelengths, producing the colors of the rainbow, we do not view the colors as being in opposition or warfare, because the colors appear beautiful to us. Yet the separation of unity into its constituent spectrum of qualities, which we find so uncomfortable that we forget the underlying unity, is in some ways similar to the separation of white light. Just as white light and the various colors of the spectrum do not exist independently of one another, the oppositions that the left brain observes are part of a great unity.

Pick any quality in nature or in life—light/darkness, heat/cold, brightness/dullness, fascination/boredom—and it can be seen to be on a continuum in terms of its unification with, or its separation from, completion. Extremes of heat or cold can be life threatening or at least very unpleasant, yet heat and cold in moderation are part of the variety that makes life interesting.

When the process of separation creates such a large gap in a holon that its unity can no longer be seen, wholeness seems to become two completely separate things rather than two aspects of one thing. Of course, along with polarization, we typically experience a clash in values, which often produces emotional conflict.

Whenever the specialized functions of the left brain are allowed to run amok in culture, polarization is common—as can be seen in the extreme polarization that exists around many public issues, or in the predatory behavior of large corporations (where corporate interests are sometimes in conflict with public interests), or in the emphasis on short-term gains and narrow selfish interests in every level of society. On the other hand, when dualistic consciousness is able to expand and embrace the holistic viewpoint, the results can be very different. Dualistic consciousness working together with holistic consciousness can give rise to a new level of holistic integration as well as a culture that honors growth and integration. A full understanding of ourselves and our world requires the consciousness of both hemispheres.

There is nothing wrong with polarization *per se*. It orients us to possibilities and expands our ability to make choices. Polarization can provide us with stimulation or even a certain amount of clarity, such as what we find in a good debate centered around real issues. Seeing the extremes can help us attain knowledge and clarity—although getting lost in these extremes can create delusion and conflict.

Typically, the problems we associate with polarization come into being because we misunderstand and mismanage polarized information. The dualistic left hemisphere, by tending toward a narrow focus, does not see the broader context of which the parts are limited expressions. Its point of view becomes self-reinforcing: its inherent tendency to dissect and deconstruct is reinforced by its narrow field of vision. In this way, the relationships between parts of a whole may be missed altogether. The antidote for this is context. By seeking context, we engage the holistic hemisphere and start to receive its broadcast.

When broad, contextual relationships cannot be seen (whether due to physical distance, cultural differences, or complex interrelationships of mind and ideas), there is less ability to find sympathetic resonance with other realities or points of view. We see cultural evidence of this type of response all around us—for example, in political parties that seem incapable of bridging the chasm that divides them, and in cultural splits between segments of our population—and we are so immersed in our own preoccupations that we are incapable of empathizing with others' problems and points of view. Witness the cultural polarization we see in the United States between "red" and "blue" states. This polarization is not the creation of dualistic-dominant individuals alone. Holistic individuals also contribute to this polarized mentality, as when they blame rationality itself for the dysfunctionality of our culture—ignoring the fact that rationality contributes to intelligent and even compassionate decisions, and that rejecting rationality outright is as dangerous as rejecting holistic harmony. Of course, people guided by the "rational" hemisphere are not always rational—too narrow a focus is not truly rational, but a kind of madness—just as those guided by a holistic hemisphere are not always holistic, as when parts of the whole (such as rationality) are arbitrarily rejected outright.

Another common source of cultural polarization comes about as a result of the left brain's mission to put self-interest first. Individuals guided by their left brain, fearing the power of unity itself, resist integration into holistic systems unless it is on their terms. As such, left-brain-dominants tend to be skeptical of efforts to get them to cooperate for the good of the greater whole. They see survival value in maintaining the distinct identity characteristic of dualistic systems and their ways of doing things. We see an example of this in sex-role identification. Most males in our culture, in defense of male sexual roles, would not be caught dead in women's clothing, even women's shirts and jeans, for example, whereas holistic women tend to wear anything they like, from formal dresses and high heels to clothing from the men's department.

In addition to being *externally* polarized, such as we find in political and gender opposition, we can be *internally* polarized. Internal polarization occurs when we fail to respect or hear the advice of our nondominant operating system. Because it is usually easier to recognize the inconsistencies of others than it is to recognize our own, the general tendency is to focus on the polarized behavior and positions of others, and ignore our own.

Cognitive Consequences of Separation

In order to better comprehend the actions of people and cultures operating under the influence of polar-based systems, it is important to understand the cognitive consequences of separation. To get a better sense of how separation works at its most fundamental level, we will go back to the point where oneness becomes separation.

As we have discussed, in response to encountering the overwhelming complexity that is characteristic of wholeness, the left brain, with its system that is specialized to look into holons, breaks them down into smaller, more comprehensible parts. Typically, this process starts with a division into two parts—for example, hot and cold, good or bad, right or wrong, black or white, yes or no. These dualistic divisions then get broken down in more nuanced ones.

Keep in mind that the left brain is trying to do the impossible when it tries to separate a holon from its context, or from other aspects of itself. When we divide a holon, it loses its wholeness. We can, however, separate holons *conceptually*. For example, we can ignore conflicting elements in our mind, or through rationalization move them to a position of irrelevance. And holons can be *arbitrarily* separated, as when we cut a cake or judge a performance. In this case there is no fixed way of doing it. In the example of a cake, we simply choose how many pieces we want; in judging, we can choose the number of points to use in our scale. The same pattern of division applies when trying to separate concepts like goodness into parts. We can choose to divide goodness into *good*, *better*, and *best*, but we can also divide it into *good* and *bad*, or make any number of other divisions.

A first step in advancing the process of cognition might involve the polar hemisphere's dualistic system in a constructive role. The first thing we need to know as we set out on a quest into the unknown is the nature of any extremes that we might encounter. As holistic teacher and author Gregg Braden asks in his video *Beyond Zero Point: The Journey to Compassion,* "How can you ever find your balance in life until you know what the boundaries of that balance are all about? How can we know our balance until we find our extremes?"[6]

The two extremes of a polar system frame the stage for the unfolding of knowledge that occurs as we explore different positions between those extremes. In order for polar consciousness to divide a complex holon into its two most fundamental parts (or, put another way, to dissect a unified holon into a set of polar opposites), a certain amount of insight or information is necessary. For that reason, we sometimes make mistakes when we try to separate holons. For example, we have traditionally separated love into two parts: love and hate (with gradations in between). But the absence (or opposite) of love is actually fear—hate is a response of fear, an aspect of fear.

For the brain to divide a holon into three or more parts, even more information is needed. An example of a primal three-part separation is the famous truth/beauty/goodness triumvirate. These, it has been suggested, are the three aspects of love—or perhaps even its ancestor.[7] In any case, at this fundamental level of reality, evidence of the oneness of the three comes through. Truth is both beautiful and good. Beauty is both true and good. Goodness is equally true and beautiful.[8]

When divisions are made in a holon in an attempt to achieve clarification (in contrast to an act like cake cutting), *the more we come to know, the more parts we find.* And of course, the more parts we find, the more we know—at least in the dualistic sense of knowing. As science clearly demonstrates, you can learn a lot about something by looking at its parts.

The Disruptive Nature of Separation

When we analyze challenging ideas in an attempt to find their values or errors, we often discover helpful information. Thus, the cognitive process of separation can be very useful. However, *by itself,* lacking the proper context, this process often leads to flawed conclusions and destructive outcomes.

We see the destructive results of separation when someone's words are removed from their context in order to create an advantage for another person, such as we so often find in political wrangling and personal disputes. When we take someone's words out of context, we are arbitrarily separating the whole in a way that destroys its integrity for the sake of some perceived personal advantage.

Viewing a holon apart from its context can result in its being misunderstood. An example is when we look at one element (such as light) that has variable expressions along a continuum and instead see it as two irreconcilable, opposing things (light and dark). This kind of mistake has been known and described since antiquity. Ancient Hermetic teachings, for example, state that

> love and hate are generally regarded as being things diametrically opposed to each other; entirely different; unreconcilable. . . . [But when] we apply the Principle of Polarity [the Fourth Hermetic Principle] we find that there is no such thing as Absolute Love or Absolute Hate, as distinguished from each other. The two are merely terms applied to the two poles of the same thing. Beginning at any point of the scale we find "more love," or "less hate," as we ascend the scale; and "more hate" or "less love" as we descend, this being true no matter from what point, high or low, we may start. There are degrees of Love and Hate, and there is a middle point where "Like and Dislike" become so faint that it is difficult to distinguish between them. . . . Where you find one thing you find its opposite.[9]

We would all prefer to make separations based on factual information, but when our consciousness is dominated by our dualistic operating system, lacking the facts, we will separate based on assumptions or to benefit our goals, or use some other criteria that serve us. Since our protective dualistic brain thinks it knows the answer, it will always come up with a rationalization. When this happens, our underlying assumptions or goals can then seriously get in the way of our ability to discover what is true.

Because a separative response is so common in our culture, people have learned to create ideological moats around themselves, their ideas, and their actions. They have learned to build philosophical defenses to wall off and hide the philosophical inconsistencies that reveal the errors in their beliefs and actions. And since so few people seek to achieve deeper unity in their ideas and understanding, people (including many governmental and business leaders) are able to separate and hide parts of the truth from one another in such a way that internal ideological contradictions go unnoticed and, as a result, often go unchallenged.

The left brain's selfish, separation-based perspective leads us to believe that separative activities and processes are there to solve all of life's problems. How this actually plays out in life is a function of integrity. Need more than you earn? To some (including many white-collar criminals), the solution is theft—separating money or possessions from the rightful owner. Is someone a major problem? Murder separates, as does capital punishment. Bribery separates us from the system of law and justice. Corruption, lack of transparency, and favoritism all separate honest government from the people and from accountability. The purpose of jails and prisons is, more than anything else, to separate us from problem people.

The peaceful effects of separation drive us to live in the suburbs or the country, or perhaps a monastery. We retreat as a way of separating from the collective and from the conflicts that our neighbors present us with. That way, we don't have to make some of the difficult internal spiritual adjustments that are necessary if we are to live in peace among the other members of our culture. *And these spiritual adjustments may be exactly what we need as individuals and as a society—and might even (according to many sources of spiritual wisdom) make up our deeper purpose for being here.*

The Connection between Separation and Feeling

Because we have pointed out the importance of feeling as a way of more fully understanding our experiences, you might be wondering, does separation have a feeling?

Separation has many feelings. If you want to know how separation feels, remember how it feels to be jealous. Remember how it feels to be lonely. Remember how it feels to be separate from something you want really badly. Remember, if you dare, how it feels to hate.

To describe the attitude of a dualistic person or culture that has been separated from the context of unity and thus lacks a holistic-augmented perspective, we need only look to the synonyms of separation: *withdrawal, alienation, segregation, disconnection, isolation.* True to form, this was left-brain-dominant America's response to the rest of the world when given the opportunity to go to war in Iraq. We *withdrew* our respect for the opinion of our allies and acted against their strong protests. We *segregated* ourselves from their criticism and choice of action, and ignored the feelings that these actions provoked. In taking these actions, we *alienated* much of the world, *disconnecting* from the strong bond of unity created by the events of 9/11, thus *isolating* ourselves from our traditional friends.

The Dynamics of Brain Dominance

Given that the two hemispheres are so different in their visions and in their approaches to problem solving, the only way to maintain unity and avoid a possible deadlock between the two when their information is in disagreement is for one hemisphere or the other to dominate and act as manager of operations. But since each hemisphere, when operating alone, has its cognitive advantages and disadvantages, this raises problems. An advantage in one circumstance may be a disadvantage in another.

A holistic-dominant individual will not assert dominance in the same way as a dualistic-dominant individual. For the dualistic hemisphere, dominance is a way to maintain control and ensure survival. This effort is supported by an operating system that is impersonal and aggressive. Our dualistic system must include the ability to separate and dominate if it is to protect us against powerful collectives such as cultural and societal influences, governments, and businesses. In contrast, its peaceful partner, the holistic system, is designed to be inherently harmonious, cooperative, and supportive. Our holistic side is not inclined to exert its dominance overtly, but instead it reveals, through its actions and persuasion, the attractiveness of its point of view. For example, holistic consciousness instinctively knows that it is easier and more conducive to peace if we draw people in and get them to volunteer to serve rather than to take on the job of trying to dominate them.

The Continuum of Perspective:
Center versus Extremes

In terms of our genetic inheritance, some of us end up viewing the world from an extreme position on the continuum of perspective; we are not just dualistic or holistic, we are *extremely* dualistic or holistic. Most likely to fall into that category are people under the direction of genetic complete dominance living in a cultural setting of the same dominance. In the West and Middle East, with their strongly dualistic cultural settings, the extreme dualistic viewpoint is by far the more common one.

Other individuals, positioned closer to the center of the continuum, such as people with genetic incomplete dominance (and thus hybrid consciousness), can be expected to have a less intense experience of the poles than those experiencing complete dominance. Because people guided by hybrid consciousness are positioned somewhere within the continuum at a distance from the energetic extremes of the poles, the individual poles exert less power over the direction they take.

Even with all its potential dangers, an extreme viewpoint also has its benefits, and they are substantial. Consider that when our viewing location originates from a central position on the continuum of perspective, our interaction with the two defining extremes occurs from a distance, and this has consequences. For example, if we were to be raised in an environment where the temperature of everything was always constant, the idea we have of heat and cold would not exist. Similarly, persons who have not experienced the extremes of life may sometimes seem rather blank or lacking in depth compared with those who have. Thus, our balanced view of reality may come at the expense of a fuller understanding of the energies and values of the polar and nonpolar extremes.

Another example of the consequences of failing to understand the extremes is found in our experience with war and peace. If we lived on a planet where violence was unknown, where there was always peace, we would have no occasion to delve deeply enough into ourselves or our world to understand the value of peace. Having had no experience with violence, we wouldn't know what peace meant. We would *have* peace, but we wouldn't understand peace, its value, and the cost of not having it—and that could actually be a block to a deeper, heart-centered appreciation of peace.

Wherever we might find ourselves on the continuum (or within the sphere) of perspective, most of us only become conscious of the existence and nature of our nondominant perspective over time, often as a result of living with or otherwise being close to someone whose dominant perspective corresponds with our nondominant perspective—as is most obviously the case with heterosexual married couples.

We believe and act based on the information we encounter. And, whatever our genetic inheritance, most of our information comes from a polarized worldview that sees and discusses reality from a dualistic viewpoint, giving us a cautious attitude that often demeans and ignores nonphysical values such as are embedded in holistic ideas. When we act based on this worldview, the loss can be substantial, because the harmonious combination of the parts is always greater than the sum of the individual parts.

CHAPTER 10

Dualistic Operating-System Patterns Revisited

The day science begins to study nonphysical phenomena, it will make more progress in one decade than in all the previous centuries of its existence.

—Nikola Tesla

We first introduced the brain's polar and nonpolar operating systems as individual systems in chapters 2 and 3. Since this book is focused on the integration of these systems, and we have control over this process through our choice of perspective, it is essential that we understand the options that they give us. Considering the extreme importance these systems have in our lives, I believe that this subject is worth revisiting. We will not try to cover all of the same ground again. Instead, in this chapter and the following chapter, we will freshen our understanding of those areas of the dualistic and holistic systems, respectively, that can most inhibit—or best contribute to—the achievement of inner and outer peace. Then, for the remainder of the book, we will apply these findings to specific social, cultural, and political contexts that illustrate the brain's polarizing effects on our cultural experience.

The way that we feel is mostly a consequence of our mental state, a condition that depends heavily on our physical, mental, and spiritual "diet"—what we consume in the form of food and other chemicals, ideas, and feelings or emotions. That diet, of course, is a product of choices made, choices strongly influenced by the nature of the relationship of the two operating systems as they impact us individually and culturally. In *Why We Believe What We Believe*, Dr. Andrew Newberg and Mark Robert Waldman explain the relationship between the two brain systems in this way: "We are born with two hemispheres that will, over time, develop two distinctly different worldviews, and our consciousness does not seem to like this very much. The right side of the brain wants to exclaim, 'This is it—this is the whole picture.' But the left side intrudes, saying, 'No, you're wrong—look at all the inconsistencies and differences and pieces of the puzzle that have been ignored.' Neurological studies seem to confirm this inner conflict by showing that each person is capable of thinking both ways, though not necessarily at the same time."[1]

The brain's left hemisphere, Newberg and Waldman explain, "turns reality into sets of ideas that can be communicated through language to others," whereas "the right side spatially grasps the wholeness of the world through feelings." But—and this is a key point—"both halves of the brain, when working together, give us a sense of reality that is clearly different from the sense formed when either side acts alone."[2] For this reason, it is not possible to accurately describe the character of the brain's holistic system without describing the dualistic system—and vice versa—due to the complementary and symbiotic nature of their relationship.

Dispositions of the Left Hemisphere

The demands of life require us to respond to matters of spirit (feeling/emotion), mind, sociology, geometry, energy, and the acquisition of the necessities of life. We will therefore look at some of the spiritual, cognitive, social, geometric, energetic, and acquisitional dispositions of the two operating systems. In reviewing the brain's dualistic operating system, we will now focus on those unity consciousness characteristics that tend to generate conflict in our lives and thus play a major role in disturbing our inner peace.

Until now most (though not all) of our exploration of the two operating systems has been skewed toward an examination of the brain's information *input*—our *perspective*. From here on we shift our principal focus toward the brain's information *output*, which can be observed through our *response*. An example of a response is *perception*. Perception is our first response to information.

So let's look again at dualistic behavior within the operating-system output categories that we examined in chapter 3 (and that were introduced in the list of unity consciousness characteristics at the end of chapter 1).

Spiritual Disposition

Keep in mind that *spiritual disposition* refers to the *spirit* with which an operating system responds to information. Think of an operating system's spiritual disposition as its temperament, or as an aspect of its persona.

As we have discussed—and this is important to remember when trying to understand the behavior of dualistic-minded men—the brain's dualistic operating system focuses on the *impersonal* aspects of life. Although a disposition toward the impersonal does not force us to behave in an impersonal manner, it does point us in that direction. Of course, holistically directed people can be impersonal too. But still, as a whole, men tend to be more impersonal than women, and this is because of the predominance of the dualistic operating system in males.

Another disposition of dualistic consciousness is to focus our attention on the *physical* world. In other words, the spiritual disposition of the brain's dualistic operating system is physical. If that sounds paradoxical, it's because it is: in a physical-spiritual duality, when we shift our attention away from the spiritual end of the continuum, our attention is naturally left to monitor the physical end. The left brain's focus on the physical probably explains why males tend to be more physically oriented than females. We see this tendency to focus on the physical revealed in the selection of a mate. For example, typically physical appearance plays a large role in men's attraction to women, and less of a role in women's attraction to men.

The dualistic hemisphere's attention on the physical gives us a perspective and response geared toward serving our physical needs, and comes with a supportive spirit that is *materialistic, competitive*, and *insecure*. It wants more (a characteristic that in excess becomes greed). In contrast, the holistic hemisphere's godlike perspective and response is loving, cooperative, and secure. It wants to help people. The idea that the operating system of the brain is divided up into physical and spiritual halves might seem radical to most Western cultures, but it is traditional to native people. According to Ohiyesa (1858–1939), a member of the Sioux nation, a medical doctor, and author of 11 books on Native American life, "Indian people have traditionally divided mind into two parts—the spiritual mind and the physical mind."[3]

Because job one of our dualistic operating system is to secure and safeguard us, another of the left brain's spiritual dispositions is to be cautious. A cautious spirit makes us a conserving spirit (a characteristic discussed below in the "Social Disposition" section). We conserve out of a spirit of caution. As part of being cautious, the left brain is also skeptical and intolerant of things that might pose a threat.

The issue of security, the concern of having enough of whatever it is that we think we need, also makes us aggressive and competitive. Of course, in excess—if not also in moderation—being skeptical, intolerant, aggressive, or competitive in spirit can lead to conflict.

The left brain's protective spirit can contribute to personal (internal) and social (external) conflict. Science tells us that the left brain knows and the right brain believes. But what happens when Mr. Know-It-All doesn't *really* know? It turns out that he guesses. As a result of this, we are sometimes deceived—and, by extension, unknowingly deceive others. The disposition to be protective is a natural response of the left brain's role of looking after our security: we ask for an answer and the left brain gives us its best. Nevertheless, when the left hemisphere guesses, when it makes up answers, its misinformation tends to generate conflict. In doing split-brain research (in which the hemispheres were isolated), Michael Gazzaniga found that "though the left hemisphere had no clue, it would not be satisfied to state it did not know. It would guess, prevaricate, rationalize, and look for a cause and effect, but it would always come up with an answer that fit the circumstances. In my opinion," he says, "it is the most stunning result from split-brain research."[4]

Selfishness is a spiritual disposition of the brain's dualistic operating system. Because our dualistic system is focused on our survival, it naturally focuses us on ourselves. While an excess of selfishness can obviously be bad, to the extent that it protects us, selfishness is good and necessary.

This is not to say that those under the influence of dualistic consciousness never put others first. "Me" often transitions into "my," by which I mean that our selfish tendencies can be expanded to include areas with which we selfishly identify: *my* family, *my* tribe, or *my* country. This is why we are sometimes willing to give our lives for a collective in spite of being strongly left-brain-directed. Although it can appear as selflessness to others or to oneself, even this is an act of selfishness. The apparently altruistic act of helping someone—even to the point of giving one's life for that person or cause—is rooted in selfishness to the extent that it is done with the goals of being a good citizen and building self-respect, or in order to gain the respect of others (even posthumously), or even in order to assure one's place in heaven or paradise after death. We might appear to sacrifice our own interests for family, company, country, or God but actually do it for a promotion we want, or to prove to ourselves or to others that we are brave or loyal or righteous—or for some other reason that satisfies the dualistic self. In contrast, people informed by holistic consciousness or one of the genetic integrations (hybrid or unity consciousness) inherently understand that we are all one, and therefore they support their collective self, even at the expense of their individual self.

Reflecting the aspirations of the left brain's dominating spirit, when dualistic consciousness is dominant, we experience a need to be in control. Having control of things adds to our sense of security. But of course the need to be in control is another source of conflict, since our attempts to control and dominate people often lead to rebellion.

Dualistic consciousness, because it is narrowly focused, gives us a spirit that is *exclusive* in disposition. When we focus on certain parts, we can't help but exclude others; thus the left brain's narrow focus is naturally separative and limiting. Of course, when we are exclusive, we can create a climate of conflict around us, as those we exclude will protest our actions.

An iconic example of such exclusivity can be seen in the wearing of special attire by certain groups. Sometimes a uniform is necessary for public identification; this is obviously the case with police or fire department uniforms. In other cases—such as religious attire—the main purpose of such clothing is often simply to set one apart by highlighting and rewarding the status of one's religious attainment and perhaps dividing the more advanced from the less advanced—and the insiders from the outsiders—in a hierarchical manner. (An exception might be individuals such as ordained clergy and nuns whose attire has a more functional aspect relating to their specific duties—although there is sometimes not a clear line of demarcation between duties and spiritual status.) Within the religious environment, religious clothing is fully accepted and thus harmonious, but outside of that environment, it often provokes conflict. From the perspective of an outsider, we see this as a "holier-than-thou" statement. The competitive spirit of dualistic consciousness ensures it. The insider wearing the uniform will more often than not share this view but, rather than find its statement of piety objectionable, interpret it in a positive light. Thus the "insider" and "outsider" views are mutually reinforcing and polarizing.

The left brain's exclusive, limiting response can be very helpful when properly applied. For example, by being more exclusive with respect to what we eat, we might eat less and eat more healthful foods with the result that we feel better. Similarly, by cutting out extraneous things in our lives and forcing a discipline of limitation, we create the conditions to have more free time and save money. Limitation, including self-limitation, is to people what brakes are to a car. Limitation slows us down and allows us to avoid dangers. A limiting and exclusionary perspective can be a valuable tool when used in concert with the holistic, big picture of which it is a part. Dualistic consciousness is a problem only when we become identified exclusively with its processes and mesmerized by its narrow focus, thus losing sight of the relevant context.

As a result of hemispheric connectivity and cultural influences, we cannot help but receive some input from both perspectives, and therefore the polarized patterns of behavior we are suggesting are usually somewhat modified in practice. So, for example, although it might be characteristic of holistic consciousness to be caring and peaceful, holistically guided individuals can still be highly protective and respond violently if they sense that someone is a threat. When it comes to our security and the security of those we love, the left brain instinctively kicks in and responds to the dualistic imperative, which is to protect us and the things we fear the loss of. Otherwise, life comes at us, and in response the two operating systems give us a yin/yang choice and we are compelled to find the right balance to fit the moment—a choice that often takes place at the unconscious level.

Cognitive Disposition

The *cognitive disposition* of the two hemispheres refers to how the two brain operating systems dispose of the information they receive—in other words, how they process information.

Research suggests that both hemispheres think and that both feel, but that they also specialize. Much the same is true of the process of thought. From our left brain we receive *rational* thought, a type of limited, linear reasoning (limited, since it is a closed system). Classical Greeks referred to this type of thought as *logos*. Our right brain, on the other hand, having the big picture, gives us a more complete development of thought, referred to as *reason*—the Greek *nous*.[5] The main difference? To develop reason, we bring all of our information together, including rational thought, feelings, and intuition, and integrate it. In other words, reason is a response of unity consciousness.

Compared with the rapid mental response of the right brain, the *sequential* processing of the left brain tends to be slow. Perhaps that is why most men tend to speak more slowly than most women. In any case, that is not to say there are not some very quick left-brain-dominants, or slow right-brain-dominants—after all, there will always be variation. Ironically, as a whole, women tend to take longer to make important decisions than do men. Perhaps that is because they see more options from which to choose and are not as practiced in accessing the details as dualistic men, who are natural specialists in that area. And holistic women are likely more willing to take time to try to understand how their decisions might affect other people.

As has been made evident in our previous discussions, the left brain's analytical approach to thought is probably its most well-known disposition. Indeed, the terms *analytical* and *left-brained* are often used synonymously. We have seen that the left brain takes holons apart and studies (or analyzes) their parts in an attempt to understand how they work, in order to see what "makes them tick"—to see if they are what they appear to be. Analysis, whether its target is physical, mental, or spiritual, always attempts to disassemble or deconstruct in some manner as a way of gaining understanding.[6] This characteristic often engenders conflict.

Social Disposition

Social dispositions reflect personal relationships, which are of course spiritual in essence. Therefore, the following social characteristics could also be listed above in the "spiritual dispositions" category. Nevertheless, because of the widespread and profound role that these characteristics play in shaping our social environment, I have chosen to highlight their social aspect.

As we have seen, the social characteristics that we so often see in extreme male behavior—controlling, selfish, competitive, aggressive, and violent—all are left-brain responses, in contrast to the right brain's concern with the needs of others—characteristics more often associated with a feminine spirit.

Another social (and spiritual) disposition of the hemispheres is to be either *conservative* or *progressive*. Our conservative impulses originate in the dualistic operating system of the left hemisphere. There, the brain monitors personal security, a characteristic concern of political conservatives. In keeping with its cautious demeanor, the brain's dualistic system has a tendency to use separation when solving problems, an act that keeps us at a distance from danger ("keep the refugees out")—as opposed to the right brain's response, unification ("let some refugees in"), which often exposes us to risky elements. While these same conservative values are widely viewed as important by those who are holistic-dominant and focused on collective needs, the latter see themselves in others and consequently are trusting. The progressive side of the brain is lacking the conservative side's strong regard for caution and may therefore sometimes unconsciously lead us into danger. We will discuss conservative and progressive forces in more detail in chapter 12.

Geometric Disposition

The geometric disposition of the left brain is two-dimensional and linear, and this can be seen in some of its responses. Its focus, for example, is based on a linear form. Its process of thought is sequential, which is an aspect of linearity; and it views ideas in a linear continuum, in which people and their ideas range from one polarized extreme to its opposite. In contrast, the holistic system's geometric form is a three-dimensional sphere. Holistic structures are built around an underlying linear framework that shows the transition from linear to holistic and can be seen in the progression of the five platonic solids, from the four faces of the tetrahedron to the 20 faces of the dodecahedron.

The linear activity of focusing can produce an emotional intensity that is not present when our dominant viewpoint is holistic. Since focusing tends to put certain things in our face and exclude all others, we are especially susceptible to being emotionally drawn into the world of our focus and, once there, if conflict is present, find our passions leveraged and emotional pressures building. In general, we maintain a healthy relationship with focus simply by keeping things in context. By maintaining awareness of the context, we position ourselves a step away from our focus and mentally ground ourselves.

We've previously mentioned that another geometric disposition of the brain is to divide our attention based on the relative sizes of things. Discussing the system that feeds our consciousness, Robert Ornstein concludes in *The Right Mind* that it "divides into the large elements of perception and action and the small [elements of perception and action]."[7] Ornstein's studies suggest that "the right is much quicker and much more accurate at detecting very large waves of visual information, whereas the left is much better at detecting the very short waves."[8]

In keeping with this pattern of division, it should come as no surprise that in studying auditory patterns, Ornstein found a similar response: the left is "specialized for hearing the high auditory frequencies"—the details—whereas the right hemisphere seems to be specialized for hearing low-frequency sounds.[9] (Low-frequency sounds produce larger waves, whereas higher frequencies produce smaller waves.)

We see this same characteristic response to size in the hemispheres' interactions with ideas. To restate what has been expressed here many times in a somewhat different context: the dualistic left hemisphere, being narrowly focused, seeks out and sees the details, the facts, the smaller constituent elements of truth; whereas the holistic right, being focused on the big picture, sees an overall pattern that reflects an aspect of truth but must rely on the left brain's facts to give its big-picture understanding the clarity of detail. The holistic approach is problematic from a dualistic perspective, as the holistic's broad perspective is often open to interpretation and is sometimes seen as too vague to be useful, or possibly harboring unseen danger.

Energetic Disposition

We saw from the list of unity consciousness characteristics in chapter 1 that fear energizes the brain's dualistic system, and love powers its holistic system. Whereas the energy of love pulls us toward the object of our attention (and the object toward us), the energy of fear pushes us away. These dynamics serve to keep our mind and our environment in a state of energetic tension.

Considering the left brain's sequential processing style and the limitations of focus, we should not be surprised to find that the left brain uses its energy to *jump from focus to focus*. Like a bee that must constantly move from flower to flower in order to satisfy its needs, when our mind is flooded with dualistic consciousness, we are never able to find satisfaction in our partial view. As a result, we change our focus relentlessly. We see this "jumping" behavior in the stereotypical TV channel-surfing of left-brain-dominant males. We also see this in male sexual behavior.[10] Holistic consciousness, being fully connected, sees and experiences everything (meaning everything in sight, everything within its range of experience), and doesn't have that need to jump around.

Another energetic disposition of the brain's dualistic operating system is its aggressive, reductive, analytical approach to dealing with holons, the purpose of which is to get us to the heart of things. Incoming data, for example, is automatically examined in terms of security in an attempt to detect error and deceit and prevent us from being misled. To carry out this action, incoming ideas are met with a skeptical, destructive attitude intent on exposing hidden problems.

Although the dualistic approach to problem solving does not necessarily lead to destruction, destruction is a common response. Whether it is a car that moves too aggressively to change lanes on a crowded highway, or the use of dismissive or obstructive conversational strategies, when one individual or object moves into the space of another, we can at the very least expect a degree of destruction to someone's peace of mind. Because of the left brain's commanding role in generating conflict, we are going to take a closer look at its aggressive, reductionist approach to dealing with things.

Whether or not the dualistic turns destructive depends on many factors, including the nature of the object or process to which destruction or deconstruction is applied, as well as the *manner* in which analysis is approached. Take an engine apart, and no harm is done. Unless we break or lose a part, we can reassemble it. Ideas too, can be reassembled. But investigate the internal workings of an animal or a tree, or even a rock, and the result is some degree of destruction.

We see the destructive character of the dualistic operating system expressed graphically in the much greater frequency with which young men destroy lives and property than do their female counterparts. This destructive tendency continues through male adulthood in many ways—such as in men's use (and belief in the effectiveness) of war and weaponry as means of effecting change, and, in the corporate world, their almost psychotically obsessive focus on short-term profits at any cost. In these examples, the outcomes on the future and on the broader collective are almost invariably disastrous and unsustainable—but from the narrow focus of dualistic consciousness, we tend to overlook this because of our fixation on immediate, narrow gains. Our dualistic hemisphere also has a fascination with technological fixes as shortcuts for real understanding—an example being "smart bombs" whose accuracy in destroying a given target is erroneously confused with effectiveness in accomplishing ultimate goals. In such cases, the left brain is so mesmerized by its own ability to view things in isolation that it forgets the big picture altogether.

Force, when determined enough, almost always prevails—look at how water is able over time to erode rock. The left hemisphere, focused on security, sees domination over people and things as a way to ensure it—but, with its partial perspective (that is impersonal as well), can easily overlook factors such as future consequences. The fact that many of our global allies opposed the United States' war efforts in Iraq and refused to help us invade should have caused us to take pause, but we did not. Instead, we chose to ignore this external feedback. As a result, we created a breeding ground for terrorists—one of many unintended consequences. We created in Iraq what we went to war in Afghanistan to destroy, a school for war. Radicals went to Iraq, fought, learned their craft, and went home to spread their knowledge. Opponents of the war pointed out this obvious response for years, but their unpopular views were dismissed as partisan or unpatriotic until they were finally vindicated by a leaked secret National Intelligence Estimate.[11]

Our collective left brain, having a narrowly focused, force-oriented, go-it-alone perspective, naturally led us to ignore our old international allies and rush ahead with our plans for war. When our dualistic operating system is dominant and something stands in the way of our goals, typically we are willing to use some degree of force — or at least to sanction its use by others. The weapon of choice might be a gun, a threat, innuendo, or a vote, but whatever the tool, the intent is always to remove obstacles to the attainment of our goals.

The destructive methods of our dualistic hemisphere are there for *good* uses. They are there when we need to break a habit; or when we need to destroy obstacles in order to make a fresh start; or when we need to expose deception. The destructive nature that arises from the use of dualistic consciousness is part of the yin and yang of reality. The destructive option is a choice. It is a force that we have available to us. We are gods in that we have access to all creative and destructive forces present on this planet. We are not compelled to use coercive means to solve our problems. Coercion is a conscious choice that people sometimes make.

A Course in Miracles describes the energetic disposition of dualistic systems in terms of *fragmentation*: The ego (a fear- and separation-based thought system[12]) "believes in 'solving' conflict through fragmentation, and does not perceive the situation as a whole. Therefore, it seeks to split off segments of the situation and deal with them separately, for it has faith in separation and not in wholeness."[13] Elsewhere, the Course states, "Obsessed with the conviction that separation is salvation, the ego attacks everything it perceives by breaking it into small, disconnected parts, without meaningful relationships and therefore without meaning."[14]

Acquisition Disposition

When it comes to the acquisition of information, the holistic, with its omnidirectional perspective, serves as lookout, seeking information that might be valuable to us in some way. Our dualistic hemisphere, on the other hand, which looks *into* things, has direct access only to what the right has brought in. As we have observed, the dualistic hemisphere's information is limited to what is already known.

If our dominant mind-set is dualistic and we see something we wish to acquire, our natural tendency is to pursue it — to expend energy in an attempt to obtain it. And whether our quest is for information or for something else, when barriers get in our way, our dualistic system prompts us to use force if necessary, starting with some degree of coercion. The brain's holistic system uses the reverse approach to acquisition. Being integral in function, the holistic is cohesive; it pulls toward us whatever it is that we want. For example, in holistic consciousness we often seek to attract what we want by appealing to shared values.

The Challenge of Living with Dualistic Dominance

Those of us who inhabit a body that is guided by a polar-based, dualistic brain—most men and many women—face a unique challenge. We find ourselves in a body with a dominant mind-set that sees and seeks separation and polarization, and has a narrow focus that ignores or even sabotages the broader collective as well as long-term interests. The result is a tendency to perceive everything, including God, as being separate from us. That is what it means to be separative: to see the separation between holons (to the exclusion of their oneness) and to respond with separation as a method of achieving goals (divide and conquer).

Under the guidance of our dualistic hemisphere, we experience a greater separation from love, and from its connections, insights, and nourishing qualities, than we do under the guidance of our holistic hemisphere. Our dualistic operating system, because it channels our consciousness into a focus, is essentially blind to oneness and love, and apparently even blind to God (it is, after all, impersonal and focused on the physical). On a planet where many people feel abandoned by God, the ones most likely to feel this way are surely those individuals operating under the genetic direction of dualistic complete dominance, individuals that are led by their brain dominance to perceive the world from a perspective of separation. Only to the degree that we have holistic brain input do we escape the limiting extremes of dualistic perception as described.

A dominant dualistic operating system is obviously valuable to have when our cultural environment is dualistic, as it so often is in the Western world. As for its limitations, they are mostly those we place on it by failing to understand, respect, and accept the enormous value of our holistic operating system and unity consciousness—or even, through our reflexive habits, failing to notice our holistic side altogether. If dualistic (or holistic) dominance has been limiting up to now, it need be no longer. Once we recognize that we have two distinct ways of viewing the world, our limits are primarily those we choose to retain through inaction.

CHAPTER 11

Further Considerations of the Holistic Feminine

Everything we call real is made of things that cannot be regarded as real.

—Niels Bohr

The widespread exclusion of holistic consciousness at the cultural level is a recipe for cultural disaster. An absence of holistic influence produces a culture with a near-total reliance on one brain operating system for guidance, a limited understanding of the other system and its information, and a tendency to resort to some degree of force if necessary in order to get what is wanted. We see the attitude that this mind-set produces most dramatically demonstrated in males, since most males are left-brain-dominant and guided by dualistic consciousness, with its virtual inability to understand the broad vistas of its holistic complement. Among males, we see the extremes of this behavior most dramatically illustrated in warring cultures and where women are widely suppressed.

Right-brain-dominant women, since they are holistically guided, are inherently focused on spiritual values such as we find in personal relationships and feelings or emotions. Right-brain-dominants intuitively recognize spiritual energy as the mother energy and as being real in a way that other energies are not. Unlike other energies, spiritual energy does not dissipate over time but endures and strengthens. We all experience it, but the dualistic mind may not acknowledge it because, paradoxically, spiritual energy is everywhere, as water is to a fish. Thus we occasionally read that some spiritual teacher, philosopher, or scientist has made the seemingly irrational suggestion that what we see around us is unreal. What we see around us is mediated by mind in a way that spiritual energy is not.

Holistic Consciousness

Our brain's holistic operating system gives us our connection with the energy of love, and with the energy of truth, beauty, and goodness. It is inherently nurturing and receptive to the needs of others. It is harmonious, peaceful, and cooperative, and thus it is gentle in disposition. The holistic right brain sees and knows that everything is part of a wholeness that is, by definition, *holy*, as is implicitly recognized in the common root of these two words.

The complexity of the Whole, in the sense of All That Is—or (expressed in dualistic language) God and God's creation—is such that it is impossible to comprehend in any detail except over time. Either one already lives it and understands it in a godlike way, or this understanding evolves over eons. For such an understanding or comprehension to manifest, layers or waves of experience must be added and integrated. We refer to this process of assembly as *synthesis*.

Synthesis is a connective, integral process that holds together and builds toward greater oneness. This process may be appropriately described as *constructive*, as it is a process of evolving toward unity through growth. Since it is oneness-oriented and integrative in action, our holistic side is naturally oriented toward acquisition. In a consumer-based culture heavily focused on physical reality, one might reasonably expect this trait to lead to a predisposition to shop.

We have pointed out that the holistic hemisphere is virtually instantaneous in its information feed. We refer to this download as *intuition*. Our culture tends to exalt the rational above the revelatory mystery of the intuitive. But in *Stalking the Wild Pendulum: On the Mechanics of Consciousness*, Itzhak Bentov reminds us that "meaningful breakthroughs in science, art, and technology come not by 'figuring out' things to the nth degree, but through intuitive leaps or insight, which are later rationalized." When operating in uncharted territory, "intuition is the only thing we can rely on."[1]

In his discussion of meditation and gender responses, Drunvalo Melchizedek casts light on the operational character of the brain's holistic system:

> In the Shiva religion there are 113 ways to meditate. They believe that there are exactly 113 ways and no more. They feel that no matter what way you meditate or what you call it, even if you invent a new form, your way will fit into one of these 113 ways. The first 112 ways are male, and the last (or first) way is female. The male ways are pathways that can be written down or verbally described to another person. Exact descriptions are possible and logic is the rule. . . . The single female way has no rules. It is never done the same way twice (it could be, but that would not be known beforehand). The female pathway has no logic in the normal male way of thinking about things. The pathway moves according to feelings and intuition. It is like water in its movements, following the path of least resistance.[2]

The Role of Relationship in Holistic Systems

Since holistic relationships bind dualistic elements together in the cosmic dance of unity, let us take a closer look at the role of relationship in holistic cognition.

When we choose to understand something—whether it is matter (physical energy), a perspective or idea (mental energy), or a feeling (spiritual energy)—only by viewing it in terms of its *relationships* can we hope to correctly understand it. To get a sense of the fundamental role of relationship on our perception, let us return to our example of Russian nesting dolls, which can be nested inside one another (concentrically, vertically nested) so that only one is visible, or be placed side by side in a line, a circle, or some other shape (nested horizontally) and be seen as a set. They can also be positioned in an unorganized or extreme manner— as when they are scattered so far apart, for example, that only one of them can be seen at a time. And except for the smallest one, individual dolls can be separated into two parts.

What we can gather from this simple example is that tremendous changes can be made in a holon through changes in relationship. And when relationships change, values change—and they can change dramatically. Complete and undamaged, a set of dolls achieves its maximum value.

Relationships are felt. Relationship is spiritual in energy, and as a consequence, changes in relationship create changes in feeling. If a doll goes missing from a set, the change in relationship is felt as loss. This is of course all the more true with people, whether they be family members, loved ones, or members of a tight-knit group. When a long, close marriage ends in the death of one partner, it is common for the surviving partner to feel as if a part of himself or herself has been ripped away.

Like all holons, the holon of relationship displays the four fundamental aspects of wholeness—*individual* and *collective, internal* and *external*— each of which offers unique insights into what is happening in our sphere of interest. For example, in exploring our *internal* environment of thought and feeling, we might ask, are my beliefs in agreement with my feelings? Is their relationship harmonious? Or we might focus on *external* relationships. We might compare our thoughts and feelings with other people's thoughts and feelings to get a sense of where we stand emotionally and ideologically, relative to the cultures we interact with—those of our family, friends, work, and the like. Or consider the relationship between morals and ethics. A *moral* response reflects the internal response of an *individual* with respect to values. An *ethical* response reflects the same fundamental concern with values, but as exercised in relationship to others, a relationship that is external and collective.

We can also gain insight into the importance of relationship through physical examples such as building blocks. Building blocks obtain their individual shape—that of a square or rectangle, for example—from the relationships of the various cuts to one another. Individual blocks connect with one another to form a collective block through connective relationships; the more harmonious the connections, the stronger the resulting structure. Depending on how we relate the blocks to one another, we can create a purely utilitarian box, an architectural masterpiece, or something in between.

When attempting to assemble mental elements such as words and facts into ideas, we encounter similar developmental patterns. Close-fitting relationships are harmonious and tend to be strong and durable. Beauty and integrity are functions of the relationships we create.

Relationships play a major role in the understanding and believability of information. For example, to understand an idea through the medium of print, we depend on a whole series of nested relationships to inform us: relationships of small dots that nest together to create letters, relationships of letters that nest to form words, relationships of words that nest together to create sentences, and so on. Believability, likewise, is dependent on relationships. When our relationship with a source of information is strong and trusted, for example, we are more likely to believe it and thus make use of it.

Many in our culture would have us believe that relationships are secondary in importance to elements. However, looking at our examples, we see that it is not the elements, the pixels, that are indispensable to understanding—it is pixel *relationships*. We could express these same pixel relationships using large objects such as pumpkins or trees or airplanes, and given the proper perspective and a sufficiently distant viewpoint, we could read whatever their arrangement might spell out. Reality is found most profoundly in relationships. An element of relationship is an integral part of everything we see and say and do.

Perceptual Problems Associated with Right-Brain Dominance

It is important to avoid the impression that right-brain-dominants have the answers to all of our problems. Although the brain's holistic operating system nests its dualistic system, and thus technically has access to both perspectives, there are a number of reasons why a holistic-dominant system can fail to give us clear and accurate perception. One major reason for this—which applies regardless of which brain hemisphere is dominant—is that the quality of our interpretations and answers depends on the accuracy of our facts. To be fully informed, our dominant hemisphere must receive information from our nondominant side. Thus, if our holistic system is insufficiently or inaccurately informed by its dualistic partner, it will be fundamentally restricted in its ability to guide us to make informed holistic decisions.

An example of holistic-dominant individuals actually turning against holistic principles can be seen in the all-too-frequent attempts to suppress free speech and diverse viewpoints. This may take the form of shouting someone down who expresses an opinion different from one's own—often a conservative opinion or simply an opinion that runs contrary to a particular agenda. Ironically, free speech may be suppressed in the name of holistic values if those values have been corrupted though misunderstanding. Suppression is the response of dualistic consciousness and can occur even if the individual is otherwise holistically guided. Although those who overtly disrupt free speech are a relatively small minority, in a more covert way this same intent to suppress the free expression of opposing ideas has widespread support among those who are otherwise liberal or progressive.

This tendency is especially notable in the academic community, where the overt tradition of freedom of expression is—or should be—strongest. John Hasnas, a professor at Georgetown University's McDonough School of Business, commenting on university faculty hiring policies in the *Wall Street Journal*, pointed out that there is one area—the world of ideas— where diversity is not permitted. Basing his view on his 20-plus years of doing hiring searches there, he said that every search "begins with a strong exhortation from the administration to recruit more women and minority professors. . . . Yet in my experience no search committee has ever been instructed to increase political or ideological diversity. On the contrary, I have been involved in searches in which the chairman of the selection committee stated that no libertarian candidates would be considered. Or the description of the position was changed when the best résumés appeared to be coming from applicants with right-of-center viewpoints." He went on to state that research data indicate that "only 12 percent of university faculty identify as politically right of center," and "only 5% of professors in the humanities and social-science departments so identify." He concluded that "surely the robust exchange of ideas is enhanced by exposure to and interaction with people who have diverse political and philosophical viewpoints, not only cultural or ethnic backgrounds. Actually engaging with those with whom one disagrees can break down stereotypes and promote understanding across ideological divides."[3] And, as we have observed, this understanding is critical to the creation of a sane, peaceful, world.

Most intelligent people would not willingly suppress truly conservative ideas if they understood the valuable contribution of these ideas to the whole picture. In the case of both conservatives and liberals, responses that go against the fundamental values those positions espouse suggest dishonesty. But ultimately such responses can perhaps best be rectified by learning how to recognize some important details, starting with the understanding that we are cocreators with our opponents and thus infinitely valuable to one another (again, acknowledging the crucial difference between true conservative—or liberal—responses and the often-flawed political agendas that have co-opted those labels).

In addition to the suppression of opposing ideas, another restrictive practice that appears to be spreading within the holistic community is the suppression of certain words, a response that threatens to create additional conflict by chipping away at our freedom to speak openly without retribution. The widespread nature of this practice gives us another example of the flawed perception of some holistically led individuals and helps us understand why those led by holistic consciousness don't necessarily have a more accurate perception than those led by dualistic consciousness.

"Use of racist, sexist, homophobic, transphobic, xenophobic, classist, or generally offensive language will not be tolerated," read the syllabus for a class to be taught by Professor Selena Lester Breikss of Washington State University. "This includes 'The Man,' 'Colored People,' 'Illegals/Illegal Aliens,' 'Tranny' and so on—or referring to women/men as females or males." Any infraction of the rules would be a learning experience, she cautioned. "Repeated use of oppressive and hateful language will be handled accordingly—including but not limited to removal from the class without attendance or participation points, failure of the assignment, and—in extreme cases—failure for the semester." (Following some resulting bad publicity, the school quickly announced that no one would be punished for free speech.)[4]

This story caught my eye because "male" and "female" are words I have used frequently in this book, and they were being forbidden! I wondered why. Upon reading the article, I immediately saw that this instructor understood that human sexuality is too complex to be limited to two categories. She recognized (correctly) that individuals who do not clearly fit into traditional models can experience some conflict as a result, and, being holistically informed, she wanted to support them. However, the exclusion of any mention of traditional males and females, and the desire to control the situation through coercion and punishment, suggests a reliance on *left*-brain solutions. (Remember our observation that women typically see reality from a right-brain perspective but often respond to it from a left-brain perspective.) In focusing on the rights of one group, it is often easy to infringe on other rights, including free speech, and that seems to be what was happening here. While the instructor's intent seems to have been holistic, it is clearly not holistic to exclude the majority and suppress free speech in order to support a minority.

The suppression of opposing views clearly transcends political ideology. It is an act of fear that can affect us all, but the fact that liberals are not immune from such fear-based responses gives us another example of why we cannot simply turn over leadership of governmental or political systems to right-brain-dominant individuals and expect to automatically achieve a better result—especially in a cultural environment where many of the systems they must work in have been corrupted by money and power. Regardless of their well-intended zeal to make the world a better place, right-brain-dominant individuals, as we have often pointed out, have a tendency to fail to appreciate small details—details that are sometimes extremely important—and in doing so, they can unknowingly veer off of their progressive course, take us with them, and end up actually harming the greater good that they seek to serve. But the examples above—involving the exclusion of philosophical and political diversity, or even prohibitions of free speech, at the university level—hardly involve insignificant details, since the role of philosophy is to help unify the various contributions of the many parts of a whole, and that of politics is to point out their differences.

The accuracy of our holistic perceptual abilities can also be distorted by our cultural conditioning. Something as common as conventions of speech can distort reality and mislead us. To get a feeling for how this happens, let us look at the widespread use of the term *drugs and alcohol* (or *alcohol and drugs*) when referring to alcohol and other drugs.

Alcohol is a drug. Alcohol is vertically nested within the whole that we categorize as drugs. Saying "Drugs and alcohol are a problem in my neighborhood" is the equivalent of saying "Dogs and beagles are a problem in my neighborhood," as if beagles were not dogs and thus belonged in separate categories. Nor would we say or think something like, "My neighborhood would be more attractive if we had more trees and elms." If we choose to include alcohol when addressing the issue of drugs, just as we might say "beagles and other dogs" or "trees, especially elms," we can say "alcohol and other drugs," or "drugs, including alcohol."

This is not a matter of memorizing phrases in order to be politically correct. The goal is to discover and acknowledge what is true, not to be applauded for saying something in the proper way. Unless we recognize these relationships for what they are, our ability to perceive and understand accurately—and thus to relate to each other in a way that promotes our highest values and aspirations—is severely compromised.

Language has power. Improper uses create conflicts that divide people. The ways in which we pair words (and the ways in which we use words without inspecting meaning) can profoundly distort our perception of reality and lead to erroneous or even tragic consequences. In this case, the words are a symptom of another problem. What we have here is a lack of holistic vision, resulting in level confusion, confusion between an element and the greater context that is nesting it, something that contributes to a misapprehension of reality and flawed responses.

Drugs such as alcohol, nicotine, and caffeine are so much a part of our culture that they are irrationally placed in a more legitimate category on that basis alone. In the fog of a "war on drugs," the fundamentals of science and logic have been widely dismissed. The left brain's aggressive, impersonal management system, which relies on separative processes to solve problems, naturally supports war as a solution to a drug problem and is unconcerned with conventions of speech if they threaten to interfere with the war effort. Holistic consciousness, which gives us the big-picture view, sees no love or peace gained from locking up our children or other loved ones. Nevertheless, holistic individuals can be misinformed of the details on which they act, and in their lack of discrimination, they can take on the cultural baggage and belief systems (including belief in war) that our left-brain-dominant culture has created and promotes.

The issue here is not our choice of words. The issue is integrity and accurate perception, both individually and culturally. *Integrity*, for our purposes, means integrating the facts of the left brain and the wisdom of the right brain in an atmosphere of honesty and mutual respect—something that is widely missing in our highly polarized cultural and political wars. Do we have accuracy and integrity or not? On this issue, the evidence suggests that as a culture we do not.

Naturally, certain individuals and cultures benefit from this situation. In the case of the drug war, maintaining confusion in the minds of voters helps to maintain prohibitions against politically incorrect drugs while maximizing the profits of other drugs (whether alcoholic beverages or over-the-counter or prescription drugs) by ensuring their availability, even if at grossly inflated prices. And, whether intentionally or not, these efforts further suppress holistic perspectives and holistic processes. Both cannabis and psychedelics, for example—as objects of our war on drugs—are known to shift individuals into a more holistic perspective and perception, something discovered in the hippie culture of the 1960s.

Paradoxically, the peaceful, cooperative side of holistic perception can get us into trouble. Its inherently noncritical, nonviolent quality allows it to be easily dominated by the dualistic forces of left-brain cultures, leading holistic individuals to sometimes act against their natural instincts. And so, for example, although we might expect holistically directed individuals to be inclusive and nonjudgmental, they often succumb to the dualistic urge to be separative and judge. Even if our dualistic left brain is not dominant, considering that it is aggressive and in charge of security, it still has the potential to exert a powerful influence on our perception and consequent behavior.

Comparing the Hemispheres

Viewing life from the left brain's competitive, dualistic perspective, we compare things as a way of getting to know them better. The left brain's take on our current discussion can be phrased as, "Which system—the holistic or the dualistic—has the advantage?" But, in fact, there is no advantage to be had either way. It makes no more sense to say that one type of consciousness (linear or holistic) is better than it does to say that a particular type of vehicle is better than its engine, or that Earth is better than the solar system in which it resides. It is nonsensical to mix categories by placing items that cannot truly be separated on a linear scale of value. Without consideration for the whole, the parts are meaningless.

Judging and comparing is useful when it helps us to sort out our options, but brain dominance is not an option we can choose. Taken alone, both systems are limited. One is a part of the other. The right brain sees on a macro scale but is lacking critical information. It sees the map of reality and knows where to end up but needs help obtaining the details required to discern how to get there. The linear left brain has the ability to figure out how to get there but is often lost in terms of *why* it needs to get there. It performs very well within the rules of the game—it can "crunch the numbers" that show how to get from point A to point B—but it is a very poor judge of why the game is being played in the first place, or whether it needs to be played at all. It can miss the big picture altogether and needs the right brain's holistic context for guidance.

From the broad view of our holistic perspective, there is no disadvantage to having left-brain dominance. All viewpoints are valuable. Viewed holistically, the ideal operating system is the one that best serves the physical, mental, and spiritual challenges served up by our particular life. Holistically, we recognize that the narrow focus of dualistic consciousness is disadvantaged only when trying to understand something it is not equipped to understand. And as split-brain studies have shown, much the same can be said of a holistic operating system that is lacking its dualistic viewpoint.

I have been suggesting that it is most advantageous to use *both* sides of the brain when viewing a problem or situation, and it so happens that women are more likely to do this than are men. As Rita Carter explains in *Mapping the Mind*, "There is a tendency for women to bring both sides of their brain to bear on [a] problem, while men often use only the side most obviously suited to it. This pattern of activity suggests that in some ways women take a broader view of life, bringing more aspects of the situation into play when making decisions, for example. Men, on the other hand, are more focused."[5]

The belief or the acceptance that we can do or be a particular thing contains an energy capable of moving us along the path to success. But we must shape and guide that energy, which we appear to do through the trigger of intention. And that energy needs to be nourished, which we do by focusing our attention on it.

The development of internal harmony and peace is enhanced by finding and removing conflict from our mental body, our body of beliefs and assumptions, our programming. As mental relationships are changed for the better, physical and spiritual relationships will also change for the better. And as spiritual conflicts are resolved, physical harmony will follow. (Happiness promotes healing—as exemplified by the well-documented positive correlation between laughter and healing.)

Happiness is a companion of peace. Happiness is being at peace with what we have, at peace with who we are, and at peace with the Now. Happiness and peace are built on a foundation of giving and having freedom, which means not being at war with ourselves or with others. The happiness that comes when we have the peace of freedom is a function of the harmonious relationships we develop—relationships that are both internal and external; are both individual and collective; and are physical, mental, and spiritual in energy. It is a lot to manage, but the brain was designed for this job. Sometimes we just need to get out of its way. Often that is as simple as being honest with ourselves.

PART THREE

How Brain Dominance
Shapes Culture

CHAPTER 12

Understanding the Cultural Brain

Never trust anything that can think for itself, if you can't see where it keeps its brain.

— J. K. Rowling,
Harry Potter and the Chamber of Secrets

To this point in the book, we have focused most of our attention on how the two brain operating systems affect the behavior of individuals. In the remaining chapters we are going to shift our emphasis somewhat and direct our attention more toward the collective domain of our consciousness and behavior. We will briefly survey the political, military, economic, and social spheres of our culture and consider how our perception and evaluation of each of these areas of collective action changes depending on which of the two fundamental systems of operation feeds the attention of those involved.

The Conservative and Progressive Nature of Operating Systems

In previous chapters, we have pointed out the inherently self-protective, conserving characteristics of the brain's dualistic operating system. When our dualistic operating system is dominant and our holistic is recessive, we tend to be conservative because our primary source of information comes from an operating system that emphasizes scarcity—giving us the compulsive perception that "the glass is half empty." Dualistic consciousness cautions us not only to conserve our resources, but to be conservative in everything we do—whenever possible—such as in our movement (walk with care) or in our choice of words (speak carefully).

In previous chapters, we have also pointed out the inherently selfish, or self-protective, characteristics of the left brain. The social, cultural, and political vantage points that we tend to associate with conservative responses reflect these same characteristics. The selfishness of "me" is extended into the arena of "my" and "mine"—my family and my country; the interests and groups with which I identify, such as my religion and my sports teams; or the policies that protect my freedom, my property rights, my lifestyle and values.

Exercising control over our choices and destiny is a fundamental goal of our dualistic operating system, as is the goal of securing (or conserving) our hard-won advantages. The protection of that which is "mine" is perhaps most strongly reflected in the notion of property rights—hence the importance of home ownership ("my home is my castle") in the American Dream. It is also reflected in the sanctification of gun ownership and of the Second Amendment to the U.S. Constitution (interpreted as establishing the right to bear arms); both of these symbolize the protection of self, family, and property, even though these "protections" might come at the price of a more violent culture.

Because the conservative side of the brain is tasked with protecting us, people who rely on it for guidance tend to support a strong military and robust law enforcement, and will also favor laws protecting property rights, gun ownership, and the like. At least theoretically, this secures us from hostile influences and ideologies.

This attention to individual values and needs, at the expense of collective values and needs, forms the core of the agenda of political conservatives, even though some policies of the political right contradict these values. We will examine the inconsistencies of conservative as well as liberal positions as we proceed.

Obviously, when we associate conservatism (or the political right) with dualistic consciousness, we must also recognize that there will be exceptions. Not all people informed by dualistic consciousness are politically conservative. Nor are all political conservatives the result of dualistic dominance. Our experiences with our teachers, parents, peers, and others, as I have said, exert a powerful influence over our attention, which in turn affects our beliefs and our behaviors. As a result, individually we range across the spectrum from extremely conservative to extremely liberal and occupy all areas in between. However, in spite of the exceptions, what the relationship between politics and the brain tells us is that the self-protective "me and mine" orientation of dualistic operating systems is reflected most consistently in the conservative political agenda—and in the United States, that usually means the agenda of the Republican Party.

In contrast to the tightly focused conservative political agenda, the liberal agenda appears to have a softer focus and embrace a greater diversity. This reflects the difference between the limited but intense focus of the brain's dualistic operating system and the broad, unlimited holistic focus of its holistic operating system. Being broad in scope, the holistic consciousness of political liberals is inclusive and tends to possess and project a relatively unstructured, "free-for-all" nature such as we find in many fledgling democracies.

In keeping with the great diversity of creation that we seek to understand, holistically oriented individuals have a wide range of interests. But beyond the diversity of individual interests, they also have a set of deep underlying values. These include concern for elements like guaranteed education, universal health care, and the minimization of poverty that make for a healthy culture; concern for the environment as a way of supporting health, well-being, and collective survival; and strong stances on civil rights. Note that the emphasis on rights among liberals tends toward civil rights—the rights of everyone to full participation in the benefits of society—whereas conservatives tend toward the right to be left alone and pursue happiness without interference. Obviously, both sides of the equation are necessary.

Whereas the consciousness of an individual takes one of four possible forms—dualistic, holistic, hybrid, or unity—in terms of the collective, consciousness contains a mixture of the four in which two dominate. The polarizing effect of genetic complete dominance gives us dualistic or holistic consciousness and makes most of us into natural conservatives or liberals.

We will generalize and refer to conservatives and liberals as if they were operating from a perspective of complete dominance and able to see clearly only one perspective. My respect goes out to the many conservatives and liberals who have transcended the limitation of a single perspective and therefore make use of both perspectives and respond accordingly, but as a whole, political behavior tends to bear these generalizations out.

Of course, as individuals we have and use both operating systems, and so conservatives and liberals are fully capable of seeing the complementary nature of their viewpoints and responses. Conservatives know that it costs money to fight their almost endless wars and that this is accomplished only through more taxation, which they vigorously oppose. Liberals know that generosity has a cost, and that it is often unreasonably high when filtered through the inefficiencies of government. Conservatives, because they tend to focus on individual-oriented issues, are somewhat naturally blind to the legitimate claims of the common good. And keep in mind that the dualistic operating system is focused on nonliving things such as corporations, whereas holistic systems are focused on living things. Perhaps this explains why conservatives can sometimes be talked into taking untenable positions such as those favoring the rights of giant corporations (which are fictitious entities) over individuals.

Holistic ideas are sometimes viewed as inherently threatening from the polarity-based, individuality-oriented perspective of our conservative hemisphere. Conservatives tend to view the collective as aligned with big government against the individual. Lowering (or not raising) taxes is often viewed as sacrosanct, even when the collective need for tax dollars is dire, even when the very survival and well-being of certain individuals depends on sufficient collection of taxes to fund programs, and even when tax dollars fund programs to minimize fraud (an expenditure that actually saves them money). Liberals, on the other hand, perceiving reality from a largely holistic, collective perspective, see everyone as part of the whole that such government programs address—and so they do not easily recognize a conflict between their own interest and the larger good.

Because cultural influences often alter our natural impulses, and can alter our perspective and our political response as well, exceptions to these broad classifications are common. Conservatives are not always conserving in their beliefs and actions, just as liberals are not always progressive. Whatever our political orientation may be, propaganda, education, and other pressures are likely to draw us away from our natural path. And we sometimes change as a result of our experiences. It is common to start out as a liberal and become more conservative as we age. We eventually recognize that our idealistic cultural energies are not sufficiently supported: we share, for example, but people do not share with us, and so we watch our resources deplete. Eventually, we conclude that our idealistic behaviors are not going to be accepted by society, and fear starts to work its way in. We start thinking that we will be out on the streets unless we shift to a more conserving mode. We start paying more attention to the alternative voice in our head. This process doesn't change our overall dominance, but as we shift our attention, we shift certain aspects of our perspective, and, consequently, we experience shifts in our perception and behavior.

Since the conservative side of the brain takes the aggressive, "bodyguard" side of things, conservatives inherit a crucial and sensitive job in society. Because the selective focus and methodology of the conservative agenda can be destructive, it is especially important that conservatives be true to their highest values when choosing whether to resort to force. Yet, with so much of the world at war, it is fair to say that conservatives as a whole have not responded conservatively in recent times, in terms of either money or lives. Instead, they have responded fearfully. Liberals have reacted similarly. War is a total violation of liberal values, yet until recently, a majority of liberal voters have tacitly supported a war on cannabis users (by doing little to oppose the war—which is all that the warriors ask). As conservatives so often do, liberals have responded to misinformation with fear. Holistic values cause us to be fundamentally opposed to war—they seek harmonious and constructive solutions rather than divisive and destructive ones—but the powerful influences of politics and culture often override our natural response.

Remember that our holistic hemisphere, having its attention on the big picture, the context, *includes* the individual-based stance of our dualistic hemisphere. Collective-oriented and inclusive, the progressive side of our brain does not view individual freedom as being at odds with collective interests. Consumer-protection laws, which are usually championed by liberals and often opposed by conservatives, are an example of a case where the holistic stance of liberals is friendlier to the rights and freedoms of individuals than is the conservative's dualistic stance. The freedoms gained by consumer protections—which involve protecting real people against corporate abuse—clearly outweigh the freedoms lost through some degree of government regulation over corporate life (in which the beneficiaries of such freedoms lost through regulation are largely limited to stockholders and CEOs).

Some frequently held conservative positions reveal not merely myopic vision (as above) but blatant contradictions. As David J. Burge, a Georgia attorney and a Republican Party leader, points out, "Capital punishment runs counter to core conservative principles of life, fiscal responsibility and limited government. The reality is that capital punishment is nothing more than an expensive, wasteful and risky government program."[1]

Since conservatives are natural defenders of the individual's right to be left alone by government and to be responsible for his or her own path, gay rights and drug freedoms should be natural conservative causes. However, conflicting religious beliefs, fear of the unknown, and the self-protective tendencies of conservatives (and other left-brain-dominants) can lead to such powerful identification with their own life that a kind of fortress mentality takes over. As a result, any outside forces that propose to initiate changes—from government to alternative lifestyles—appear threatening. Thus, for much of the conservative rank and file, their primal respect for freedom is overridden by a primal fear of the unknown. Many conservative politicians may not personally share these fears, but political considerations make them reluctant to act in a way that is contrary to their most vocal constituencies.

Terry M. Clark, chairman of the journalism department at the University of Central Oklahoma, suggests that the words *conservative* and *liberal* are now so overused and abused that they've become mere labels— propaganda devices employed by politicians who are more interested in politics and winning elections than in principles. Labels, Clark says, are nothing but words that keep people from thinking. For example, he points out that *conserving* our resources is an inherently conservative act, yet those most interested in conservation are labeled "liberals." Because the so-called Patriot Act subverts our liberties, it should be consistent with conservatism to oppose this act in the name of individual rights, yet it was supported, drafted, and passed by "conservatives."[2]

Another example of the state of mental confusion in American political culture is the conservative reaction to the notion of civil liberties—especially as embodied in the foremost watchdog of their protection, the American Civil Liberties Union (ACLU). Although the common perception is that the ACLU is a liberal organization, it can in fact be viewed as embodying core conservative values.[3] What are these values? Traditionally, and at their core, conservatives are the defenders of the individual and individual rights. Conservatives are engaged in battle against the more powerful collective for individual freedom. And fundamentally, that's what the ACLU does. It protects individuals from collectives—from cultures, from their governments, and from other powerful organizations that seek to usurp individual rights.

Because the ACLU openly works to conserve individual rights, conservatives should applaud its efforts. Instead, among conservatives, the ACLU is widely viewed as an enemy. Perhaps that's because a holistic ACLU respects and defends the rights of *all* individuals, not just conservatives, and this creates conflict in the dualistic consciousness of conservatives, which sees things in terms of black or white, right or wrong, us versus them. From the defensive/offensive stance common to dualistic consciousness, the logic goes something like, "The ACLU is assisting liberals and groups that oppose us; therefore the ACLU is the enemy." While conservatives have no problem standing up for their own rights and the rights of those with whom they identify, they too often fail to see that if *my* rights are to be protected, *everyone's* rights must be protected.

We can be liberal with respect to certain belief positions and conservative where others are concerned. Depending on our experience, our focus, and our beliefs, we might respond to economic realities as from a conservative perspective, and respond to social realities as from a liberal perspective, a common combination. The choice between a liberal and a conservative response can even apply to the various experiences of our life such the amount of time we spend in service to others or on entertainment, or even something as simple as regulating our consumption of chocolate. Of course, the definition of liberal and conservative varies geographically. Whereas, in a conservative culture a person might be considered a liberal, from the perspective of someone in a liberal culture that same person might be viewed as a conservative.

Liberals, philosopher Ken Wilber observes, "believe primarily in objective causation of social ills (i.e., inequality is due to exterior, unfair social institutions); conservatives believe primarily in subjective causation (i.e., inequality is due to something in the character or the nature of individuals themselves)."[4] In contrasting the weaknesses of the liberal and conservative approaches, he points out that "the typical, well-meaning liberal approach to solving social tensions is to treat every value as equal, and then try to force a leveling or redistribution of resources (money, rights, goods, land) while leaving the values untouched. The typical conservative approach is to take its particular values and try to foist them on everybody else."[5] In some areas, liberals and conservatives can disagree among themselves. For example, as Wilber points out, "both have 'freedom' and 'order' wings, depending upon whether they value most the 'individual' . . . or the collective."[6]

Nevertheless, with the numerous caveats we have mentioned, conservatives tend to be heavily focused on the individual. So heavily, in fact, that they sometimes completely overlook issues involving the collective. Examples of this are the effect of violent video games on their kids, or the many instances in which low individual tax rates starve essential collective/cultural needs that benefit them as well. Likewise, liberals are often among the strongest defenders of individual rights where the rights of others are concerned, but in a quest to achieve their lofty goals, they may overlook important details that create unintended consequences (as when sweeping omnibus laws get passed that negatively affect certain individuals).

Liberals, like conservatives, are sometimes torn between maintaining individual freedom and preserving collective order. Because the brain encompasses both viewpoints, we naturally want both freedom and order. When we can't have both, brain dominance (nature) is likely to guide our decision unless dominance has been overridden by cultural programming (nurture).

Because our cultural environment often heavily influences both perspective and perception, our media possess enormous power. Naturally, the power of media to effect cultural change generates a great deal of emotion in a polarized political environment. Conservatives often protest that newsrooms are more liberal than the general public and complain that liberal views get more air time and more print. That is true, but it is no conspiracy. It is part of a natural process of cognitive development.

In seeking to expand their understanding of events, reporters are engaged in holistic activities. As people come up through the various news organizations, regardless of their values or the values of their employers, they are exposed to a wide variety of people, perspectives, and perceptions. This has the inevitable effect of broadening and deepening their *personal* perspectives and perceptions—making them more complete and more holistic, whatever political convictions they might have started with. Although some reporters are naturally more open to change than others, as a reporter's understanding of life progresses, the tendency is to become more liberal or progressive. Nevertheless, as a whole, movement through time is experientially expansive, which means tending in a progressive or liberal direction.

Based on the cycles of political elections and the ascendancy of many conservative political groups in the United States and the world, this tendency toward holistic growth might appear contradictory. What we are more likely to notice is that power shifts back and forth as each political party, time and time again, fails to deliver. But if we look at the broad trajectory of world history, we see that movement over time has clearly been toward the expansion of rights—as well as expansion of the *definition* of rights of minorities. We see this in the relaxation of marriage and divorce laws, the rights of the disabled, freedom of speech and religion, gay rights, the presumption of innocence of the accused, and a broad spectrum of human rights—a movement toward expansion and liberalization that is unmistakable. Even the most extreme reversals—such as the rise of Hitler and Nazism in Europe—created counterreactions that gave rise to sometimes unprecedented movement toward human rights, as embodied, for example, in the Nuremburg trials and the formation of the United Nations.

To maintain a conservative news organization, we need to somehow restrict this natural process. We have to screen people and hire only conservatives and in some way ensure that they remain conservative if they are to keep their job. But in that situation, we end up deliberately biasing the news.

Another complaint often made by conservatives involves the liberal "bias" of the entertainment industry. As actors take on new roles, they take on new lives along with new perspectives and experience new perceptions. Acting is perspective- and perception-expansive work. By expanding and accelerating an actor's understanding of life, theater creates an extraordinarily rich environment for mental and spiritual progress. All else being equal, the more enlightened the character and diverse the roles, the more progressive actors become—assuming that they are learning from their new experiences. Therefore, the nature of acting creates a veritable mother lode of liberals, but of course, openness to change varies with actors as with everyone else.

Radio, on the other hand, is a friend of conservative cultures. Conservative talk radio is successful because it can and does focus almost solely on seeing and discussing issues from a dualistic viewpoint. From its viewpoint, we develop an us-versus-them attitude that is polarizing and results in responses such as we see expressed through grassroots political and cultural conservatism. On conservative radio, life is polarized into black or white, good or bad, right or wrong—making it relatively easy for conservative listeners to find agreement and therefore bond. In this environment, the relatively complex holistic perspective of liberals becomes fodder for caricature—a situation that is hardly conducive to understanding. Liberal radio is less successful because liberals tend as a group to be less focused and less black-and-white in their outlook, as well as more diverse in their interests. Their holistic outlook cannot be easily fed from (or reduced to) a single perspective such as is common to conservative radio; rather, it is fed from a multitude of perspectives. As a result, liberal radio finds it much harder to build loyal audiences in the way that conservative radio can and does.

Perspective and Political Affiliation

In the United States, liberals tend to congregate in the Democratic Party, the more holistic of the two parties. When our dominant consciousness is holistic, we naturally look out for others. From that perspective we see oneness, and we feel a duty to help everyone, including the poor, the disadvantaged, and the uneducated. The holistic view of reality perceives a world that thrives on cooperation. Helping others, we are led to believe, is what brings harmony, happiness, and holiness to the world. These are, of course, generalizations. As a result of the power of fear to alter our holistic aspirations, there are many exceptions.

The holistic attitude that tries to come through in the liberal, grassroots perspective of the Democratic Party is often distorted beyond recognition.

Try to associate the Democratic Party with the holistic perspective and you soon come face-to-face with the *relative* nature of holistic perception. Our political systems, like most of our cultural systems, have been designed by dualistically minded males to favor those in power, mostly men. Basically, to have a chance at winning an election, you have to think and respond dualistically—be competitive, aggressive, and focused. Since the Democratic leadership is predominately male and heavily dualistic, the party is largely guided by dualistic consciousness, with its strong emphasis on individual self-preservation. This means that dualistic consciousness (which is functionally incapable of comprehending the multidimensional scope of holistic consciousness) is trying to direct a holistically leaning political party.

Most Democratic politicians, like most Republicans, will do whatever it takes to stay in office. Like most Republicans, most Democrats cooperate with corporate lobbyists in order to obtain the money they need to get reelected. This kind of response puts self first, corporations second, and country third. This is not holistic. Although the Democratic response to the problem of drug use and abuse is changing, it has long been one of resorting to separation (jail) and other forms of punishment. This is the same solution championed by conservatives—a narrow, confining response based on fear. Similarly, Democratic Party efforts to keep third parties off the ballot are self-serving and hypocritical because they fly in the face of the principles of democracy and freedom of speech. In the 2016 presidential election cycle we saw this in the use of "superdelegates" that allowed the party elite to play an outsized role in the nomination process.

As we have noted, Democrats, to the extent that they are typical and identify with the collective-oriented principles of a holistic operating system, are naturally inclined to reach out to help others. Since they see themselves in others, they are often motivated to help, especially those who are socially and economically suffering. Since helping others in a political context usually involves government programs that are paid for by tax dollars, Democrats, by assisting those in need, have earned the tax-and-spend label. Republicans, since they are the party that focuses on maintaining individual freedoms, especially economic freedoms (even to the detriment of the collective good), naturally work to lower taxes. Their intent, as we have pointed out, is to ensure their own and their family's wealth and survival. Peter G. Peterson, a lifelong Republican and former secretary of commerce, explains the difference in perspective between the two political parties and taxes in this way: "Democrats push benefit hikes while pretending that they're unrelated to a government that collects taxes. And Republicans push tax cuts while pretending that they're unrelated to a government that disburses benefits."[7]

Conservative Republicans are not unsympathetic to the needs of others (a response of their holistic operating system and holistic insights acquired from culture), but if they are going to respond to that need by contributing some of their time or capital, the nature of the help needs to be consistent with their views of economic freedom (or nonintervention) and minimal government involvement. They don't want government giving away money. They know that government programs tend to be inefficient and often spiral out of control and waste money.

Reflecting the power of cultural forces to override our natural inclinations, we occasionally find Republicans who are liberal and Democrats who are conservative. Prior to giving the keynote address at the Republican Convention of 2004, U.S. Senator Zell Miller was asked by Peter Jennings of ABC News to explain why he, a Democrat, was about to address Republicans. "I've been set in my ways for a long time because I'm a conservative Democrat, and there used to be a time when there was room for conservatives in the Democratic Party, but no more. But the main reason, of course, is because 9/11 changed everything. . . . I want a president who will grab [the terrorists] by the neck and not let 'em go to get a better grip. . . . When I hear a politician talk about seeing the complexities of things, that means it's a person that sees nothing but gray. They don't see black and white. They suffer from analysis paralysis, and they have a hard time making a decision."[8]

Here Miller gives us more clues as to his brain dominance by expressing a desire to work with the party that will use the most force and by reference to his dualistic preference for black-and-white choices. To individuals who see reality in terms of two starkly different fundamental options, the choice *is* clear, so it is no wonder that Miller harbors doubts about people who can't make such a simple choice. However, when this same reality is viewed in its wholeness, we see that the answers are not as simple as dualistic consciousness leads us to believe. We see that our decisions can have widespread and unforeseen ramifications that, to caring individuals, must be taken into consideration. This concern for others and the complications it introduces is why, as Miller suggests, individuals whose perspective is holistic sometimes have a more difficult time making a decision.

Miller believes that people who "see complexities" (meaning they see holistically) are unable to see black-and-white choices. In fact, the holistic perspective *requires* the assistance of the dualistic perspective in its holistic attempts to achieve unity consciousness. Those who rely on their holistic operating system for guidance *are* capable of seeing issues in terms of black-and-white differences—though perhaps not with the proficiency of someone who is dualistic-dominant. In addition, as a consequence of living in a fundamentally dualistic world, liberals tend to be familiar with dualistic processes. In contrast, most conservatives are given comparatively little education in the use of holistic consciousness (artistic-oriented education being one exception). It is not that those who see a more complex world *fail* to see the black-and-white choice; rather, their consciousness transcends the limitations of dualistic choice, and as a result, they tend to come to more balanced and thus more holistic conclusions.

Our natural patterns of decision-making, we have said, can be culturally overwritten, either partially or wholly. We are programmed to a large degree by our parents; therefore, in spite of our natural perspective, we most often vote like them. But we may also rebel and do the opposite of what our parents do. In either case, our parents are a strong influence— to be emulated, the holistic response, or to be avoided through separation, the dualistic response. Nature sets us up with hardware and basic programming, and nurture provides us with a learning environment, but ultimately, we choose our behavior.

In both political parties, selfish dualistic forces corrupt the system and the politicians who populate it. Both parties give in to a variety of special-interest groups, fail to reflect their respective roots, and betray the fundamentals that they profess. Nevertheless, there are differences. In 2008 we saw the Republican and Democratic parties make public their operating-system dominance in their approach to selecting candidates for their presidential primaries. Democrats, exhibiting their collective right brain's inclusive, unifying, holistic perspective, mandated that states assign proportional representation in selecting convention delegates, thus ensuring that more candidates would win delegates. Republicans, true to type, chose the left-brain-directed response. Freedom-of-choice–oriented Republicans let individual states choose their delegates on either a proportional or winner-take-all basis.

Links between Religion and Political Affiliation

Religious values, because they are generally coming into our brain from outside, from a book, from leaders, from teachers, represent an especially strong case of "nurture." Members of conservative, sectarian religions often take on an us-versus-them mentality based on a rigid, exclusivist black-and-white theology. This, combined with a belief in scriptural inerrancy, or at least scriptural authority, often results in distrust of the outside world of "unbelievers," including the findings of science. The idea of evolution has long represented such a threat. Similarly, secular government is often distrusted, leading many Christians, for example, to adopt conservative political views that seek to minimize government. Such polarized values may lead to a rigid conservatism that, ironically, is in direct contradiction to the teachings of Jesus.

Christianity is of interest in our investigation, not only because the overwhelming majority of Americans are professing Christians, but also because the teachings of Jesus are so clearly holistic and "liberal," especially in the area of helping the poor. Indeed, Jesus's position concerning the poor and our obligation to help them is far more radical in spirit than even the most liberal political agenda of today. And yet, the exclusivist, sectarian nature of much religion has created a religious culture dominated by dualistic consciousness, and this sectarianism has trumped even the teachings of Jesus himself.

If we were to simply consider the peace-loving, people-serving, harmony-seeking, holistic teachings of Jesus, we might expect that most Christians would identify with liberals and that most practicing American Christians would choose the Democratic Party. It is clearly the more holistic of the two major political parties; it is the party with a strong sense of service to others, the party that is more than willing to go into debt if it might help others.[9] In spite of this, most practicing Christians in the United States are in fact self-identified conservatives and are members of the Republican Party. Although there is a large contingent of Christian liberals, and liberal activism has always had a strong Christian component, liberals are in the minority of practicing Christians.

There are at least three major influences that work to help produce this result. The first is the dominating power of dualistic systems, both individually and collectively, that leads us to focus on taking care of ourselves and our values first, which in turn means that often we vote for the party that best serves individual interests. And of course this brings up another influence, money. Conservative Christians, by virtue of being conservative, tend to be conserving of money, another trait often associated with the Republican Party. A third factor that helps to explain why so many Christians vote Republican involves a widespread rebellion against the Democratic Party because of its support for abortion. Abortion is a crime to those guided by the security-oriented conservative values of our dualistic consciousness, with its focus on protecting individuals against the forces of a much more powerful collective. To the conservative-oriented mind-set, this is a life-and-death issue, which immediately makes it worthy of war and automatically puts many Christians at war with the Democratic Party. We will explore the issue of abortion more fully in the next chapter.

Cultural Polarization

In a healthy, balanced, and unified culture, holistic attempts to achieve unity and harmony are appreciated and nourished along with dualistic efforts to protect individual rights. In a unified culture, the cultural left brain (the voice of true conservatives) criticizes holistic perceptions (those of liberals) in order to keep the liberal big-picture mind-set sharp—and liberals appreciate the criticism and its corrections, and adjust accordingly. In a healthy culture, we find a center of power made up of left- and right-brain-directed individuals cooperating and competing in an environment of mutual respect. In this situation, ideological extremists are heard, but the power they exercise is mostly limited to the power of truth (since truth will always triumph, given sufficient time). In a holistic culture, we have a central core of stability, along with two enormously valuable but potentially dangerous extremes feeding new ideas into the center.

Such a scenario works. Here is what does not work: The center splits, and we are left with two relatively equal forces in a battle for control, each seeing the other as responsible for our cultural problems. When this happens, instead of the harmony of a whole regulated by the wisdom of the center, we have two polarized harmonies, disrespectful of each other, battling for supremacy. The result is a polarized culture, and culture wars. And once dualistic consciousness gains control of culture, it is difficult to rein in due to its inherent desire for control and its willingness to use any tool available—including secrecy, deception, and violence—in the name of security, order, and its perception of individual and public interest.

When we lose our balance as a culture and lean excessively into the leadership of dualistic consciousness, then our culture becomes focused on details at the expense of the big picture, as was the case when we failed to protect the levees and marshland around New Orleans prior to Hurricane Katrina. When we lose our balance and allow dualistic consciousness to dominate, we produce a culture that is *competitive* at the expense of being *cooperative*. Dualistically oriented government officials, with their primary focus on reelection, tend to allocate funds where they will be most politically effective. In effect, government held a competition for the money that could have secured the environment around New Orleans and prevented the flooding of Hurricane Katrina. Perhaps it went to Boston's Big Dig. The dualistic operating system's competitive, dominating drive also creates situations such as we find in the unwillingness of law enforcement organizations to share information that could save lives or prevent disasters like 9/11. The consequences of such competitive behavior can be, and often have been, disastrous.

Healthy, informed, holistic cultures recognize that we are living with two very different but complementary perspectives, and they are largely at peace with the differences. In contrast, cultures rooted in dualistic consciousness, having polarizing perspectives, tend to see our two fundamental perspectives as opposites and in competition. When we act based on intelligence derived solely from the dualistic left hemisphere, we are prompted to fight to ensure that such a dualistic perception dominates. Thus, dualistically directed individuals, along with others who have bought into a dualistic version of life, view the more inclusive holistic vision as being in opposition to their cultural beliefs and values, and often respond by building walls of separation that effectively prohibit a unified perspective.

This is not to blame those whose dominant operating system is dualistic, or the resulting political conservatism, for cultural polarization. Dualistic consciousness is simply doing what it was designed to do, which is to seek separation from collective influences as a way of protecting individual freedom from the possible failings of collective domination. Being protective, individuals acting under the influence of dualistic consciousness seek to conserve individual (including family) resources such as wealth. Being competitive, our dualistic hemisphere challenges and motivates us and thus helps us to build our wealth.

The responses of dualistic consciousness are there to serve us—but we've seen throughout this book that dualistic consciousness, when acting alone without the balancing effect of the holistic, can sometimes go too far in its responses (as can the holistic). Without the moderating influences of our holistic system, our dualistic system lacks an efficient feedback mechanism (and vice versa). In addition, the cultural left brain ignores an important and fundamental idea: for all its strengths, a focused, dualistic operating system is no match for a holistic operating system when it comes to understanding broad and long-term views. One needs the inclusive viewpoint of holistic consciousness to make the big-picture decisions that will influence our lives for decades, centuries, and even eons to come.

Ultimately, if we are to blame someone for our cultural dilemma, for polarization, those most responsible are the ones we are least likely to question; these are the "good folks"—from both sides. Just as we have corrupt cops in law enforcement because "good" cops fail to remove them, so too do we have corrupt politicians in both parties who are retained by the "good" in order to protect a voting bloc or some other vested interest—and they are put there because of "good" voters who make bad management decisions. Destructive elements are present in most cultures and must be controlled if there is to be peace. Unfortunately, the polarization of our culture into liberal and conservative camps has separated the good elements of society and weakened their influence. They now find themselves relatively powerless in an entrenched, tradition-dominated, dualistic political system determined to resist systemic change, a system in which independent thinkers are often coerced into following party goals by party enforcers.

If we are to become more holistic as a culture, we must deal with those at the extremes who resist being marginalized by a powerful center. We must have the courage to embrace their knowledge whenever they are in harmony with the truth, even though their contribution is radical. And at the same time we must have the discipline to act with sufficient care before embracing extreme ideas.

Holistic consciousness makes us aware of our oneness. From the viewpoint of holistic consciousness we understand that we hurt ourselves when we hurt others. The use of violence to solve a problem makes no sense to someone looking through the broad lens of a holistic operating system. As a result, holistic individuals and cultures are naturally nonviolent, although when threatened and feeling they have no other choice, they are of course capable of responding with violence. The left brain takes over.

In one of my favorite *Star Trek* episodes, members of a race of human-like beings whose right side is white and left side is black come into contact with a race whose right side is black and left side is white. Seeing each other dualistically, they notice the differences and immediately begin to fight. Sometimes, self-understanding is best achieved by standing back and studying ourselves through the behavior of others.

CHAPTER 13

How Brain Dominance Affects Our Perception of Abortion

Being a woman is a terribly difficult task, since it consists principally in dealing with men.

—Joseph Conrad

As with many other issues, opinions about abortion not only polarize around a great cultural divide, but they also epitomize the differences between the holistic and dualistic consciousness. Cultural liberals and conservatives might never come to agreement on the issue of abortion, but they can come closer, and even discover some common underlying values, by better understanding one another—which means understanding the differences in their brains' operating systems. By examining how the two brain operating systems bias our perception of abortion, and looking at the areas in which the two sides may actually agree, this chapter will attempt to bridge this chasm in understanding—and thus (at least to a degree) enable us to create greater justice for both the mother and the unborn.

First we will explore the brain's vision or lack of vision with respect to the four qualities of wholeness discussed previously—interior, exterior, individual, and collective—and look at how it affects our perception. Remember, each operating system views only two of those four fundamental components. So what happens if you have the gene that causes you to be governed by complete dominance? If your conscious vision is limited to one of the two operating systems, do you see all four parts of the whole? What happens when you don't? We will also look at several pairs of complementary (or, from another point of view, opposing) characteristics—element and relationship, text and context, security and service, scarcity and abundance, aggression and submission, living and nonliving—and try to determine what happens to the quality of our perception when we see clearly only one of the two parts of each inseparable pair.

I once lived near a religious bookstore. A marquee above the entrance to the building read, "Pray to stop abortion." For years, as I would pass by and see the sign, I would always have the same thought: "Pray to stop unwanted pregnancy" would accomplish the same goal but be more effective. I still believe this is true, because the second prayer would involve neither the loss of life nor the coercion of women. Nor would it involve a loss of individual rights or invasive medical procedures, among other things. The change in attention—addressing the problem earlier in the process—would make life easier for everyone, make this kind of prayer more attractive to more people, and as a consequence, enlarge the circle of prayer, which, in the beliefs of many traditions, gives the prayer more power—a position confirmed even by some scientific studies.

Of course the general consensus among conservatives is that abortion is murder, so many individuals feel obligated to stop it however they can. When our attitude is dualistic—meaning we identify with only one of two "sides"—if our side is attacked, we feel entitled to respond in kind. Thus medical personnel are sometimes threatened and even killed when legal actions aren't effective in stopping abortion. One thing is certain: the conflict has its origin in a difference in beliefs. So let's look at the underlying forces that shape our beliefs and see what we can learn that might help the two sides better understand each other. We will look at how our operating systems are influencing our behavior toward abortion, which arises out of the beliefs we choose or are culturally given. We will start with how the brain perceives wholeness.

Our brain's dualistic operating system is focused on the interiors of things—that is, on things that must be discovered or deduced and thus are ordinarily hidden. In the earlier stages of pregnancy (when abortion is widely considered as a legal option), the woman's relationship with the fetus is more abstract, and the nonviable fetus itself bears relatively little in common with the human being it is later to become. From the abstract, relatively "hidden" point of view that is accessed by the dualistic operating system, the continuity of the fetus with the human being and the fact that a fetus is a human being *in potentia* are the critical issues, even at this early stage of development. From the more expansive viewpoint of the holistic OS, the health and welfare of the mother as well as the economic, health, and societal issues surrounding the raising of a child (which relate to the welfare of the child, the mother, and society) become the paramount issues. Those governed by a dualistic OS will insist on enforcement of pregnancies being carried to term, even at the expense of the mother's, society's, and (sometimes) the future child's welfare. For those governed by a holistic OS, on the other hand, the dualistic point of view, since it is recessive, is often *overlooked in the broad vision of their dominant perspective.* Now we will further explore how this plays out.

When genetic complete dominance locks us into our holistic perspective, we are given an exclusively big-picture view without interference from the recessive dualistic side—unless we consciously choose otherwise, or circumstances require dualistic control. What does that mean to us in looking at the issues of abortion? It means we see the entirety of the situation, with special attention to the context—but primarily, we see the mothers, their environments, and their needs, which are the most accessible, immediately apprehended components of the issue. We can add to that the ability of the mother and society to successfully raise a child—and that includes economic and health-related issues. Thus liberals (governed by a holistic OS) naturally tend to support the woman's interests and choices—which include the interest and ability to raise a child. For the holistic hemisphere, the fetus does not come up so much as a separate concern, except as it relates to the mother and issues that could affect the fetus's later development as a child. While the well-being of the future child is important, the "right to life" of the fetus in itself is mainly off the holistic radar. The dualistic hemisphere, being more concentrated on the fetal right to life, acts as a balancing agent to the broad-picture holistic view.

In practice, the brain hemispheres work together to some degree, not in isolation—even in the case of genetic complete dominance. So, in practice, the holistically oriented individual is of course fully aware that the issue of abortion involves the fetus as well as the woman—all the more so because holistic complete dominants have a good connection to their dualistic hemisphere when they choose to pay attention it. In fact, the dualistic OS is the source of much of their information. Nevertheless, an individual with holistic complete dominance may well identify overwhelmingly with the mother and the mother's interests (including whether to raise a child) rather than with the fetus. (There has not been sufficient research into those individuals whose genetic inheritance is *codominance* or *incomplete dominance* for us to draw conclusions relating to the present discussion.)

While social liberals—who tend to be holistic complete dominants—may seem to be uninterested in the welfare of the fetus (perhaps "out of sight, out of mind" is at work in the case of the "hidden" fetus), we also find what appear to be unexplainable blind spots and inconsistencies among social conservatives. Conservatives know, for example, that the least capable among us—such as young children in poor households—often suffer the most when taxes and programs are cut. Yet, even as conservatives extol their love for children, they often seek to cut programs that benefit the most needy among them while cutting taxes on those individuals and corporations who can *most* afford to pay them.

Conservatives also tend to favor a large military budget and support expensive systems even when the relationship between those systems and national security is tenuous at best. Often military systems are supported based less on proven need and more on the basis of supporting weapons manufacturers and the jobs they create. When perpetuating a bloated industry for the sake of profits is more important than preserving or enhancing the quality of children's lives, bedrock conservative values are contradicted. When the quality of children's lives is not addressed, the bedrock of our personal and national security—a primary conservative value—is undermined. Charities that rely on voluntary donations can do magnificent work, especially when locally based, but they cannot begin to address the magnitude of poverty, health issues, poor educational opportunities, and dysfunctional environments that many children face. The problems resulting from ignoring these issues can hardly be overstated—from increased criminality to a reduced, less-skilled workforce to the need for increased assistance: a vicious cycle that cannot be ignored forever. This kind of blindness to obvious need suggests that many social and political conservatives are not seeing something. If liberals fail to see the fetus, conservatives fail to see the need to protect the child after birth. It appears that individuals in both groups tend to overlook the view from their nondominant hemisphere, and in doing so fail to receive its information—or, having noticed it, fail to understand its value.

The illogical behavior of large groups, which are populated by individuals who may be very intelligent, suggests to me that the blocking out of our recessive hemisphere—collectively as well as individually—can create a huge mental blind spot. Although we always have the conscious ability to engage with our complementary perspective—thus dominance is not an excuse for ignorance—we also clearly have the ability to block things out; and we often block, or try to block, things that are uncomfortable. Of course, blocking is often an unconscious behavior.

Other than interior and exterior, the other aspect that every whole in the universe exhibits is to be both an individual unit of wholeness and a part of a greater wholeness. We have said that our dualistic hemisphere is oriented in such a way that it shows us *individual* aspects of wholeness, whereas our holistic hemisphere is oriented to the *collective*. So how does this affect our ability to see and respond to the abortion issue?

When our perception is fed a diet of dualistic-based information, we are led to focus exclusively on individual aspects of our environment, in this case individual rights. This interest in individual rights includes the supporting of individuals who are either like-minded or evoking sympathy through the perception of innocence; the fetus is clearly an example of the latter. Because the activity of focusing is by definition limiting (what is not focused upon is ignored or simply not seen), collective needs and rights are not normally within the sphere of our dualistic conscious attention (nor do they need to be, since our collective system supports them). Focusing brings on a certain intensity (think of what visual focusing does in the case of a close-up photograph or movie scene), as it puts things in our face. As you might imagine, this intensity can arouse our passion for an issue or argument.

On the other hand, when our dominant operating system is holistic, we come from a perspective that sees life as a whole event or process, which includes all that we have experienced, learned, and believed, plus other dimensions that we dream about and imagine. From this perspective it is clear to us that the collective is made up of individuals and that caring starts with caring for individuals. And from a holistic perspective it is clear to us that when individuals are not happy, the collective is not happy. As holistic-minded individuals, we have our own personal interest in and respect for individual rights. And yet, should a conflict exist between the individual and the collective, we know that the greater whole—the collective body, mind, and spirit—is the more important of the two. Those of us who are directed by a holistic perspective care about the freedom of the individual, but our perspective leads us to consider the rights of all of those involved. So, in making decisions, the harmony and freedom of the greater whole—in this case the woman and the network of individuals who are emotionally connected to her—are likely to be given more value than any single factor.

The dualistic brain of a conservative, which is focused on protecting individual rights, cries out that every single individual is precious and must be protected. But the holistic brain of a liberal looks at the whole of the situation and perhaps sees the continuing destruction of our planet due to pollution brought on by overpopulation, and asks question like, is this really God's will? We know what happens when overpopulation occurs in the animal kingdom and don't want to contribute to doing that with people. Holistic systems spawn questions like, does God really want every woman to be a mother? Perhaps some women are born to focus their attention on something else. Holistic systems notice that we don't care for many of the children we have, and respond by prompting us to ask whether it would be conserving—and thus *conservative* in the true sense of the word—to take care of what we have before demanding more.

Having looked at how the brain's separation of wholeness into two parts affects our perception of abortion, let us consider some of the brain's other characteristic responses and observe their influence on our perception.

Another way of viewing the individual/collective relationship that we have just seen is to think of an individual holon as an *element*, and a collective of holons as a *relationship*. We know that one of the responses of our operating systems is to divide the perception of unity into elements and the relationships that bind them. So how does this relate to our perception of the abortion issue? The same way it affects our perception of individual and collective aspects. The focus of dualistic attention in an abortion is the fetus (an *element*), whereas from the holistic perspective our attention is on the collective *relationship* between the woman, her body (including the fetus), her beliefs, the support systems (family, community, legal, and institutional) available to her for exercising options including motherhood, her ability and desire to raise a child, and societal and global impacts.

If we then add more specificity to element and relationship, we come to *text* and *context*. It is not that conservatives aren't aware of or don't care about context; in fact, they often care passionately when the context is within their focus. But when someone's focus is on a particular issue, or a passionately held belief, that focus becomes *the* defining issue—as we clearly see in those who would let a woman die (something that is blatantly *anti*-life) rather than have her abort. When an issue is perceived as important enough, it tends to demand our full attention and can cause us to overlook other important issues. Because the sanctity of innocent life arouses such strong beliefs, adding more context is often mightily resisted, as it can be seen as a lure leading us away from the central issue. A mother can never be as innocent as an unborn child, because she can make decisions for herself (such as whether or not to have a child). *Innocent* then becomes almost synonymous with *unborn*, and with *helpless*. For perhaps the same fundamental reason, conservatives tend to resist the taking of the life of individuals who have lost virtually all of their human capacities—even those who are brain-dead. This includes not only opposition to assisted suicide, but even insistence on the artificial and extremely expensive prolongation of life through mechanical means when there is little or no hope of recovery. In such cases, biological life can trump dignity and choice.

The brain's division of the process whereby we see and respond to *abundance* gives us another peek into the brain's role in helping us to understand the issue of abortion. As we have seen, the dualistic, or conservative, operating system sees *scarcity*, and is naturally concerned that a precious resource is being lost; thus, it has a tendency to cause us to want more children. You see this tendency expressed around the world in conservative cultures where large families are viewed as important for survival. In contrast, the holistic, or liberal, OS encompasses everything; thus it gives us a view of abundance. Where there is abundance, the need for fulfillment is lacking, so liberals don't react to the loss of embryonic life with the passion of conservatives. From a holistic perspective we recognize everything as ours and that everything living is eternal, so we are not upset if a mother somewhere decides that she does not want to carry her fetus to term. From a holistic view, it is not essential that every attempt at emerging life survive. The holistic view includes the insight that children are wonderful, but that they need a whole system of love and support—something that is often lacking in situations where the woman is considering abortion. To the liberal mind, the abortion decision is ultimately to be made by the woman (in conjunction with health professionals, supportive intimates and friends, and perhaps counselors); this decision may be based on her relationship with a Creator or higher power, but not by the government or by voters who wish to enforce their sense of what the Creator wants.

As we have said, our conservative system serves up our *aggression*. It helps us to reach out in an attempt to change life in a way that suits us. Our holistic system, being complementary, is *submissive*. The holistic mind knows that the things we want will come to us if they are good for us—the universe gives us what we need. As a result, holistic individuals don't have a visceral response to abortion in the way that conservatives do. From a conservative perspective, considering that life and death are involved, the restrained response of liberals doesn't appear to give the proper respect or energy to this issue, a response that puzzles and angers many conservatives.

Another characteristic of the split brain that we have established is its separation of our perception into a system that works with the *living* aspects of our constantly changing environment and a system that focuses on its *nonliving* aspects. The holistic hemisphere attends to living systems, whereas non-living aspects of life are handled by the dualistic hemisphere. This might seem paradoxical or contradictory to conservatives, since they tend to be much more passionate about life in the case of abortion and end-of-life issues; yet here we see that the holistic love of concerned conservatives for children (something that no system of response can suppress) is combined with their dualistic commitment to provide security, especially for defenseless individuals. Liberals, with their respect for freedom and concern for the adults, seek the freedom of adults to make their choices rather than have government make them.

What we have seen is that the dualistic operating system guiding the responses of most conservatives has a vastly different perspective on the issue of abortion than does the holistic OS of liberals. The two systems see the issue in terms of different values and come to different conclusions, yet both systems offer us valuable information. Where we position ourselves on the continuum of belief regarding this issue is greatly influenced by our genetically acquired brain dominance, but it is also subject to cultural influences, our unique personal experiences, and how successfully we integrate our perspectives, as we have often discussed.

Finding Common Ground

A relatively small number of us will have to struggle with the decision of whether to abort or not. Nevertheless, the issues it brings up are crucial for everyone. What do we do with the women who refuse to manage their lives based on our beliefs? Do we impose penalties through our support of like-minded legislators and laws? We must also decide what to do to those who support the women. Those with dualistic views naturally tend to demonize those who offer assistance, as a result of the left brain's polarizing "you're with us or against us" attitude.

The educational route—when applied effectively and compassion-ately—offers a much better solution than force, but education takes time. Education begins by placing emphasis on an area where we can all agree—stopping unwanted pregnancy before it happens. Education must also be humane; it must supply a large dose of open-mindedness and tolerance for opposing viewpoints. Teaching the built-in differences between the brain's operating systems can do much to further those objectives. If training is added that can help us access and integrate our non-dominant OS, then we will no longer be slaves to our own mental processes.

The dualistic system's solution—relying on aggressive (force-based, separation-based) processes such as threats of imprisonment to accomplish its goals—has the advantage of being much quicker and easier. As with any cultural mandate, all we have to do is convince a majority of voters and then let law enforcement apply the pressure, out of our sight. On the other hand, such a solution is disastrous, not only for those individuals whose lives are destroyed, but because it fosters a permanently polarized society in a perpetual state of ideological warfare.

We started by suggesting that liberals might not always see the conservative perspective, or at least see it well, as a result of the tendency of their dominant operating system to specialize in the big picture. But at least the holistic system has the ability to see the dualistic perspective. However, studies show that this ability to see the perspective of the opposite OS is not strictly reciprocal. The focused, detail-oriented dualistic system typical of conservatives simply does not see the context—which includes the collective and its opinions. Obviously, that does not mean that conservatives cannot obtain holistic information; it only means that they must get it from their holistic brain (or their culture's holistic brain), and many are either unwilling or (due to lack of training) unable to open up to other ways of thinking or reacting. Often one's ideology—especially when that ideology is dualistic—can cripple the ability to access one's own recessive brain hemisphere. If one consciously despises progressive, liberal values, can we expect them to value the insights of their *own* progressive hemisphere? The dualistic left hemisphere, being competitive and hier-archical, and associating effective and appropriate actions with black-and-white choices, tends to make choices based on narrow (though often important) values. While these values should be respected and integrated, conservatives often exclude the broader, more inclusive (and often more important) holistic view.

We need both holistic and dualistic perspectives and processes in order to arrive at the truth—but we need them cooperating. When we fight rather than cooperate, we create conflict within ourselves—our personal self and our cultural self. To achieve peace in any arena, we have to be at peace ourselves. This means we must understand ourselves. And to understand ourselves means we must understand the battle of the brains, because once we shed light on the two sides, their oneness can be seen. There is no value in being angry with anyone for his or her opposition. The opposition within them is within you. Once you remove yours, how others respond will be largely irrelevant to your peace and happiness.

CHAPTER 14

The Brain behind the Military-Industrial-Congressional Complex

Fascism should more properly be called corporatism because it is the merger of state and corporate power.

—Benito Mussolini

America's spiral into debt began in the 1970s when the balance of trade turned negative and debt began to climb. By 1987, foreigners owned more of the U.S. than Americans owned foreign properties.[1] At the time of writing, our gross national debt is close to being equivalent to the total value of our economy. With the exception of a brief period after World War II, our debt levels have never been as high as they are now. Rates of income inequality have also reached crisis levels in recent decades. In his sweeping history of the American economy, Kevin Phillips reported that "in just a little over two centuries the United States went from being a society born of revolution and touched by egalitarianism to being the country with the industrial world's biggest fortunes and its largest rich-poor gap. . . . Real disposable (after-tax) income for non-supervisory workers peaked in the late 1960s. Debt taken on by the bottom two-fifths of the population rose so sharply that by 1995 their inflation-adjusted net worths had fallen below 1973 levels."[2] Since 1995, inequality has risen more sharply than ever, and political polarization has not been this severe since the Civil War. In this chapter, we explore the many factors that have produced our current political and economic predicament, with special reference to what I call the military-industrial-congressional complex. What we will find is a series of events and policies driven by dualistic left-brain values directing cultural behaviors in an atmosphere where the moderating influences of the holistic right brain have largely been ignored.

Following the Money Trail

In *New World New Mind: Moving Toward Conscious Evolution*, Robert Ornstein and Paul Ehrlich report, "Cultures did not spontaneously develop the ability to deal with long-term trends because they had no need to until very recently." Ornstein and Ehrlich point out that politicians, who provide our leadership in the economic arena, "are the ultimate creatures of the moment," confronted with a "constant stream of problems that must be solved *now*. . . . At most their time horizons reach [no farther than] the next election, which in most Western democracies means a maximum of six years. . . . As a result, politicians have little incentive to tackle or even to identify and analyze long-term trends."[3] I point this out so that everyone might recognize that long-term planning, which is vital, is almost always ignored by election-minded politicians and must be imposed by the electorate.

Engaging in wise policies for the regulation of business, for example, requires such a long-term view. Under reasonable regulation, risks can be managed and losses kept under control, advises nationally recognized consumer advocate Jamie Court. But during President Reagan's leadership, corporate regulatory and tax structures were dismantled. This freed risk takers from their traditional oversight. President Clinton then followed up by championing governmental partnership with private industry and, with his permissive consolidation policies, concentrated power into the hands of a few big corporations.[4]

Conservative cultures, being dualistically oriented, are naturally protective of individual freedom and feel oppressed by regulation. Intelligent regulation is holistic, because it exists to protect the whole from individual excesses over long periods of time. Paul Volcker, chairman of the Federal Reserve Board when Reagan took office, supported strong regulation. He was then replaced by Alan Greenspan, who supported deregulation and went on to preside over the inflation of a tech bubble that popped in 2000–2001, followed by the housing and derivatives bubbles that burst in the great recession of 2008–2009.

When we imagine an economic system in which debt is highly concentrated, highly leveraged, and managed with few regulations by dualistically oriented (and therefore naturally competitive and destructive) young men on a long leash held by other dualistically oriented older men, we start to understand how empires managed with so little respect for holistic consciousness are ultimately doomed.

Congress: Ground Zero of the Crisis

"The crisis in American capitalism isn't just about the specific details—about tricky accounting, stock options, loans to executives, and so on," Paul Krugman observes. "It's about the way the game has been rigged on behalf of insiders."[5] Rigging the game so that it benefits the individual instead of the collective is, of course, a dualistic response. As Kevin Phillips points out, wealth becomes more and more concentrated among ever fewer people "with the help of the corruption of politics on one hand and the persuasive efforts of market idolatry and economic Darwinism on the other."[6] The chief mechanism for rigging the economic game in the United States is the U.S. Congress.

Congress has a number of serious problems. Primary among them is that it has lost sight of its most fundamental values. We see this when Congress makes decisions designed to strengthen the power of one's own political party or weaken the opposition, rather than basing decisions on the long-term welfare of the nation and its citizens.

Congress is facing a *systemic* crisis, which is a holistic problem—one that calls for holistic insight. It has a systemic problem because, rather than a well-thought-out unified system designed to help manage a complex modern economy, the rules Congress has set for itself are a self-serving collage based on protecting vested interests. In a holistically crafted system, the process is designed to get things get done efficiently and effectively. For example, a well-designed system of government would be constructed so that an individual would be unable to disrupt it and hold legislation back, deny a vote, or otherwise delay the business of the American people. But in the system we now have, our employees, the members of the House and Senate, make their own rules, rules that benefit them and their partisan goals. We send good men and women to Congress, only to have their hands tied by the flawed system in which they are forced to work. Take, for example, Vermont Senator Bernie Sanders's attempt in 2008 to find out how the Federal Reserve had been spending the money it prints. Sanders asked then Fed Chairman Ben Bernanke if he would tell the American people who the recipient was of a $2.2 trillion loan the Fed had arranged. Bernanke's simple answer: "No." Nor would Bernanke provide the information confidentially and off the record to Congress.[7] As we will discuss a bit later, the Federal Reserve is a private, independent organization that regulates our money supply as it sees fit.

We see the dysfunctional attitude of Congress revealed in the fact that it doesn't even allow itself sufficient time to read some of the bills on which it votes. Congress is in charge of the rules and the laws that guide the rules. It could change this dysfunctionality if it wished, but there is a dark reason for limiting access to some bills. Ramming through a bill and forcing a quick vote allows amendments and "riders" that otherwise would not pass to be inserted into bills that have a likelihood of passing. Through this technique, members of Congress are able to obtain favors for themselves, their party, their districts, and their friends—and the taxpayer gets the bill. A system that does not allow every bill in its final form to be examined by the public and *all* members of the deliberative body before being voted on comes from a selfish, separative dualistic-based power structure that often has something to hide. And this is just one example of a system that is designed to benefit the insiders and the powerbrokers at the expense of the people. We see this same masculine consciousness at work in Congress's patchwork approach to improving or evolving how it operates, including such issues as campaign finance reform. The system needs to make a quantum leap into something that would be altogether more effective and responsive, but would require a holistic approach—an approach that corporate interests seem determined to undermine. In fact, a dysfunctional or nonfunctioning government is very much in the interest of certain large corporations and politicians. If you are doing well and are selfish, you want to avoid change. You want to keep things the way they are.

Many leading Democrats are also defenders of the corporate status quo, in opposition to the party's progressive wing. Writing a decade ago, David Sirota (author of *Hostile Takeover*) commented on this intra-party division, reporting that the Democratic Party is split into two groups—one that represents citizens and one that represents corporate interests. As an example of the latter, he pointed to the Democratic Leadership Council (DLC), an organization funded by large corporate interests and supported by a number of high-ranking Democrats. Sirota, quoting the DLC's president, Al From, reports that From's goal is "to give Democrats 'a game plan to try to contain populism.'" "Populism," wrote Sirota, "is defined as 'supporting the rights and powers of the common people in their struggle with the privileged elite.'" In other words, the DLC was at the time attempting to "contain" a fundamental value of the Democratic Party— its focus on protecting and supporting holistic interests. The DLC, Sirota goes on to say, "bills itself as quasi grassroots, holding so-called 'national conversations' in an effort to create the impression that its corporate-written agenda has some semblance of public support." Nevertheless, Sirota reports, the *Rocky Mountain News* checked into one of the DLC's "national conversations" and found out that it was at the time, "in fact, 'not open to the public.'"[8] Nonetheless, the holistic and populist side of the Democratic Party, long suppressed by DLC and other elite forces in the party, reasserted itself in the 2016 presidential campaign.

Congress, reflecting the consciousness of the people that elects it, is a culture dominated by separative, force-oriented, dualistic thinkers. As a result of their aggressive mind-set, congressional actions, rather than being determined by bipartisan solutions, are often based on what the stronger of the two sides wants. Most actions are determined by a majority vote rather than by engaging in dialogue to get relatively harmonious agreement. The results are then imposed (a dualistic response) on the opposition: a coalition of the most powerful decide; the rest are forced to go along.

As a result of having only limited access to their right brain's perspective, members of Congress as a whole do things that would surely embarrass them if they could see themselves holistically. We see ample evidence of Congress's selfishness and lack of concern for the average American where we find American schools that lack basic materials and children without access to the most basic health care or even clean water, while members of Congress give themselves and their families everything they need and more—in spite of their doing what most Americans agree in poll after poll to be a substantially below-average job of managing the country's business. For example, in 2009, with the economy clearly tanking and with record numbers of Americans losing their jobs, most members of Congress received a $4,700 pay raise. To try to separate themselves from any responsibility, they made pay raises automatic so that they would never have to vote on them. Now when they say to their constituents, "I was against a pay raise, but there was nothing I could do," they have cover.

Members of Congress need lots of money to get reelected, and much of it comes from powerful interests who have an interest in how laws are written. Obviously, laws that reduce taxes are popular with such donors. But what the big corporations don't pay, others must—or the amount must be added to the debt. In his book *Perfectly Legal: The Covert Campaign to Rig Our Tax System to Benefit the Super Rich—and Cheat Everybody Else*, Pulitzer Prize–winning *New York Times* reporter David Cay Johnston explains, "When governments set tax rates, they are making decisions about who will prosper and by how much. A government that takes in 90 cents out of each dollar above a threshold, as the United States did in the Eisenhower years, is deciding to limit the wealth that people can accumulate from their earnings. Likewise, a government that taxes the poor on their first dollar of wages, as the United States does with the Social Security and Medicare taxes, is deciding to limit or eliminate the ability of those at the bottom of the income ladder to save money and improve their lot in life."[9]

Johnston reports that "some of the biggest tax breaks for the rich are not even in the tax code." He found that "the IRS was completely unaware of many widely used tax fraud schemes." What surprised him the most, he said, was "the realization that our tax system now levies the poor, the middle class and even the upper middle class to subsidize the rich."[10] This game-the-system attitude, which in effect steals from the vast majority of citizens in order to benefit a powerful few, reflects a near-complete dominance of dualistic males over management of the nation's governing systems.

For the largest players, the legislation that Congress enacts is viewed as an investment opportunity or a mere business expense, as pointed out by Kevin Phillips and many others. To those with sufficient wealth, legislation is seen as just another investment—and often a very lucrative one. Through lobbyists, who are the corporations' version of stockbrokers, those with money are able to invest in laws through campaign contributions. Contributions buy access, and access gives you the opportunity to promote your ideas. If you manage the process well, if you contribute enough, a member of Congress will create a provision beneficial to your investments and insert it into some law that is about to be passed. And you can strike it rich. Phillips gives the example of a $30 million tobacco industry "investment" in lobbying Congress that produced $50 billion in revenue, for a return on investment of 167,000 percent; and a $5 million contribution made by the broadcast industry to secure free digital TV licenses worth $70 billion, a return on investment of 1,400,000 percent. And investment in legislation is not limited to big corporations. Big donors have similar opportunities.[11]

Between 1993 and 1995, Congress's enactment and implementation of the first of the North American Free Trade Agreements (NAFTA) and its new commitments to the World Trade Organization (WTO) "seemed to push democratic precepts aside," in Phillips's words. Soon after, he says, "the transnational deliberations of NAFTA, the WTO, and the European Union began to yield rulings that set aside local and national legislation and regulatory decisions." Phillips sums up the impact of the monumental agreement by remarking that "survival of the fittest had jumped onto an international stage."[12] In his book *Where the Right Went Wrong: How Neoconservatives Subverted the Reagan Revolution and Hijacked the Bush Presidency*, Patrick Buchanan said of the agreement, "Congress's surrender of its constitutional authority over trade has been total. In 1994, Congress was allowed only a yes or no vote on a twenty-three-thousand-page GATT treaty. No amendments were permitted. With its yes vote, Congress put the United States under the jurisdiction of an institution of world government, the World Trade Organization, whose dispute panels operate in secret. . . . The WTO was also granted power to . . . demand the repeal of American laws. And this it has repeatedly done."[13] Here again we see selfish perceptions of dualistic consciousness limiting the freedoms of the majority in order to concentrate power and promote the agendas of a relatively small power elite. At the time of writing, similar "free trade" legislation concerning other regions of the world is also moving through Congress, and all of these proposals further erode our sovereignty.

The Media: Controlling Information Flow

The military-industrial-congressional alliance naturally includes media. Powerful corporations, driven by forceful dominance-seeking males, go to great lengths to control what people see and hear. At the very least, they know that this gives them an economic advantage in a highly competitive marketplace.

In 1981, under the Reagan administration, media deregulation began in earnest, and wealthy and powerful interests quickly began an unprecedented power grab. Between 1981 and 1985, the number of TV stations any single entity could own grew from 7 to 12. In 1985, guidelines for minimum amounts of nonentertainment programming such as news and public affairs were abolished, and limits on the amount of advertising per hour were eliminated. In 1987, the Fairness Doctrine, which required the balanced and honest presentation of controversial public issues, was eliminated. In 1996, under President Bill Clinton, unprecedented consolidation took place in radio after a 40-station ownership cap was lifted. One company, Clear Channel Communications, eventually came to own 1,200 radio stations.[14]

Corporations dominate culture, Jamie Court suggests, by dominating the media. "By gaining power over what is and what is not told, media corporations can control what is sold both commercially and culturally. . . . [In recent years] corporations [have] become far more aggressive in making demands of the media and attacking it for coverage that is too critical of corporate interests." And if your only interest lies in maximizing corporate profits, why not? "The power to control the individual's and the public's perspective is the ultimate political power."[15] At the same time, "the majority of press releases and new pitches received by newsrooms across America come from public relations firms working for corporations that pitch their news all the time." And this is occurring in an environment in which newsrooms have been downsized, creating conditions that make reporters "more receptive to ready-made stories and satellite-fed video news releases."[16]

When media corporations encounter subjects that conflict with their ideological goals, they sometimes attempt to suppress the news. When the ABC news program *Nightline* chose to honor those who had given their lives in the Iraq War by broadcasting their names and photos, Sinclair Broadcasting, which controlled or maintained 62 local television stations in 39 markets, made news of its own when it told its local ABC affiliates not to air the special broadcast.[17] Sinclair, being supportive of the war in Iraq and fearing that showing the war's true cost might diminish support for it, responded separatively (dualistically) by withholding some of the facts.

But even big media can suffer setbacks. On January 18, 2002, a train derailment spilled 210,000 gallons of anhydrous ammonia and left a killer cloud threatening Minot, North Dakota. Time was of the essence. To quickly warn residents of the deadly toxic cloud, local authorities turned to Minot's seven commercial radio stations. But authorities were unable to contact six of them by phone—there was no answer. No one was on the air. Live people had been replaced with recorded programming. The six stations were part of the 1,200 owned by Clear Channel Communications.[18]

After that, many people, even some members of Congress, came to the conclusion that media deregulation might have some flaws. In response to what could have been a major disaster, Congress started questioning consolidation—but of course it eventually caved in to corporate pressure, and in an omnibus spending bill it raised the ownership cap enough to cover the giant media corporations that had already ignored the rules and exceeded the cap. By 2004, three-quarters of Americans watched channels that were owned by just six companies.[19]

Senator Bernie Sanders has long argued that media consolidation is one of the most important political issues we face. "We're not going to be able to address the major economic and foreign policy problems facing this country," he suggests, "unless the people have an opportunity to hear all points of view and learn the truth about what's going on in their country, and at the moment, they are not doing that."[20] Institutions such as Congress and big corporations, because they see reality through the lens of dualistic consciousness, need to control the media if they are to keep people from knowing the truth about their activities. And so far, they have largely been successful, although the holistic energy that springs from the Internet seems destined to change that. Nevertheless, keep in mind that a typical dualistic response to a challenge from the Internet would be to gain greater control over it, and legislative attempts are made periodically in an attempt to do just that.

Congressional Betrayal

In the discussion of corporate influence, particularly that of multinationals on government, one of the strongest voices of criticism has come from the political right, in the voice of Patrick Buchanan. His opinion of Congress is equally critical. While he has often taken separative and divisive positions concerning cultural issues, his brilliant no-holds-barred critiques in other areas—such as Congress's abdication of its traditional role, as well as the corporate oligarchy that this country has become—have proven very much a service to holistic consciousness.

In his book *Where the Right Went Wrong*, Buchanan minced no words in condemning actions taken by his own political party in Congress, where he states, "The Republican Party, which had presided over America's rise to manufacturing preeminence, has acquiesced in the de-industrialization of the nation to gratify transnational corporations whose oligarchs are the party financiers. . . . The Republican Party has signed off on economic treason."[21]

Another area where, in Buchanan's view, Congress has passed the buck—and thus created an unaccountable system—is in the creation of money. "Congress is an institutional coward," Buchanan has written. "The Constitution gives Congress the power to coin money, but in 1913, this power was transferred to a new Federal Reserve," a private bank that refuses to answer to Congress. (Or should we say the bank that Congress refuses to regulate?) Buchanan also points out that Congress has separated itself from responsibility in its central role—lawmaking. "Congress has, for half a century, been surrendering its lawmaking power to judges and justices. . . . Congress prefers to let . . . the courts make the decisions on issues that divide us deeply and emotionally." Reflecting the default response of the left brain to dealing with problems, the use of separation, Congress prefers to let someone else take the heat. "The dirty little secret," as Buchanan sees it, "is that Congress no longer wants the accountability that goes with the exercise of power. It does not want to govern. Both parties prefer to make only those decisions that will be applauded by constituents and rewarded at the ballot box, and to pass on to others decisions that deeply divide or roil the public." As a result, "congressional powers granted in the Constitution [have] been seized and subdivided between presidents and a Supreme Court that is now the final and binding authority on what new laws Congress may enact and what Congress meant when it enacted the old laws."[22]

In trying to avoid responsibility for the dysfunctionality of Congress, its members like to blame the other political party. In addition, members of Congress will tell you that their hands are often tied, that the system is outdated. And it is. But the truth is that they don't want it fixed because the system in place provides them with security. Most members of Congress, regardless of party—and in spite of any patriotic rhetoric—are inclined to put self first. Examples of their selfish drive abound, and in many cases these examples are quite obvious.

The Culture of Big Business

In 1936, Standard Oil of California, Firestone Tire and Rubber Company, B. F. Phillips Petroleum, and Mac Manufacturing, under the leadership of General Motors, formed a holding company, National City Lines. National City then proceeded to buy electric trolley lines and tear up the tracks in cities all across the nation. In *Gangs of America: The Rise of Corporate Power and the Disabling of Democracy*, Ted Nace takes us through the unsavory details. "Each time it destroyed a local trolley system, National City would license the rights to operate a new system to a local franchisee, under the stipulation that they convert to diesel-powered General Motors busses. By 1949 more than one hundred electric transit systems in forty-five cities had been torn up and converted." Hit with antitrust actions in 1949, General Motors eventually paid a $1 fine, and the holding company paid a fine of $5,000 per company. "After the conviction, the companies [resumed activity]. By 1955, 88 percent of the country's electric streetcar network was gone."[23]

The power of big business to control our environment and shape culture can be overwhelming. And naturally, what big business wants is a consumer culture. Thus, we find ourselves essentially led by a business system focused on moving product through our lives in order to enrich the (mostly) dualistic males running the system. Under dualistic leadership, the pursuit of money and consumer goods becomes the fundamental goal of our culture. What business represents at the level of consciousness was brilliantly fleshed out by sociologists Don Beck and Christopher Cowan, whose extensive research led them to formulate an eight-level system called Spiral Dynamics. In this system, which is designed to map the evolution of consciousness and culture, corporations operate out of fifth-level consciousness—a level that values science and technology, business, and competition over all other options.[24] Thus, from a cultural-consciousness standpoint, we have a fifth-level system of government and commerce leading a culture of people, many of whom are at the sixth, seventh, and eighth levels of consciousness, according to Beck and Cowan's analysis. Quality, beauty, and goodness do sometimes come through to a substantial degree, as they always have, as a result of good, talented individuals working within the system, but the system's prime directive is to make money and to make the people running the system rich—at the expense of the rest of us.

The indifference of the corporate culture to the human culture is "nowhere more evident than in the exporting of American jobs to cheap overseas labor markets," Lou Dobbs states in *Exporting America: Why Corporate Greed Is Shipping American Jobs Overseas*. "The rising debate over the outsourcing of hundreds of thousands of American jobs has revealed a fundamental imbalance in our economy and society."[25] On the other hand, corporate managers will tell you that if they don't go where the cost is lowest, they will become uncompetitive; they will be unable to sell their products and will be driven out of business. And they have a point.

American consumers bear a much larger portion of responsibility for the loss of American jobs and its devastating effect on the economy than has generally been acknowledged—and don't overlook the security risks associated with shipping our manufacturing overseas. When American consumers choose to focus on price exclusively (a dualistic response), they are unwittingly *pushing* manufacturers into cheaper labor markets—which usually means overseas markets. Ultimately, in consuming imported products and thereby supporting foreign economies at the expense of their own, American consumers have collectively pushed many of their neighbors out of their jobs.

Most of us are aware of the importance of economically supporting our neighbors. Nevertheless, if our dualistic operating system is dominant, since it is focused on us and ours, its natural tendency is to do what best serves our needs, rather than those of our neighbors. Remember, our dualistic side is focused on our security and on physical reality, which drives us to save money; and it is impersonal, leading us to value things over people. Ultimately, the decision to support our neighbors comes down to how we define *self*, as revealed by what we value—people and a vibrant local economy, or money and material things.

Marjorie Kelly, cofounder and editor of the journal *Business Ethics*, explains in *The Divine Right of Capital: Dethroning the Corporate Aristocracy* that corporations are dominated by an attitude of economic aristocracy that trumps the democratic principles on which the country was founded. "That more people own stock today has not changed the market's essentially aristocratic bias."[26] In the construct of a free market, "everyone scrambles to get what they can, and keep what they earn. In the construct of the corporation, one group gets what another earns."[27] Kelly points out that capitalism, as practiced by modern corporations, "embraces a predemocratic concept of liberty reserved for property holders, which thrives by restricting the liberty of employees and the community. . . . In the predemocratic mindset, people without property were not permitted to vote. And so it is with corporate employees today, for stockholders alone govern corporations. . . . The public corporation is a kind of inverted monarchy, with representatives of the share-owning aristocracy hiring and firing the CEO-king," she explains. "Stockholder privilege rests on the notion that corporations are not human communities but pieces of property, which means they can be owned and sold by the propertied class. . . . The free market reserves liberty for property holders, even as it denies liberty to employees and the community."[28] This is another example of how dualistic consciousness focuses us on nonliving aspects of life, whereas holistic consciousness focuses on the living.

In speaking of corporations, we are primarily referring to *large* corporations, and in particular, those that practice some of the invasive behaviors that are becoming increasingly troubling. Small corporations, we acknowledge, often struggle for survival along with individuals. Size matters. With size comes power. The growing power of the corporate system is allowing the corporate world to redefine the basic rules of society, law, and ethical customs to the detriment of traditional rights and individual freedoms. In his introduction to *Corporateering*, Jamie Court quotes the response of an editor to whom he was pitching his book prior to publication, who said, "Corporations are not just impacting culture, they *are* culture."[29]

Due to the size and influence of corporations, the rights of corporations frequently outweigh not only the rights of individuals, but also the rights of whole communities. Corporations have become "super-citizens" driven by competition to use their super-powers to try to influence political decisions that ultimately work against the good of the whole. Thomas Linzey, the attorney for a Pennsylvania group called FROST (Friends and Residents of St. Thomas Township), discovered this when he tried to stop the establishment of a limestone quarry near St. Thomas, a quarry that would have been located a thousand feet from an elementary school. "Decisions made by corporations and the corporate few that run them every day are trumping the rights of the majority at the local level to make decisions about what they want their communities to look like in 20, 40, or 50 years," Linzey concluded.[30]

As corporations have grown in size and gone transnational, we have seen a shift in the nature of the corporate structure. John C. Bogle, founder and retired CEO of the Vanguard Group, points out that as ownership has been diluted, owners have grown less and less powerful and less connected to their investment. Corporate leadership, Bogle says, has increasingly shifted to management, and now, instead of *owner*-based capitalism, we have *manager*-based capitalism. "The classic system—*owners'* capitalism— had been based on a dedication to serving the interests of the corporation's owners, maximizing the return on their capital investment. But a new system developed—*managers'* capitalism—in which [in the words of journalist William Pfaff] 'the corporation came to be run to profit its managers, in complicity if not conspiracy with accountants and the managers of other corporations.'"[31]

When Wall Street's corporate bears go hunting for meat, they head for Main Street, their claws being an economic system designed, Marjorie Kelly says, "to enrich a few at the expense of many." It is a system that exalts rising share price as the definition of corporate success, a system that tends to see culture as little more than a PR investment. Citing an egregious example of such abuse, Kelly asks whether achieving a 15 percent return for a billionaire is more important than paying employees a living wage.[32] When competitive, thing-oriented dualistic consciousness dominates our thinking, it might well be.

Stockholders, too, can be demanding, and like most of management, most stockholders are driven by separative dualistic forces. In *Gangs of America*, Ted Nace describes how Henry Ford, in a holistic gesture, wanted to plow his company's retained earnings into building more factories to employ more people and "help them build up their lives and their homes." Shareholders took him to court and forced him to pay dividends. "Since Ford defended his reinvestment plans in terms of social goals rather than in terms of maximizing shareholder returns, he lost the case."[33]

Making a profit requires that corporations minimize their expenses. Nace, repeating an observation made by Ralph Estes in *The Tyranny of the Bottom Line*, warns that in corporate culture, "the goal of profit maximization requires corporations to off-load their negative impacts [onto society] wherever possible"—pollution being one of the most egregious examples.[34] Nace further points out that "particularly in the areas of labor law, pollution control, and government contracting, some corporations regard complying with the law to be more expensive than breaking it." Through their close partnership with Congress, corporations lobby to weaken laws that work against them so that when they break the law, penalties are minimal or eliminated. Nace explains that in contrast to citizens, who, if they have a felony conviction, are prohibited from voting in certain states, corporations with a pattern of repeated legal violations are able to maintain their political power. They can still actively lobby Congress.[35]

When corporations can't weaken laws or get them crafted to their advantage, their managers, led by powerful legal teams, find other creative ways to boost the bottom line by taking advantage of small businesses and individuals. When giant Texaco Oil Company was found to have underpaid for natural gas they had withdrawn from a section of land in which I held a mineral interest, Texaco refused to pay us, the mineral owners, citing statutes of limitations. The company claimed it owed nothing to the royalty owners, mostly family farmers like myself, based on the fact that we had not discovered their underpayment until more than two years after the gas had been withdrawn. Later, in a separate incident, Burlington Northern Santa Fe (BNSF) resorted to this same law when I made a claim against them. To compensate for the railroad's damage to my property, the BNSF roadmaster in charge agreed to replace a fence—but instead, for more than two years, he repeatedly delayed taking action. Eventually a company claims representative refused to honor the agreement, citing statutes of limitations—knowing full well that company representatives were responsible for the delay. Rather than accept responsibility and settle, the company offered me a small nuisance amount to try to keep out of small claims court.[36]

Consumer advocate Jamie Court reports that another disturbing corporate tactic is "the growth in deception by corporate groups who hide their identities from the public." Court says that, of the corporate-funded groups he battles, "all claim to represent individuals, not corporations." He cites as an example Citizens Against Lawsuit Abuse, a group that "fights to limit the individual's legal rights to challenge corporations in court. . . . It places letters to the editors in local newspapers and lobbies legislators under the banner of a 'citizen's' organization." Other examples he gives are Californians Against Higher Taxes and Higher Electric Rates, an organization operated by the utility companies with the goal of blocking deregulation, and the Civil Justice Association, whose "only goal is to limit liability for large corporations."[37]

Not only do some corporations practice deception in order to boost the bottom line, but some even claim the *right* to lie! Journalist Thom Hartmann reports that in response to a public relations blitz intended to quell consumer concerns about subcontractor sweatshop practices, Nike was sued by a consumer advocate, Marc Kasky, who thought Nike had gone too far, "citing a California law that forbids corporations from intentionally deceiving people in their commercial statements. . . . Instead of refuting Kasky's charge by proving in court that they didn't lie, however, Nike instead chose to argue that corporations should enjoy the same 'free speech' right to deceive that . . . citizens have."[38]

Management of the military-industrial-congressional complex relies heavily on dualistic consciousness and can be summarized as follows: *Focus on self* (on what is good for the individual manager and his individual corporation). *Maximize profits and power* (even if at the expense of holistic goals such as the good of the community). *Offload negativity* (separate from it, deny responsibility). We find a disturbing example of the effect of this manner of thinking in the book *An Air That Kills: How the Asbestos Poisoning of Libby, Montana, Uncovered a National Scandal*, coauthored by Pulitzer Prize–winning journalists Andrew Schneider and David McCumber. They report a case in which W. R. Grace & Company managers discovered that the vermiculite ore they were mining and processing contained tremolite, an especially lethal type of cancer-causing asbestos, but kept on mining and processing it for years. No one knows how many hundreds or thousands have died or will die as a result of exposure. Several U.S. government agencies also knew of the problem and for years dragged their feet and failed to act.[39] Only individuals out of touch with the values of their holistic hemisphere are inclined to respond in such a blind, selfish way as to continue to produce a product that is killing their workers.

That something like this could possibly happen might be explained in some part by the synergy of two things that we know about the lateral split in our brain and its effects on cognition. First is the power of complete dominance to effectively shut down one half of the brain's management team, leaving us with only one of the two aspects of consciousness to guide us. Second, as we've seen, is the hemispheric division of our attention into a focus on either living or nonliving aspects of life. Of course, being dualistic does not exclude us from consciously visiting our holistic viewpoint and responding to its insights and values, or considering what our holistic culture believes; nevertheless, if we are unaccustomed to consulting our holistic hemisphere, its unusual responses can be difficult to understand and trust. When we consider the situation holistically, it is clear that harming employees or the surrounding community does not serve the company's best interests, but incident after incident tragically suggests that the importance of human values often gets overlooked in the minds of thing-oriented individuals—people guided by dualistic consciousness.

The military-industrial-congressional complex we are examining not only creates problems for citizens of the United States but also creates international problems.

For example, in 1999, after years of pressure from the World Bank, Bolivia's government agreed to privatize the public water system of

Cochabamba, its third-largest city. The water utility was subsequently taken over by an international consortium led by the infamous Bechtel Corporation. Following the change, the cost of water rose substantially more than was promised. By some accounts, collecting rainwater in a tank required a permit. Owners of private wells were required to install a meter and pay. "These increases forced some of the poorest families in South America to literally choose between food and water. A popular uprising against the company, repressed violently by government troops, left one 17-year-old boy dead and more than a hundred people wounded."[40]

In 2002, the *Prestige*, a 26-year-old rusting, single-hulled tanker loaded with highly toxic crude oil, sank in an area off northwestern Spain that contains some of the world's richest fishing grounds. Its cargo, estimated at 20 million gallons, contaminated 350 miles of coastline, causing one of the worst oil spills in history. The *Prestige* had spilled almost twice the amount of oil as the *Exxon Valdez* did in 1989. The subsequent investigation found that it had been known beforehand that the ship was not seaworthy. But when its captain had demanded repairs, the Greek owner found another captain—thus (in an all-too-frequent dualistic response) separating himself from a major repair bill. When the Spanish government tried to collect damages, they found that the ship was owned by a corporation that owned nothing else. A separate company had been set up to avoid any liability beyond the value of the ship—there was no cash in the company to collect.[41] A Spanish news organization reported that almost 7,000 fishermen (among others) developed respiratory damage within two years of helping to clean the region's beaches and waters. The cleanup masks given to the workers were inadequate.[42] The estimated cost to clean the Galician coast alone ranged as high as 2.5 billion euros.[43]

The 87-day Deepwater Horizon oil spill of 2010 (often referred to as the "BP oil spill") is the largest marine oil spill in history. It killed 11 workers, injured 7, and dumped approximately 210 million gallons of crude oil into the Gulf of Mexico. As indicated by satellite-image data, the spill is calculated to have occupied an area roughly equal to the size of Oklahoma. Halliburton Co. was testing the well just prior to the event, Transocean Ltd. owned and operated the drilling rig, and BP LLP owned the well. A White House commission blamed all three companies, citing an insufficient safety system and excessive cost-cutting measures. They also concluded that "systemic" problems contributed to the disaster.

Recognition of systemic problems, you will recall, is the domain of the right brain, the recessive side of the brain in most men.

The Culture of the Military

In *Waking Up in Time: Finding Inner Peace in Times of Accelerating Change*, physicist, psychologist, and philosopher Peter Russell reminds us that "our cultural condition has trapped us in a materialist mindset . . . that says that if we are not happy, something in the world around us has to change."[44] That usually means *someone* has to change. Since most people don't like to change—or at least don't like to be forced to change to suit the whims of another—to get the change we seek, we often feel required to use force or a threat of force.

The military, industry, and Congress form an interlocking, interdependent whole that functions rooted in the power associated with money and the need to control others for security purposes. The exercise of force requires offensive and defensive gear, and that requires the services of industry, which in turn is financed by its rich, gullible sugar daddy, the U.S. Congress. Money men court military men in order to boost the bottom line. Working together, they court Congress to get preferential treatment for themselves and their organizations—more freedom, more money, and more power. And of course, Congress courts the military and industry in order to maintain its privileged position, and is rewarded in the form of election funding. By courting the military and the corporate world, members of Congress also gain a large voting bloc, thus further ensuring the job security of everyone involved. Paramilitary organizations such as state and local law enforcement cultivate the same relationships with Congress and industry for the same reasons.

Taken as a whole, the military, like law enforcement and corporate leadership, tends to reward and promote the most aggressive (read "forceful") and most focused behavior. As efficient and practical as this might seem from a dualistic point of view, a holistic orientation reveals that such behavior often has negative, even catastrophic, side effects. Interventionism, a fancy word for applying force to make other people and countries do what we want, is dangerous, no matter how well intended. As Pat Buchanan has observed, "Interventionism is the incubator for terrorism."[45] People fight back. As a whole, left-brain-dominant males apparently don't understand this or they would not have, for example, allowed behavior such as occurred at Abu Ghraib prison. One of the brothers who massacred 12 people in the attack on the satirical newspaper *Charlie Hebdo* in Paris credited American treatment of prisoners at Abu Ghraib for starting him down his path.

Viewing the world from a dualistic perspective, we see ourselves as separate from others. Likewise with our most valued cultural spheres— *our* family, *our* team, *our* country. And of course, if it belongs to us, we are probably going to be willing to defend it. Even some of our most extreme actions are done to achieve what is generally acknowledged as a noble objective: self-defense, which also includes defense of one's family, country, and religious beliefs. From that perspective, our acts of defensive war are not necessarily mean-spirited. Rather, they are a real requirement of the business of protecting what is ours. But of course, this response can get out of hand.

For example, a group of former military officers hired by the Pentagon to analyze the cost and effectiveness of weapons systems found that the Defense Department was spending more money than before but for fewer weapons, and underestimating their costs. They found that, rather than shifting the focus to the war on terror, the military was spending most of its money on legacy systems designed during the Cold War to deal with the Soviet Union. In an interview for the PBS series *Now*, Bill Moyers reported that one of the officers, Franklin C. "Chuck" Spinney, warned that the system was out of control, pointing to the Defense Department's own inspector general. The Pentagon's financial books bordered on pure fiction, Spinney told Moyers.[46]

This seems to be common knowledge in the military community, but then, we might expect members of the military to know about this after Secretary of Defense Donald H. Rumsfeld's stunning speech of September 10, 2001. Most taxpayers, on the other hand, missed this story, since the tragic events of the following day consumed news cycles for months thereafter. In his speech, Rumsfeld told the nation, "The technology revolution has transformed organizations across the private sector, but not ours, not fully, not yet. We are, as they say, tangled in our anchor chain. Our financial systems are decades old. According to some estimates, we cannot track $2.3 trillion dollars in transactions. We cannot share information from floor to floor in this building because it's stored on dozens of different technological systems that are inaccessible or incompatible."[47]

The Pentagon is the only federal agency that has not complied with a law that requires annual audits of all government departments. Since 1996 the Pentagon has been required by federal law to be audited. Yet, according to a Reuters investigation, between that year and 2013, $8.5 trillion in taxpayer money was doled out by Congress to the Pentagon and has never been accounted for. In 2009 Congress passed a law requiring the Defense Department to be audit-ready by 2017. Researchers at Reuters doubt that the Pentagon will meet its deadlines due to its "continuing reliance on a tangle of thousands of disparate, obsolete, largely incompatible accounting and business-management systems. Many of these systems were built in the 1970s and use outmoded computer languages such as COBOL on old mainframes. They use antiquated file systems that make it difficult or impossible to search for data. Much of their data is corrupted and erroneous."[48]

Spinney reminds us of what most of us already know: "The Pentagon still spends more than the rest of the world's military spending combined. . . . Contractors funnel Pentagon dollars through a corrupt procurement process that kicks back a significant percentage to politicians who sign off on the spending and reward insiders with lucrative jobs in the defense industry the insiders are supposed to oversee."[49] Patriots using a holistic approach would do what was best for the country as a whole, the military as a whole, and its soldiers as a whole, and they would seek to do this while respecting the rights of the hardworking individuals who must part with their money to help fund the military.

What We Can Do

When something does not work, the traditional, conservative approach is to try to repair it, especially when dealing with something that has historical value. Buckminster Fuller taught an alternative approach: "You never change things by fighting the existing reality. To change something, build a new model that makes the existing model obsolete."[50] To propose such a model is beyond the scope of this book, so none will be attempted.

However, there are some things that we need to keep in mind as we collectively work to develop a more functional approach to our economic and political dilemmas.

Congress is divided and appears incapable of fixing itself. From the left brain's dualistic perspective it is hard to see how Congress can break itself out of its dysfunctional system of management as long as voters are polarized and sending two messages.

But from the perspective of holistic consciousness, our next move is obvious. We need to come together and speak with one voice. The divisions in Congress reflect the divisions in the electorate. We need to find our center and govern Congress from a position of unity, something that starts with a degree of acceptance. We simply accept that most people on both sides in our political theater, no matter how wrong they might be about something, are fundamentally well intended and not responsible for the condition of our country. It is not a lot to ask, and acceptance is a powerful spiritual antidote for conflict and division. In fact, neither conservatives nor liberals are responsible for the polarization of culture. And certainly, no single individual is. *The system is responsible.*

Since the systems of work rules that govern the House and Senate have so much influence over the lives of individuals and their cultures, the first place we need to direct our attention in the collective sphere is to the rules that frame the system. For each of us individually, the system that is in most need of fixing is that of our brain's operating system, since it is the management system that orchestrates the brain's responses. It too can harbor disruptive elements—a prime example being flawed beliefs. After all, this is the system we use to try to figure out how to fix the other systems that are causing us trouble—including those that regulate the functioning of government. Because our brain's two operating systems are complementary, so are many if not most of the perceptions, ideas, and other responses that spring from them. But rather than see the unity of our brain's two sets of responses, we often see them as contradictory. And, failing to see their unity, we see their relationship as conflicted, and we sometimes end up thinking that we need to defend one or the other. Ultimately, the root of this confusion is the failure to get in touch with the insights of our own recessive operating system. If we understand only one viewpoint, it is going to prove difficult to harmonize with people who hold complementary ideas. People are not necessarily unintelligent, insane, or enemies simply because they have opposing views. They might be expressing a perspective that is being repressed in our own brain! When we understand the reasons for people's responses, they are more easily accepted.

In trying to work together politically, we find ourselves separated into different camps in an ideologically poisoned environment in which, if we support virtually any idea coming from the other side, we may be considered a traitor and subject to mean-spirited reprisals by people who are supposed to be on our side. This attitude limits communication, flexibility, and transparency.

Let me be clear. This chapter has not been a criticism of left-brain values. We have simply explored some of the ways that the dualistic operating system can mislead us when its holistic context is suppressed. The solutions to our problems are not going to be found in turning the military-industrial-congressional complex over to right-brain-dominants to manage. The right brain alone does not hold our answers. The solution lies in unity consciousness, a harmonious marriage of dualistic and holistic consciousness. Either hemisphere, when accurately informed and fully assisted by its partner, is capable of giving us a glimpse into unity consciousness.

CHAPTER 15

Making War: The Default Response of Left-Brain Dualism

The more prohibitions you have, the less virtuous people will be. The more weapons you have, the less secure people will be.

—*Tao Te Ching*, verse 57

Why do we wage war? We could rattle off many reasons—greed, revenge, impatience, and desperation, among others. It is also true that, for millennia, nations and cultures and religions have assumed imperial ambitions, and over and over again they have proved themselves willing to sacrifice the rights of anyone who gets in the way of their success. But in this chapter we will look beyond the obvious battlefield conflicts, which for many of us in the First World seem remote, in spite of the ever-present specter of weapons of mass destruction in the news. Instead we will examine war in its larger dimensions, which go far beyond conflicts between nation-states, and even far beyond the new dangers that terrorists and rogue powers represent. Indeed, war is being fought in our own neighborhoods and communities—and, as we shall see in this chapter, I am not using hyperbole here.

War in one form or another is a constant of human history, its roots springing from deep within our dualistic consciousness. By uncovering and understanding the roots of war, we can come to a deeper understanding of its underlying forces, and as a result, our longed-for goal of greater peace may finally be within sight.

War requires at least tacit acceptance of force as a way to achieve a result. Force may involve physical harm or killing, or it may involve lesser forms of coercion, but it always results in denying (or intending to deny) another person his or her free will and freedom of action and substituting our own. In other words, it always involves enslavement in one form or another.

When our freedom is threatened, conflict is produced, fear is generated, and the experience is felt in the whole of our energy body. The instant our energy body connects with conflict-based energy, the conflict *becomes* one with us. This shocks our nervous system and is felt throughout the body's various physical, mental, and spiritual centers. Naturally, the degree to which this experience affects the course of our behavior depends on the intensity of the conflict and the resources and insights we bring to its management. Once we are able to recognize this energy for what it is, we can understand it and move beyond it.

Our true nature as children of God is to be cooperative and gentle. Operating from holistic consciousness, under normal circumstances we don't use force to achieve our goals. In fact, when governed by this consciousness, we tend to do the opposite: through the power of attraction, we *entice* people to help us achieve our goals. We know that when we apply force against another in order to obtain the outcome we desire — whether that force is physical, mental, or spiritual — we are interfering with someone's creative freedom. Numerous spiritual revelations teach that such interference is a serious infraction of one of the universe's most fundamental rules: *As children of God, we are free to chart our own destiny.*

Nevertheless, we live in a planetary environment characterized by such high levels of selfishness, ignorance, and confusion that even many of our spiritual leaders are conflict zones, a topic we will discuss in the next chapter. These limiting qualities are characteristic of an egoic, dualistic system, which is energized by fear and focused on our security. However, dualistic consciousness, being separative in action, can also be destructive. Our dualistic system supplies and manages our defense and offense, and from it we receive the skills to fulfill our need for a protective "bodyguard."

To maintain a mental refuge for peace, a place where we can go to escape the conflict inherent in a dualistic environment and express our true nature as peaceful beings, our warlike, dualistic propensities must be held at bay. This is what the lateral split in our brain does for us. Lateralization results in a split in consciousness wherein we can be the peaceful people we naturally are, even while our dualistic system, with all its tendencies to violence and aggression, acts to protect us. The means by which our peace is separated from our conflict is the thin layer of brain that connects and divides the two hemispheres, the corpus callosum. When we meditate, we go into our peace-loving side.

In exploring and discovering the roots of war (or the roots of any issue of major importance), it is necessary that we consult both of our primal perspectives. We want to search *internally* for conflict within ourselves—a task that dualistic consciousness is designed to handle—and to search *externally* for areas of conflict between us and others—a task that we accomplish through holistic consciousness supported and supplemented by dualistic consciousness.

To understand the character of war, it is essential that we keep in mind the impact of variability. In other words, there are *degrees* of war, and war's intensity varies depending on the amount of energy behind it. While this might seem like a rather obvious statement, nevertheless the dualistic consciousness that guides so many of us tends to see war as an all-or-nothing proposition, while overlooking or failing to notice the subtler manifestations of war that set the stage for more extreme situations. When the energy of war expresses itself in subtle ways, its effects can be overlooked; but, like a low-level poison, it can slowly eat away at life and relationships, including our energy.

Not all forms of aggression are necessarily forms of war. Unintended aggressions—often referred to as *microaggressions* when group sensitivities are involved—belong in a separate category from war, although they can certainly *trigger* the forces that lead to war. For example, in a conversation one might use the term "sexual preference" rather than "sexual orientation," unaware that this use of "preference" in that particular context might be considered a microaggression. This might lead to certain people being micropissed, but this is not necessarily the beginning of a war. The roots of war have an aggressive energy behind them that is attempting to get something from someone or do something to them that is selfish. War—which involves knowingly seeking selfish goals at the expense of others, and without their consent—is usually intended. Typically we know when we are pushing against someone, although an unintentional slight might be mistakenly perceived as intentional by the other individual.

Peace is our birthright, yet for many of us it has been lost or severely degraded and needs to be reestablished. Generally, we recover our peace by removing impediments to peace, principally conflict, that have come into our space. This work that we need to do is obviously a personal endeavor, mainly in the mental and spiritual dimensions.

We regain our peace by looking closely at ourselves and our relationships and finding *honest* ways to eliminate internal conflicts. Internal conflicts might include contradictions between two of our beliefs (something typical of inconsistent or contradictory sets of beliefs) or contradictions between our beliefs and our behavior (as in hypocritical actions). In seeking to bring internal conflicts to an end, it is important to recognize that most cultures practice and teach us dishonest or hypocritical ways of resolving conflict.

From a dualistic perspective, dishonest ways of resolving conflict—methods involving the use of suppression, denial, distortion, and violence—often appear to offer the easier path and might even be helpful in some social situations. The problem is, if these techniques work on others and we become comfortable with them, we may end up using these dishonest techniques on ourselves!

When our view of life comes to us through holistic consciousness, we see these dishonest responses in their context. In context we are able to recognize them as work-arounds that may seem easy or even necessary at the moment but create greater problems down the road and do nothing for our internal peace and integrity. Think about the meaning of suppression, denial, and distortion. Do they imply an end to conflict to you? What they do is create another job, another issue to manage. You will have to *work* to suppress, to deny, and to distort. And in the end, the conflict will still be there. The appropriate action—which most of us know at some deep level—begins by diving into the conflict. Once there, we then make the appropriate adjustments, knowing and confident that the process ends in peace.

Of course, the chaos around us—and the chaos inside us—make the attainment and maintenance of our peace a challenging project. Not only is internal conflict often difficult to detect, but external conflict can be difficult to keep out, especially when it involves our livelihood and our personal relationships—or the larger-scale processes in the world to which our survival seems connected. For example, we acknowledge that some wars must be fought—we would feel justified, even required, to repel an enemy invasion of our country. Large-scale *internal* wars, on the other hand, tend to get resolved relatively quickly (assuming it is possible to do so), simply because they tend to be so profoundly unsettling. But minor internal conflict, like minor external conflict, can hide below our conscious radar; and thus the subtleties of war—including the precursors to open conflict—can sometimes be overlooked. It is therefore always wise to examine our individual (internal) and collective (external) relationships to determine whether we are supporting (actively or passively) the processes that lead to or perpetuate unnecessary conflict.

Intent is another factor that comes into play when seeking to understand war. Whereas we might consider an attempt to impose our will on another a harmless "nudge" or a form of "encouragement," in our attempt to impose our values on another, we start down a path to conflict that can quickly lead to war (in all the senses of this word we've discussed) unless someone submits or backs off—which is what usually happens and why war is usually avoided. Of course, people sometimes wish to get nudged or encouraged, especially when they can't decide. Parents, for example, sometimes need to help young children choose. Sometimes that requires a nudge. The key questions are these: Are we going against someone's will? Are we denying others some part of their physical, mental, or spiritual freedom in order to support goals of our own? What do we get out of our efforts to "help" someone?

Intent is not always clear. We should not underestimate our capacity for self-delusion. In Neale Donald Walsch's book *The New Revelations*, God says to Walsch,

> There is not a country and there is not a group of people on Earth that imagines itself to be an aggressor. Everyone who enters into war does so saying that *they are defending something*. . . . On your

planet there are no "attackers," only "defenders." You achieve this interesting paradox by simply calling all attack a defense. In this way you are able to change your basic values from moment to moment as it suits you, without seeming to change them at all. You get to kill people with impunity to obtain what you want by simply saying that you had no choice. You had to *defend* yourself.[1]

In *The Unfolding Self: Varieties of Transformative Experience*, Ralph Metzner, professor emeritus of psychology at California Institute of Integral Studies, looks at war and concludes that the conflict and destruction of war arise out of "a mixture of judgmentalism and violent rage." (Recall that judgment is one of our most fundamental acts.) When war is the product of judgment, Metzner found, it is because judgment "is expressed, acted upon, in a destructive and aggressive way. That which is judged to be bad is attacked and destroyed." Metzner suggests that, "for transformation to take place, we need to learn to become wise, impartial judges of ourselves, not punitive, vindictive judges." We start "by realizing that the opposing enemies are all within us: we are both judge and accused, both jailor and prisoner, both executioner and condemned."[2]

In seeking to explain our addiction to war, *A Course in Miracles* refers to an ego voice focused on the self and a nurturing voice focused on the greater collective good (which is a description of the functions of the brain's holistic and dualistic operating systems). The Course explains that "the body exists in a world that seems to contain two voices fighting for its possession."[3] And further, "Every response to the ego is a call to war. . . . Those whom you perceive as opponents are part of your peace, which you are giving up by attacking them. How can you have what you give up?"[4]

The Drug War

We usually think of war as armed hostile conflict between nations or states. Although every such war has been justified (or rationalized as just) by its perpetrators, there is general agreement that such wars are inevitably destructive of innocent lives and of culture. When we speak of other kinds of wars—wars against disease, class wars, culture wars, the war on drugs—we often take the term *war* to be a generalized metaphor. And yet, when we look at some of these wars—in particular the war on drugs—these are true wars in just about every sense. In fact, the war on drugs (or "drug war") includes armed militias, innocent civilian casualties, clearly unconstitutional procedures by law enforcement and courts, and more instances of incarceration in the United States than for all serious crimes combined—making our U.S. prison system a de facto prisoner-of-war camp for drug dealers, drug users, those living with or associated with drug users, and many innocent "collateral" cases in which an individual's only crime was to be in the wrong place at the wrong time. In fact, it can be said that the drug war is the most destructive war in which 21st-century America is engaged. (This is still true in spite of promising recent legalization or decriminalization efforts in parts of this country.) This war is being fought on our home turf, can potentially affect every family in this country (whether or not it includes illegal drug users), forces ordinary citizens to become informants (even against family members), and is (like many other wars) even based on a largely manufactured "problem."

The drug war is unusual in that it is overwhelmingly one-sided. One group attacks aided by the full force of the law and backed by a powerful military-industrial-congressional complex, sophisticated modern technology, and a largely supportive media; the other side, lacking the support of law enforcement or the community, mostly hides. Caught in the middle is everyone else—mostly a large group that neither actively wages war nor actively works for peace or justice—many of whom are afraid to object for fear of reprisal. We may set out with good intentions to protect our culture; but then, by default, we choose intimidation and force as tools, all the while ignoring the greater whole, which includes inputs like science, honesty, and compassion.

For all the reasons we have mentioned, we are devoting most of this chapter to an examination of the drug war in America. The lessons to be gained from this examination are instructive not only for what they say about *all* wars, but also for what they say about the split brain's contribution to the beliefs and belief systems that lead to such destructive, unholistic behavior.

In contrasting the way the two operating systems handle the issue of drug abuse, I will frequently refer to Oklahoma, one of the most socially conservative of American states. The manner in which Oklahomans have responded at the voting booth to the issue of illegal drugs shows us how a largely unrestrained conservative system based on dualistic complete dominance leads us to behave. My insights come from the perspective of an insider. I grew up and went to school in Oklahoma. The majority of this book was written there.

"Drug Sentencing Questioned," the *Daily Oklahoman* headline read on December 7, 1992. "Prosecutors and drug agents say the punishment fits the crime. Defense attorneys and, privately, some judges call it draconian." The newspaper's front-page article reported that "more than 90% of the convictions on drug offenses in the U.S. Western District of Oklahoma carry more than a ten year sentence. . . . Many defendants get sentences of 20 to 30 years, and in the last month in Oklahoma City federal court, four individuals were sentenced to life, including a 25-year-old woman with no prior convictions."[5]

This old headline from a large conservative paper in a heavily conservative state shows that as a society *we know* how extreme our drug war has become, and we have known this for a long time. When some judges call the law draconian, people should probably pay attention. Are judges not the proverbial canary in the coal mine of justice?

Although a wave of change in the laws is slowly ushering in an end to the war on cannabis users in some states, the war is still raging in many areas of the country. Politicians don't want to look soft on crime. In 2011, even as penalties were easing elsewhere, Oklahoma legislators voted 119 to 20 in favor of a bill that set sentencing guidelines allowing life in prison for hashish (concentrated marijuana) manufacturing. A blog by Paul Armentano, deputy director of NORML, names Oklahoma number one of the "five worst states to get busted with pot."[6] As of November 1, 2016, penalties for the second possession of cannabis in Oklahoma are halved, meaning that a second offense requires a mandatory minimum sentence of one year, with the possibility of five years and a $5,000 fine. A first offense still stipulates up to a year in prison and a $1,000 fine.

When Congress passed the Rohrabacher-Farr amendment in December 2014, newspaper headlines reported that Congress had legalized medical marijuana. But the laws have not been interpreted as intended by the authors. Dispensaries, growers, and producers of precision-dosed extracts continue to be the targets of DEA-led law enforcement raids that profit from the seizure of assets. And state laws, while seeming to accept marijuana as a medicine, are often excessively restrictive and apply only to minors. As of March 2016, of the states that have some form of medical marijuana, 16 limit its use to some form of oil that is often lacking in THC, the psychoactive ingredient that works synergistically with the CBD component. Oklahoma's entry into medical marijuana was limited to 0.3 percent CBD oil for individuals aged 18 and younger with severe forms of epilepsy or other serious seizure conditions.

Since Colorado and Washington became the first two states to legalize the possession of cannabis for widespread use, several states have joined in relaxing their laws, and the trend is likely to continue. Therefore, some might conclude that this chapter is soon to be irrelevant. But keep in mind that even though the drug war is our immediate focus, the ultimate goal of this chapter is timeless: to understand what it means to have and approach problem solving with a holistic perspective. War is what happens when we are not holistic. The stories that follow are presented as a way of revealing some of the stark differences in the two broad mind-sets that are struggling for control of cultures all over the world. Notice the differences in how the brain's two operating systems lead us to comprehend the events of our world and how they typically prompt us to respond when we are caught up in our fears—as we often are in war.

Scientific and Commonsense Perspectives on the Drug War

For decades, we have been fed a prohibitionist diet of propaganda through corporate-owned media, law enforcement, and grassroots "antidrug" forces. In addition, governmental entities have been promoting this perspective by giving big bucks to big media. The intent here will be to gain a more holistic and inclusive view of the drug war, and thus one that is more balanced. Since the conservative prohibitionist perspective, with its focus on the damage done by drug abuse, has enjoyed extensive and enduring coverage, there is little point in going into detail on all the ways that drugs can damage or destroy lives, especially the lives of children. It is beyond argument that unless medically warranted, *all* drugs should be kept away from children. Children should not be able to buy drugs, illegal or not, just as they are not allowed to buy guns. We allow adults to do many things that are harmful to children. Our discussion here will focus on adults.

Nor will we discuss drug abuse generally. We surely all agree that illegal drugs, like legal drugs and almost everything else, can be harmful if used in an excessive or otherwise unwise manner. Instead, our intent will be to achieve a more balanced understanding of the costs of the drug war. To do this, we will look at some of the consequences of the drug war that the military-industrial-congressional complex and its supporters have failed to tell us about.

Since more arrests involve cannabis than any other drug, we will dig deeper into the war on cannabis and discover the real reasons for its existence. And although these wars are very expensive, costing taxpayers many billions of dollars per year, the financial cost pales in comparison with the human cost. So, for the most part, we will focus on the human cost and ignore the financial.

Why do people use drugs? Ronald K. Siegel, an associate research professor at the University of California, Los Angeles (who has been referred to as the Leif Eriksson of psychopharmacology), has described our demand for drugs as the "fourth drive."

> History shows we have always used drugs. In every age, in every part of this planet, people have pursued intoxication with plant drugs, alcohol, and other mind-altering substances. . . . Almost every species of animal has engaged in the natural pursuit of intoxicants. This behavior has so much force and persistence that it functions like a drive, just like our drives of hunger, thirst, and sex. This "fourth drive" is a natural part of our biology, creating the irrepressible demand for drugs. In a sense, the war on drugs is a war against ourselves, a denial of our very nature.[7]

In his book *Waking Up in Time: Finding Inner Peace in Times of Accelerating Change*, Peter Russell says that people take drugs because "they want to feel better. They want to feel happy, high, relaxed, in control, free from fear, more in touch with life. In this respect, the drug user is seeking nothing different from anyone else — it is just the way in which he or she is doing it that contemporary society finds unacceptable."[8]

We face many of the same issues in our addictions to material things. In acquiring things, Russell explains, "we are trying to make ourselves feel better. But any happiness we get is usually only temporary, so as soon as one high wears off we go in search of another." We thus "become psychologically dependent on our favorite sources of pleasure."[9] These may include food, music, shopping, games, TV, violence, sex—we can become dependent on many things, and in the process harm ourselves and others.

Whatever our focus might be, we tend to seek to repeat responses we enjoy. Things that make us feel better can develop into an addiction in some people, spiraling out of control into abuse and giving off ripples of negative energy that are absorbed by the collective. Consequently, culture (or the collective self) then feels abused and may respond, just as an individual would—first by requesting or demanding that the abuse stop, and perhaps waiting patiently for a response, but soon moving toward use of force to bring the world back to our ideal—or at least back to what it was before the problems showed up. Eventually, we pass laws and employ people to enforce them in order to *force* compliance, and war is born. And, as is so often said, the first casualty of war is truth.

When we become overreliant on receiving guidance from dualistic consciousness, we are at special risk when it comes to apprehending the truth, due to our tendency to home in on separate parts at the expense of the whole. In *Marihuana, the Forbidden Medicine*, Lester Grinspoon, MD, describes how this separation from truth can play out in our lives. Grinspoon, who had been of the attitude that cannabis, or marijuana (its Spanish name), is a very harmful drug, set out in 1967 to define scientifically the nature and degree of its dangers. After three years of research, Grinspoon found that cannabis had "long been used as a medicine in India, China, the Middle East, Southeast Asia, South Africa, and South America," and that early "evidence for medicinal use of cannabis [includes] an herbal published during the reign of the Chinese Emperor Chen Nung five thousand years ago," as well as evidence of medical use in Europe. Grinspoon found that cannabis was considerably less harmful than tobacco and alcohol, and concluded that he, like many others, had been brainwashed. In 1971, Grinspoon predicted that cannabis would be legalized within a decade, based on the evidence he had discovered. Instead, he encountered a political climate in which it was difficult to discuss cannabis openly and freely. "It could almost be said that there is a climate of psychopharmacological McCarthyism," Grinspoon wrote.[10]

To understand the truth about the effect of cannabis on those who use it, how much more thorough and credible does the evidence have to be than this? In 1988, the Drug Enforcement Administration's (DEA's) own "administrative law judge, Francis Young, after taking medical testimony for 15 days and reviewing hundreds of DEA [and] NIDA [National Institute of Drug Abuse] documents posed against the evidence introduced by marijuana reform activists, concluded . . . that 'marijuana is one of the safest therapeutically active substances known to man.'"[11] Granted, this didn't make many newspaper headlines, and perhaps many small newspapers failed to carry it since it wasn't what most of their readers wanted to see—but the information got out, and people who craft drug policy certainly noticed. Indeed, many must have been shocked. And most of the nation's legislators must have noticed. Considering that all of these groups have paid staff whose job it is to make such items known to them, these groups must have also been shocked in 1995 when the prestigious British medical journal the *Lancet*, in an editorial, observed: "The smoking of cannabis, even long term, is not harmful to health."[12]

These legislators also must have noticed in 1994 when the *New York Times* published a comparison of six drugs based on the findings of Jack E. Henningfield, MD, of the government-sponsored National Institute on Drug Abuse (NIDA), and Neal L. Benowitz, MD, of the University of California, San Francisco. The two researchers, in independent studies, had compared nicotine, heroin, cocaine, alcohol, caffeine, and marijuana. Their studies focused on problems associated with withdrawal, reinforcement, tolerance, dependence, and intoxication. They evaluated the six drugs in terms of the five problems and assigned a numerical value to each problem, the values ranging from 1 to 6, with 1 being the most problematic. When we average Henningfield's results, we find caffeine and marijuana tied at 5.4, the highest score, meaning the *least* problematic of the six drugs. Benowitz's numbers show marijuana to be even *less* problematic than caffeine, caffeine earning 4.4 and marijuana 5.2. (As a comparison, Henningfield gave nicotine and cocaine equal ratings of 3.0, alcohol 2.4, and heroin 1.8. In Benowitz's study, nicotine averaged 3.6, alcohol 2.6, cocaine 2.2, and heroin 2.0.)[13]

Among other things, this information tells us that American drug laws are in conflict with science—so much so that they are nothing less than a deliberate flouting of facts arrived at through painstaking methodologies. People often fear certain truths. Since truth by its nature challenges those of our ideas that deviate from truth, truth can interfere with our power, with our love of wealth, and with the harmony of our ideas.

When we are guided by dualistic consciousness, we can find it difficult to accept facts that threaten our established beliefs. An example of this is found in the true story of a woman who had moved to the Solomon Islands to set up a business collecting old gold to resell. All of her life she had heard the phrase "passing the acid test," but it had been meaningless until she discovered that people would try to pass off brass as gold, and that nitric acid would reveal the truth. Her very first experience with pouring acid over brass took place in a room with 10 potential gold sellers. Naturally, upon contact with the acid, the brass immediately turned green and boiled up like a witch's cauldron, forcing everyone in the room to run for a door or window to escape the awful smell. Once the woman felt it was safe to breathe again, she looked over at the little man who had tried to pass off brass as gold and exclaimed, "That's not gold!" "Acid lie," the uneducated man replied, offering an excuse in a futile effort to hide his attempted deception.[14] Uneducated individuals and those in extreme denial of the implications of what they know still fail to appreciate the strength of science's contribution to truth and goodness. They still fail to recognize how transparent their ignorance and closed-mindedness is to those individuals who understand and accept science's role in keeping us informed and honest.

Antidrug warriors often contend that even if marijuana is not dangerous itself, it is dangerous in that it leads the user to try dangerous drugs. This is sometimes called the *gateway theory*. But just as "alcohol, tobacco, and caffeine do not cause people to use marijuana, [marijuana] does not cause people to use heroin, LSD, or cocaine," write Lynn Zimmer and John P. Morgan in *Marijuana Myths, Marijuana Facts: A Review of the Scientific Evidence*.[15] According to a review of scientific evidence by Zimmer and Morgan,

> In the end, the gateway theory is not a theory at all. It is a description of the typical sequence in which multiple-drug users initiate the use of high-prevalence and low-prevalence drugs. A similar statistical relationship exists between other kinds of common and uncommon related activities. For example, most people who ride a motorcycle

(a fairly rare activity) have ridden a bicycle (a fairly common activity). . . . Bicycle riding does not cause motorcycle riding, and increases in the former will not lead automatically to increases in the latter.[16]

A quote from *A Course in Miracles* bears repeating here: "Seeing adapts to wish, for sight is always secondary to desire."[17] When we desire to believe the gateway theory to justify our support for the drug war, we find it easy to see as fact.

If the gateway theory is going to be used to guide our laws and behavior, then why not add caffeine, the world's most popular psychoactive drug? Roland Griffiths, a neuroscientist at the Johns Hopkins University School of Medicine, says that he is "concerned that impressionable adolescents exposed to marketing messages that promote caffeine as a performance enhancer will later turn to stronger drugs, like steroids, Ritalin, or cocaine."[18] Caffeine restricts cerebral blood flow to the brain by an average of 27 percent,[19] which is surely reason enough to try to restrict its use by adolescents, though of course, this has not been done. How would you feel if a member of your family got 20 years in prison for possession of a pound of coffee? If that sounds excessive, be advised that a pound of pot can get you more than that. And remember that Henningfield, a government scientist, found cannabis to be equal to caffeine in terms of the problems it causes society, while Benowitz, a nongovernment scientist, found caffeine to be *more* problematic than cannabis.

As justification for their violent response, supporters of the war on drugs often claim that illegal drugs cause behavioral changes in people. In *Saying Yes: In Defense of Drug Use*, Jacob Sullum states (and most experts agree) that "drugs do not cause behaviors or changes in behaviors. How a person acts after taking a drug is determined by a complex interaction of variables, a process in which the user's beliefs and choices play crucial roles."[20] He goes on to say that "alcohol is more strongly associated with violence than any illegal drug, but that does not mean it turns peaceful, law-abiding people into brutal criminals. The link between alcohol and violence depends upon the drinker's personality, values, expectations, and circumstances. The same is true of crimes committed by other drug users, with the added complication that black-market violence fostered by prohibition is often confused with violence caused by drugs."[21] Sullum explains that "just as drinkers do not typically become alcoholics, users of illegal drugs . . . do not typically become addicts," and cites University of California psychologists Jonathan Shedler and Jack Block, who found that "problem drug use is a symptom, not a cause, of personal and social maladjustment."[22] Sullum also cites a government study by the National Institute on Drug Abuse that supports this conclusion. And he points out what should be obvious—that scientists who see drug use as anything other than a problem "are not likely to get funding from the government, which has no interest in raising questions about its war on drugs, or from academic institutions that rely on government money."[23]

"Outlawing drugs in order to solve the drug problem is much like outlawing sex in order to win the war against AIDS," Ronald Siegel says in *Intoxication: Life in Pursuit of Artificial Paradise*. "In order to solve the [problems that can accompany drug use] we must recognize that intoxicants are medicines, treatments for the human condition. Then we must make their use as safe and risk free and, yes, as healthy as possible."[24]

Is the "Drug War" Misnamed?

The "war on drugs" is much more than a war on drugs; it is a war on *people* and on *families*. *People* are forcibly detained and terrorized by the physical, mental, and spiritual violence of the process. *People* spend all their savings and more on lawyers to try to hold on to their freedom. *People* are wounded and killed—many of them adolescents. And *families* are traumatized: by being separated, by having their houses and cars seized, and by being forced into poverty. In almost every imaginable way, families are damaged. From the consciousness of our holistic perspective we see the living component of reality, so rather than seeing a war on drugs, we see a war on users, a war seeking to maximize people's suffering as a deterrent to use, but resulting in *far* more suffering than the drugs themselves usually cause.

The dominance of dualistic systems focuses our consciousness on nonliving things. Drugs are nonliving things. Therefore, from a dualistic perspective, we have a tendency to see this issue as a war on drugs rather than on people. The suffering of the user is not lost when our consciousness is dominated by dualistic systems; but the suffering is seen as a consequence of a thing, drugs, and therefore, the "logic" goes, drugs must be eliminated in order to resolve the problem. As in so many areas—

from surgery and radical medical interventions to our laws and decisions to use destructive weaponry—the dualistic consciousness sees a single evil that must be eradicated, without paying attention to the fact that a new (and potentially much greater) evil is almost inevitably being created in fighting the targeted evil. While being guided by dualistic complete dominance doesn't preclude our caring greatly about people—and even perhaps considering them the focus of our work—that caring response is coming from influences originating in our holistic system.

As discussed above, to achieve the feeling of peace that we seek, it is important that we resolve internal conflicts in our beliefs as well as in beliefs versus actions. Dualistic thinking often uses forceful and therefore dishonest ways of resolving conflict, and elements of this dishonesty and conflict get imbedded in our belief systems, our mental programming. This then shows up in our responses and in how we feel. Many of us claim to be conservative in our beliefs and actions; however, some of our responses are anything but, and so we broadcast our inner conflict to the world.

In this light, we might ask if the so-called war on drugs is truly conservative as it is currently being waged. Even the most extreme social conservatives usually believe in the long-established American principle of the sanctity of one's home. Most of us in the United States grew up thinking we lived in a country where our homes were protective castles as far as the government was concerned. But thanks to the war on drugs, that is certainly not true today. In a paper written for the Cato Institute, we are given a view of this issue from the perspective of Radley Balko, a former policy analyst with the Cato Institute and a former senior editor for *Reason* magazine, specializing in drug war, criminal justice, and civil liberties issues.

> Over the last 25 years, America has seen a disturbing militarization of its civilian law enforcement, along with a dramatic and unsettling rise in the use of paramilitary police units for routine police work. The most common use of SWAT teams today is to serve narcotics warrants, usually with forced, unannounced entry into the home.
>
> These increasingly frequent raids, 40,000 per year by one estimate, are needlessly subjecting nonviolent drug offenders, bystanders, and wrongly targeted civilians to the terror of having their homes

invaded while they're sleeping, usually by teams of heavily armed paramilitary units dressed not as police officers but as soldiers. These raids bring unnecessary violence and provocation to nonviolent drug offenders, many of whom were guilty of only misdemeanors. The raids terrorize innocents when police mistakenly target the wrong residence. And they have resulted in dozens of needless deaths and injuries, not only of drug offenders, but also of police officers, children, bystanders and innocent suspects.[25]

The castle walls, it appears, have been breached in pursuit of drugs, in the name of protecting us.

Ryan Frederick's nerves were a bit frazzled on January 17, 2008, when he went to bed in Chesapeake, Virginia, according to another report by Radley Balko. The 28-year-old man's house had been broken into earlier that week. Awakened by the fierce barking of his two dogs and the sound of someone trying to break down his front door, Frederick grabbed a gun he kept for defense and went to investigate. Seeing someone trying to squeeze through a busted panel in his door, thinking it was an intruder, Frederick fired. It was a drug SWAT team looking for a marijuana-growing operation. A team member was killed. "Neighbors described Frederick as shy, self-effacing, non-confrontational and hard-working. He had no prior criminal record." Police had acted on an informant's tip. They had no evidence that he was growing or distributing, and no marijuana plants were found.[26] Frederick was convicted of manslaughter and sent to prison.

Most raids take place under cover of darkness with no cameras. When things go wrong, the police almost always blame the occupants of the raided house for the results. Juries tend to believe whatever the police say. The infamous raid in Goose Creek, South Carolina, was all caught on surveillance cameras, and law enforcement had no cover. According to a report on StoptheDrugWar.org, "Tapes show students as young as 14 forced to the ground in handcuffs as officers in SWAT team uniforms and bulletproof vests aim guns at their heads and lead a drug dog to tear through their book bags." One of the students forced to kneel at gunpoint in the school hallway reported that "they hit that school like it was a crack house, like they knew that there were crack dealers in there armed with guns." The student's father, a local deputy sheriff who had served on SWAT teams, told reporters, "A school drug raid is not a SWAT situation, but that's how the Goose Creek police handled it." He referred to the police raid as unnecessarily dangerous, explaining, "It was a crossfire just waiting to happen. If one door slammed, one student dropped a book or screamed . . . those guns would have gone off all over the place." The raid, authorized by school principal George McCrackin, "came up empty. No weapons or drugs were found and none of the students were charged with any crime."[27]

The promoters and prosecutors of the drug war know that these atrocities occur. They know their laws and enforcement activities often inflict great harm on the community—including turning people against law enforcement—yet they believe they are doing the right thing. Let's look at the drug war as viewed from their perspective and consider how people are able to do some the things they do and still see themselves as honorable people. It can get pretty bizarre. After their plot was discovered, the sheriff of Love County, Oklahoma, and another lawman confessed in taped recordings to the FBI their plans to kidnap and torture a suspected drug dealer. In spite of this, the pair was widely supported by the county's citizens (details to follow).

In the Love County story we have an example of what can happen to a culture when dualistic consciousness exercises complete dominance over decision-making. Because what we believe is so profoundly affected by what we see, when we look at the issue of illegal drugs from a dualistic perspective of complete dominance, we see a different reality than we do if we are guided by incomplete or codominant systems, both of which have the advantage of a genetic connection to the greater insights of holistic consciousness.

Since drug war rationale and the behavior of law enforcement are overwhelmingly dualistic, we will be referring to drug warriors as if they were dualistically directed and completely so—that is, operating under genetic complete dominance. But of course there are always exceptions to our broad rules. In this case, the drug war has long had strong support from the holistic community, thanks to a continual campaign of fear flowing into the holistic community from an aggressive, war-oriented dualistic community.

Of course, to the extent that you are holistic, you are peaceful. You don't want to push back against the drug warriors. Your mind-set is not mentally intended or equipped for fighting. You can fight, through the services of your dualistic system, and sometimes you do, but you don't want to. You were built to love. Holistic complete dominance makes us into pacifists. The drug war is a particularly difficult war, since you are fighting from behind enemy lines in most cases; and those you are fighting have government backing, legal protection, widespread community support, and guns.

In any case, when our holistic vision is dominant, we see the big picture and we rely on others, on the experts, to supply the details. Being holistic doesn't mean you see the truth of everything. Often such individuals believe what they are told, which is a more naturally peaceful response than doubting or contesting everything. Thus they may support very un-holistic positions in the voting booth. Their natural inclination is to establish a more holistic and free system, but this may be overridden by their fear of what might happen if drugs were legalized. In addition, holistic individuals have their own fear-based dualistic brain with which to contend. As a result, there has been little opposition to the drug war from the holistic community, and the drug warriors have largely had their way.

Of course, the job of law enforcement is to respond to the damage done by drugs and those who use them, so what law enforcement sees is, naturally enough, the harm that drugs do. Giving full value to the experiences and insights of men and women in law enforcement, we point out that the bigger picture — what we are working toward in this chapter — is quite complex and nuanced. And the full picture is relatively out of sight and out of mind unless you seek it out. Due to its scope and complexity, the information provided by the big picture is more difficult to apprehend. This is the longest chapter in the book, and still it is incomplete in describing the many damaging consequences of choosing war as a way of dealing with drug use and abuse.

Genetic Complete Dominance and the Drug War

What does the complete dominance of a dualistic system do to the behavior of people who support the war on drugs? Our dualistic operating system is *aggressive*. It is energized by *fear*. Dualistic system responses are *electric* and *dominating*. They act *independently* and tend to be *disruptive*. When dualistic systems direct us, our natural response is to acquire what we want through *coercion* or other *forceful* means. Notice that these are all characteristics that are helpful to have if you work in law enforcement. Those guided by the dualistic vision understand that they sometimes cause great pain to some people, but comparing the two options, they see tough enforcement tactics as the lesser of two evils.

Another characteristic of dualistic operating systems and those who are guided by them is to be *judgmental* in order to help us discern differences. Focused on the damage of drug abuse, dualistically oriented individuals can't help but judge it. Besides being judgmental, the brain's dualistic system is *skeptical,* a helpful quality in law enforcement; *rejective,* a quality that is useful in detecting holes in a suspect's story; and *intolerant* of those who commit crimes with their attendant harms (real or perceived).

Sequentiality is another characteristic of dualistic systems that can help to explain conservative law enforcement's response to illegal drugs. Being sequential in perspective and response, dualistic-oriented legislators and enforcement personnel view everything that occurs in their war as a secondary response to someone's drug use. Drugs are viewed as the first cause, and as such they bear ultimate responsibility for drug-related problems — after all, if people would simply stop doing illegal drugs, the drug war would stop. "All suffering caused by the drug war, including that inflicted by and to law enforcement, starts with the users. They are responsible for this war. It's that simple" — so the reasoning goes. When we see the situation from this perspective, there is little reason for us to look at the big picture and question the collateral damage that is being inflicted in waging this war.

We also said that the brain's dualistic system is *egoic* and *impersonal* in character. Both qualities help us isolate ourselves from feelings of responsibility for war damage. This point of view can be stated as, "We are the authority. We fight a thing, crime. It's not personal." This is not to suggest that those in law enforcement do not have feelings, or any of the other qualities of holistic systems. Rather, as with everyone else, their feelings do not originate from their dualistic consciousness; and when complete dominance is in force, our complete reliance on one system's perspectives will profoundly shape our behavior and lead us, in this case, to choose impersonal and egoic responses. Strongly egoic individuals do not respond kindly when their authority is challenged, especially when they are carrying a gun.

Also shaping our perception of the drug war is the *separative* nature of dualistic systems. Working from dualistic consciousness, we have the ability to mentally separate things. When our mind-set is dualistic and completely dominant, our natural tendency is to see ourselves (and therefore our concerns) as separate from the lawmakers we elect, so we feel no responsibility when their laws are excessive and things get out of hand because of it. Likewise, lawmakers are separate from law enforcement, and they tend to accept no responsibility when enforcement is excessive. And neither accepts responsibility for the violence inflicted by law enforcement or the violence that is attributable to bad laws. "We don't make the laws, we just enforce them. The voters tell us what to do" is a common response. Nevertheless, our brains are split to include both a refuge of peace and an environment of conflict, and this gives those who serve in aggressive roles the possibility of peace, like everyone else.

The Drug War Affects Everyone

Law enforcement has little pressure to change. Many people seem to believe that the drug war is a necessary evil, and that as long as they don't do illegal drugs, they have nothing to fear from the police or the law; and so, even though they might not be comfortable with this war, they do nothing to oppose it.

We don't know if that's how 92-year-old Atlanta resident Katheryn Johnston felt or not. And it's too late to ask. She was killed after opening fire on a group of police officers who had forced their way into her home on December 1, 2006. Johnston reportedly was frightened of intruders and kept a gun for protection. The raid was based on a tip from an anonymous informant, who later recanted a statement that he had purchased drugs in Johnston's house. From a police perspective, "no-knock" raids are necessary to prevent suspects from destroying evidence.[28] From a holistic perspective, the destruction of evidence in a few cases pales in comparison with the lives lost by this heavy-handed tactic and the destruction of the principle that our homes are off-limits to government intrusion. When you add to that the fact that the war effort as a whole is making no headway in combating the availability of illegal drugs, a case cannot possibly be made that this tactic is necessary in order to stem their flow. But in the absence of voter-led accountability for its actions, law enforcement has little pressure to change.

Commenting further on this case, Radley Balko tells us that

the police alleged that they had paid an informant to buy drugs from Ms. Johnston's home. They said she fired at them first, and wounded two officers. And they alleged they found marijuana in her home. We now know that those were all lies. . . . The initial arrest of the ex-con [the informant] came via trumped-up charges. The police then invented an informant for the search warrant, and lied about overseeing a drug buy from Johnston's home. Ms. Johnston didn't actually wound any of the officers. They were wounded by fragments of ricochet from their own storm of bullets. And there was no marijuana. Once they realized their mistake, the officers handcuffed Ms. Johnston and left her to bleed and die on the floor of her own home while they planted marijuana in her basement.[29]

Our dualistic operating system, being egoic, is protective of self; consequently, individuals under its direction tend to take care of themselves first. From the perspective of dualistic consciousness, one would say that since Mrs. Johnston is now deceased, she is not going to be hurt by efforts to put the blame on her—so why not fake the evidence and save oneself and one's fellow officers a lot of grief? This is war, and different rules apply.

As hair-raising as these stories are, someone not involved in the drug scene might feel detached from them in the same way that a person in a gated suburban community might feel detached from inner-city gang wars. One might say, "I don't do drugs. I don't even know anyone who does. I have nothing to fear from the American drug war. I don't even live in America." The following might give even those individuals second thoughts.

Columnist Dave Kopel reports that on April 20, 2001, a Cessna owned by the Association of Baptists for World Evangelism, having filed a flight plan as required, took off on a return trip from Islandia, Peru, on the Amazon River. Bound for Iquitos, the plane carried missionaries James and Veronica Bowers; their daughter, Charity; and their son, Cory. Just over an hour into the flight, an A-37 interceptor aircraft, flying in a joint Peruvian-U.S. counternarcotics operation, fired 7.62-caliber slugs into the plane, killing Veronica and Charity and wounding the pilot, who was also with the missionary association. According to the State Department, up to that time under the program, some 39 aircraft had been shot or forced down.[30]

You might think that at least the authorities would have learned from their mistakes so that nothing like this would happen again. In this case, however, learning from one's mistakes was apparently not an option. According to Kopel,

> The investigative team for the official report was specifically "not authorized" to either "question witnesses under oath or receive sworn testimony." Nor were they to "examine misconduct or fix blame." In other words, the investigators were prevented from conducting a real investigation. While formally barred from assigning responsibility . . . the investigators still attempted to scapegoat missionary pilot Kevin Donaldson—even though his only mistake was to occupy airspace where government agents had been given a license to kill. . . . Nor were the accident investigators merely forbidden to assign blame. They were also barred from making "a recommendation or determination with regard to the suspension or start up of counternarcotics aerial intercept operations in Peru."

Kopel's conclusion: "The message is clear: Legal accountability for killings has been eliminated, lest it hinder the work of drug warriors."[31]

How does an operation like this get created? Kopel thinks he knows. One reason for the policy, he suggests, is that Bill Clinton was gearing up for his re-election campaign. "His advisors worried that Republicans would raise 'the character issue.' Clinton needed to prove his stern morality on drugs, and so he began ramping up spending for the drug war—especially military spending. . ."[32]

"The war on drugs has turned into a war on minority communities and a war on the poor," says Fatema Gunja, former director of the Drug Policy Forum of Massachusetts. "The punitive nature of our drug laws stems from a basic premise that links drug use with morality: those who use drugs commit immoral acts and, therefore, should not be granted the same privileges afforded to those who choose to abstain. . . . In 1996, Congress passed the Welfare Reform Act. . . . Introduced and ratified in just two minutes with bipartisan support, Section 115 . . . made felony drug offenders, including nonviolent drug offenders, ineligible for welfare benefits and food stamps. No other crime, *including murder or rape*, results in the loss of such benefits [emphasis added]." Subsequently, the same punitive measures were extended to public housing, higher education, adoption, and foster care. "In theory, these laws are justified mostly on punitive or deterrent grounds. In reality, their effects delay successful reintegration of ex-drug offenders into society, leading many back to prison."[33]

Before cell phones, drug dealers often relied on pay phones to receive messages. To discourage this activity, pay phones were changed so that incoming calls were blocked. Of course, this also prevented everyone who could not afford a phone from receiving calls. Imagine how you would feel if you couldn't receive calls. What problems would that introduce into your life? The situation has changed, but the phones have not. Once the typically separative-oriented male with his destruction-based "solutions" focuses on an important issue, such as "stopping drug traffic," the competitive drive of his dominant operating system demands that success be achieved, *whatever it takes*—even war if necessary.

Until about 1965, the drug war was focused mostly on minorities. In 1965, according to estimates by the National Organization for Reform of Marijuana Laws (NORML), approximately two people per hour were arrested for marijuana possession. And though the sentences were sufficiently harsh to act as a deterrent, they failed to produce the desired results—people didn't stop using drugs just because a so-called "moral" majority wanted them to. As a result, year after year, new and more punishing laws were passed, and more and more people were dragged into the system. By 1992, for example, the arrest rate had escalated to more than 39 arrests per hour.

Jump to 2006. According to the FBI, 829,625 persons were arrested for marijuana violations in the United States in that year, breaking a record for the largest total number of arrests in one year. This brought the rate up to 95 arrests per hour.[34] The year 2007 set another record with 872,721 arrests, an increase of 5.2 percent over the previous year, bringing the arrest rate up to 99.6 per hour. Compare that with 597,447 arrests nationwide for *all violent crimes combined*, which includes murder, nonnegligent manslaughter, forcible rape, robbery, and aggravated assault.[35]

On October 10, 2008, the 20-millionth cannabis arrest took place (NORML estimate).[36] Arrest rates have since declined, and with increased legalization and the spread of medical cannabis, the trend is clearly downward, but NORML estimates that as of 2014, nearly 25 million marijuana arrests had occurred in the United States.

Legendary reporter and news anchor Walter Cronkite noted in 2004 that almost 80 percent of incarcerated women were in prison for drug offenses, and as a result, the increase in the number of female prisoners far outstripped that of male prisoners (although in absolute numbers, the overwhelming majority of prisoners are still male). "The deep perversity of the system," Cronkite explained, "lies in the fact that women with the least culpability often get the harshest sentences. Unlike the guilty drug dealer, they often have no information to trade for a better deal from prosecutors and might end up with a harsher sentence than the dealer gets." Cronkite pointed out that many of the women are mothers of young children. "Those children left without motherly care are the most innocent victims of the drug war and the reason some call it a 'war on families' as well as on drugs."[37]

From the holistic perspective of U.S. District Judge John L. Kane, we see that a broad and sometimes surprising range of people suffer as a result of the drug war.

> They are those people and businesses who can't get into court to have their cases heard. They are the victims of traditional crimes such as burglary, rape, and robbery who can't get justice because the police are tied up with drug cases. They are merchants [bankrupted] because the police no longer have time to investigate or prosecute bad check cases. They are the battered spouses whose mates are not sent to jail because there's room there only for pot smokers. They are the physicians and other medical care providers who cannot treat their patients according to conscience and the discipline of their profession. They are the sick and dying who endure unnecessary pain. They are the children whose parents are taken from them. They are the police who have given up honorable and challenging work investigating and detecting crime because they have become addicted to and dependent upon an informant-based system. They

are the families forced to select one member to plead guilty lest the entire family be charged. They are the prosecutors and defense attorneys who have turned the temples of justice into plea-bargaining bazaars. They are, most painful to me, judges who let this happen and don't say a word. . . . Our national drug policy is inconsistent with the nature of justice, abusive of the nature of authority, and ignorant of the compelling force of forgiveness. Our drug laws, indeed, are more mocked than feared.[38]

Contrast Kane's holistic perspective taken from the front lines of drug-war reality with the simplistic and dualistic perspective we so often hear: "The drug war is the price we must pay to protect our kids." Of course, the latter perspective totally ignores the damage that *war* does to kids, and only makes sense if drug use is considered the worst of all possible evils in every circumstance. It also ignores a crucial set of facts: young people are instinctively driven to experiment, and they are inexperienced in dealing with law enforcement, a deadly combination that leads large numbers of them to be caught up in the war, unjustly punished, and alienated from society just as they are beginning their independent lives.

We have already mentioned the fact that cannabis has long been used by various cultures for healing a wide range of health problems. Psychedelics are another group of drugs that have shown tremendous potential for healing and learning. According to a report written by David Jay Brown for *Scientific American*, prior to 1972, when psychedelic drugs could still be studied, "research suggested that psychedelics offered significant [healing] benefits: they helped recovering alcoholics abstain, soothed the anxieties of terminal cancer patients, and eased the symptoms of many difficult-to-treat psychiatric illnesses, such as obsessive-compulsive disorder. For example, between 1967 and 1972 studies in terminal cancer patients by psychiatrist Stanislav Grof and his colleagues at Spring Grove State Hospital in Baltimore showed that LSD combined with psychotherapy could alleviate symptoms of depression, tension, anxiety, sleep disturbances, psychological withdrawal, and even severe physical pain. Other investigators during this era found that LSD may have some interesting potential as a means to facilitate creative problem solving." As a result of the poisoned political climate, after 1972 there were no human studies of psychedelic drugs in the United States until 1990. Since then, limited research has resumed. Brown goes on to say that "psychedelic drugs affect all mental functions: perception, emotion, cognition, body awareness and one's sense of self. Unlike every other class of drugs, psychedelic drug effects depend heavily on the environment [in which they are experienced] and on the expectations of the subject, which is why combining them with psychotherapy is so vital."[39]

A highly disturbing recent trend that goes even beyond the criminal-ization of drug use is the criminalization of *pain relief* and of the doctors who provide it. Reporting for the *Washington Post*, Mark Kaufman explains that the drug war now threatens our access to *legal* drugs, especially drugs for pain control. "Official rhetoric has escalated to the point where federal and state prosecutors often accuse arrested doctors of being no better than drug kingpins or crack dealers." He quotes one of the fathers of modern pain management, Russell K. Portenoy, as saying, "Treating people in pain isn't easy, and . . . now . . . medical ambiguity is being turned into allegations of criminal behavior." In the same article, pain specialist Rebecca J. Patchin adds, "Doctors hear what's happening to other physicians, and that makes them very reluctant to prescribe opioids that patients might well need."[40]

Opioid addiction from prescription painkillers has recently been revealed to be a major public health problem in certain communities, so clearly not all physicians have been intimidated by DEA tactics—but many still are. I learned this recently when I was in so much pain from muscle spasms that I had to be driven to my doctor's office because it was not safe for me to drive. I was in otherwise good health and taking no other medications, but my doctor refused to give me anything other than Tylenol, which only causes me stomach pain. I suffered more physical pain in the two days following my failed request for medication than I have at any other time in my life.

In addition to interfering with our freedom to seek individual means of physical and mental healing, the drug war limits the options we have in our spiritual search, and as such, it directly abridges our religious freedom. Native peoples have used psychedelics in their spiritual quests for centuries. Psychedelics are sometimes referred to as *entheogens*— which literally means "that which generates God" ("theo"), or "the Divine within." Entheogens help us draw closer to our God nature. But positive news of any kind is viewed as undermining of war efforts, and therefore, a threat to drug-warrior mind-sets and goals. As a result, permission to scientifically study psychedelics, and opportunities to prove their benefits to humankind for physical, mental, or spiritual healing, are very hard to come by.

By prosecuting a war on the very people it seeks to serve (many of whom help pay police salaries through taxes), law enforcement becomes less and less respected among large segments of the population, making their job even more difficult. As one Colorado district attorney remarked about the war against marijuana, it is "the single most destructive force in society, in terms of turning our children against the system."[41] From a holistic standpoint, hearing something like that would cause us to pay close attention and investigate. From the dualistic point of view, however, we would be more likely to separate from it in some way (such as denying the allegation) or to use distortion to make a justification (perhaps dismissing it as a mindless exaggeration and of no consequence).

Because young people have a tendency to do the opposite of what they are told, it only makes sense that drug prohibition might even be *encouraging* a segment of our youth to experiment with illegal drugs. But from the point of view of egoic consciousness, we see ideas like this as a threat to our war effort—even a threat to the validity of our beliefs. Conflicting answers bring up questions that we can't answer, and this can be frightening. And since dualistic consciousness is survival-oriented, if our dominant system is dualistic, we are effectively encouraged to be defensive, an act that can quickly turn offensive. Ego consciousness, being separation-oriented in action, leads us to try to forget, to mentally separate from the conflicting data rather than engage it by allowing our beliefs to be challenged. In ego mode we attack and we retreat.

How Prohibition Feels

Albert Einstein, speaking of alcohol prohibition in *My First Impression of the U.S.A.*, remarked that

> the prestige of government had undoubtedly been lowered considerably by the prohibition law. For nothing is more destructive of respect for the government and the law of the land than passing laws which cannot be enforced. It is an open secret that the dangerous increase of crime in this country is closely connected with this.[42]

No doubt Einstein would have said the same thing about today's *drug* prohibition laws—and he would not be alone. In an interview conducted for public television, Nobel Prize–winning economist Milton Friedman said, "The case for prohibiting drugs is exactly as strong and as weak as the case for prohibiting people from overeating. We all know that overeating causes more deaths than drugs do. If it's in principle OK for the government to say you must not consume drugs because they'll do you harm, why isn't it all right to say you must not eat too much because you'll do harm? Why isn't it all right to say you must not [go] skydiving?"[43]

It doesn't take a rocket scientist or Nobel Prize winner to understand the effects of prohibition. Nevertheless, considering that the majority of voters still support prohibition in the case of certain drugs, perhaps we should remind ourselves of what is at stake. The mother of former Minnesota governor and professional wrestler Jesse Ventura lived through the alcohol-prohibition era and has a perspective that includes the benefit of hindsight. As she sees it, there are obvious similarities between alcohol then and illegal drugs today: in both cases, the gangsters get rich while the government wastes money fighting a losing battle.[44]

So far, we have looked at what people *think* about prohibition, but remember, we are *feeling* beings. What we think is extremely important, but what we feel reflects who we are. How does prohibition feel? Let's take the perspective of Tracy Ingle of North Little Rock, Arkansas, as again reported by Radley Balko.[45]

Imagine waking in the middle of the night to the sound of someone trying to break into your house. Someone is pounding on the front door, and you hear your bedroom window shatter. Thinking robbers are entering, you grab a broken gun to try to bluff them into thinking you might be a threat. As you grab the gun, you are fired upon, and your thigh bone shatters, your lower leg nearly severed. You don't know it yet, but it's a drug raid, and hearing the first shot, other officers open up on you, hitting you four more times. One bullet lodges just above your heart.

Police take you to intensive care, where you remain for a week and a half. Upon release—still in your pajamas—you are taken to the police station and questioned for five hours. You are not allowed to speak with your family. Police then take you to jail, where the pain medication and antibiotics you have been prescribed are withheld from you. Though you have been instructed to clean your wounds every four to six hours, your jailer changes them only twice in the four days that they keep you in jail, and your wounds become infected. But your troubles are only starting.

Police find *no* drugs, and you have *no* drug-related prior arrests, but your sister, a former sheriff's deputy, had stored some common jewelry-making equipment at your house that included a scale and some plastic bags. Based on this, police charge you with running a drug enterprise and set your bail at $250,000—a high amount because you "engaged in a shootout with police"—never mind that you thought they were robbers and that you were knowingly using a broken gun that was incapable of firing a shot. Having to sell your car to make bail, you walk two miles to your hearing on crutches with an infected leg.

Lucky for you, your neighbor had a direct line of sight into the bedroom and saw the entire raid. Unlucky for you, the North Little Rock Police don't question him until a month later. And when they do, they question him for four hours, alone, refusing to let his wife come home or to allow anyone else to see him. After the "interview," your neighbor reports that the police told him that he did not see what he thought he saw. This experience has resulted in your neighbor's being afraid to speak to the media. You have no health insurance, and no money to pay for medication or to otherwise treat your injuries. Eventually, a Pulaski County jury finds you guilty of felony assault for pointing your nonfunctional pistol at the officers who entered your home. They also convict you of maintaining a drug house, as well as possession of drug paraphernalia. You are sentenced to 18 years in prison and fined $18,000.[46]

How does that feel?

You are a paraplegic living in Sayre, Oklahoma. Confined to a wheel-chair, you suffer from chronic antibiotic-resistant infections in your lower body. Staying in a rehabilitation clinic, you hear about cannabis's success in treating people with spinal cord injuries, relieving pain and spasm in their paralyzed limbs; and so, in spite of your disability, with the help of cannabis you are able to support yourself as an auto mechanic. Unfortunately, you get caught with two ounces of marijuana in the back of your wheelchair—arrested by a lawman named Lawless (who was later charged with embezzling from the police property room). The cannabis was for your personal use, but at the trial, another officer claims that he has never seen anyone with two ounces who was not a major dealer. The jury believes him and gives you, a first offender, the maximum sentence for each charge, amounting to life plus 16 years and a $31,000 fine, later reduced by the judge to 10 years and $20,000. Law enforcement then attempts to seize the house in which you live, a house that belongs to your elderly mother, further increasing your legal burden. After a year in prison and nearly dying twice because of the failure of the state of Oklahoma to provide adequate treatment for the highly communicable infections, and being a medical threat to other prisoners, you are released on an appeals bond. The Oklahoma Court of Criminal Appeals affirms the distribution conviction and sentence based solely on one officer's testimony.[47]

The "justice" imposed on you is so outrageous that your story is included in an *ABC News* report. But before it runs and you can see it, you are reimprisoned, where you are frequently placed in solitary confinement and handcuffed to a prison bed without adequate medical treatment for the antibiotic-resistant infections in your lower body. After a public outcry, you are released on medical parole, which is officially protested by the district attorney. You later lose a leg from an ulcerated bedsore developed in prison.[48]

How does that feel?

Events like these don't simply happen. We create them when we support prohibition with our silence and with our energy, with our vote, and with our moral and financial support of prohibition-oriented organizations and policies.

Ironically, under American "justice," *evidence* of a sale is not required in order to convict someone of drug trafficking (selling)—if "evidence" is taken to mean any proof that a sale has taken place. As Jimmy Montgomery, profiled in the above story, discovered, you can go to prison for life based on nothing more than the *suspicion* of law enforcement and the quantity in your possession, an amount that can be as little as two ounces (as if no one ever bought or stored more than one ounce at a time). I've even seen reports of trafficking convictions for less than one ounce based on such "evidence."

The Drug War Creates More Problems Than It Solves

In the 1980s, with the drug war still not working—drug usage was climbing along with drug-war budgets and violence—many with the pro-drug-war mind-set thought that the sentences being given out by some liberal judges were too soft and were undermining the system. Oblivious to Einstein's definition of insanity as doing the same thing over and over again and each time expecting different results, they continued to pursue their original policy of the application of pain as a deterrent, accompanied by ever-greater infringements on personal liberty. In a get-even-tougher mentality, mandatory-minimum sentences were passed in the Drug Abuse Act of 1986. Sentencing discretion was taken from federal judges and replaced by a schedule of minimum prison sentences for drug cases based on the type and quantity of drug involved.

Sheila Devereux, a mother of three, devoted her time to caring for her kids and earning a business degree. After a bitter divorce and custody battle, she turned to drugs to ease the pain—a common response in our culture. After an accidental overdose of cocaine, Sheila was taken straight from the hospital to jail and charged with felony possession. Several years later, her truck broke down and police found a marijuana cigarette in it, her second felony. For a second time, she was given probation. According to FAMM (Families Against Mandatory Minimums), in 2005 Sheila's ex-husband had custody of their children, and Sheila was spending a few days with a new acquaintance until she could move into a house near her children. About a week and a half after she moved in, police burst into the house, and the resident, a man named Allen, turned over six grams of crack. According to the FAMM account,

> Though Sheila had no drugs in her possession and was not a resident of the house, she was held accountable for Allen's crack. Oklahoma law requires that if over five grams of crack is found, everyone involved is considered a drug trafficker. At trial, the police testified they had never seen Sheila participate in any illegal activities, nor was she intoxicated when they searched the house. Allen admitted that the drugs were his and Sheila knew nothing about them. However, because of Sheila's two prior felonies, she was charged under Oklahoma's three strikes law and sentenced to mandatory life in prison without the possibility of parole. Allen received 13 years.[49]

Actions like this are automatic in many states as well as in the federal system under this still-widespread type of law. Of course, the use of mandatory sentencing totally disregards the fundamental holistic, realistic, justice-oriented intent of allowing judges to use their discretion based on the variable nature of circumstances. The response that is mandatory sentencing has developed into its current form in part because:

- When our dualistic consciousness is in charge, we feel the need to be in control. We need that control in order to maintain a secure environment. Mandatory minimums give us a greater sense of control.

- Dualistic systems focus us on what we know. We know that prison is a deterrent. We don't know what will happen if drugs such as marijuana are legalized in *our* community (even if they have been legalized elsewhere). We do know that if legalization *might* pose a risk to our community, we don't want to take that risk. If moderate sentences are not creating a sufficient deterrent, we will make them more severe. If liberal judges won't impose our draconian measures, we will make them mandatory. Attitude: We just haven't gotten tough enough yet.

- Mandatory sentencing is the creation of an egoic mind-set. Knowing nothing about the context of the purported crime, a legislator cannot predict the outcome of his or her mandatory sentencing other than for one metric: time spent in prison. In contrast, a judge typically has a relative wealth of information about the various consequences of his or her court wards and thus considers a variety of factors. Judges, when allowed sentencing latitude, are able to give the justice system a much more holistic approach to sentencing.

- Mandatory sentencing is a response of war—and, by definition, sentencing that allows for no leniency, no variability, no respect for human factors, *cannot* be just. Mandatory sentencing effectively dispenses with the fundamental role of the judiciary and turns judges into high-paid law clerks. This is a pure egoic-male, aggressive, separative, destruction-oriented, single-purpose, truth-suppressing response.

It goes without saying that mandatory minimums increase the size of our prison populations. A 2013 report points out that Oklahoma ranks number one among all states for the percentage of its women that it imprisons, a rank the state has held in earlier surveys. Oklahoma's incarceration rate for women is nearly double the national average.[50] According to a research fact sheet by the National Council on Crime and Delinquency, the United States, which has an incarceration rate that is four times the world average and incarcerates more people than any other country in the world, also incarcerates more women than any other country (over three times more than any other nation, Russia coming in second). This tells that, based on reported data, as a percentage of its population, Oklahoma imprisons more women than any country on the planet.[51]

But mandatory minimums don't deter illegal drug activity, so another get-tough attitude idea that prohibitionists came up with was to create drug-free zones around schools, parks, churches, housing projects, and other public areas, where extra penalties were added. In some cities, that covered most of the territory. In New Jersey, a commission found that "instead of declining, drug arrests in the zones rose steadily after the law took effect in 1987." It also found that "96 percent of offenders jailed for zone violations were black or Hispanic." Only 2 percent of the cases they studied involved students. "A former assistant attorney general in Massachusetts reviewed hundreds of drug-free-zone cases, and found that less than 1 percent involved drug sales to youths."[52] Thus, the well-intentioned goal of deterring drugs from being peddled around schools has led to disastrous results. Rather than helping students, this law has instead become just another tool of punishment, another opportunity for prosecutors to add prison time or a fine to someone's sentence and to further crowd our prisons. An Alva, Oklahoma, man experienced the consequences of this law when cops found illegal drugs at an isolated bar that he operated on the edge of town. Although the bar was a long distance from an actual school, because it was near school-owned *farmland*, he was charged with violating drug-zone statutes.[53]

Another reflection of government's desperate get-tough attitude was to start going through people's trash. "By a six-to-two vote, the U.S. Supreme Court ruled that police may freely rummage through ordinary household trash left at curbside without obtaining a search warrant."[54] In Alva, Oklahoma, residue was found in the trash of two men after their trash was searched, and they were charged with felony possession of marijuana within 1,000 feet of a school, even though there was no evidence that they had any connection with the school. This charge called for imprisonment of up to two years and a fine of $2,000.[55] That would, of course, be on top of any other drug-related charges.

Trash searches can get you killed. In Beaver Dam, Wisconsin, police searched Scott Bryant's garbage for cannabis residue for several days before getting a no-knock warrant. According to news and eyewitness reports, the four sheriff's deputies storming the residence made no effort to identify themselves prior to smashing in the door, and they shot the unarmed Bryant immediately. Bryant made no attempt to resist and was killed in front of his seven-year-old son. Police later reported finding less than three grams of cannabis.[56]

Another major tool of drug-law enforcement is forfeiture. Glenn Greenwald, a former civil rights litigator, explains:

> Unlike English common law, which required conviction prior to seizure, American forfeiture dispenses with the need for proving the property owner guilty of anything. All that is necessary is for the state to claim a connection between the things seized and drugs, whereupon the government may confiscate the property. It is then up to the owner to prove (at their own expense . . .) that the property is "innocent." Critically, **the proceeds from the seizures go into the budget of the state or federal law enforcement agencies and prosecutors offices** [Greenwald's emphasis], creating a horrible incentive for officers to go after seizures solely for the purpose of enriching their units with a swell new fleet of fully loaded police cruisers, or lovely new desks for the DAs.[57]

We see clear evidence of the incentives for forfeiture in the fact that "as part of training for ATF [Alcohol, Tobacco and Firearms] agents and state and local task force officers, ATF purchased a number of Leatherman tool kits engraved with the words 'ATF Asset Forfeiture' and 'Always Think Forfeiture' for distribution to the participants."[58] We see evidence of the effect of incentive in the attitude of Oklahoma City police. After seizing $1.3 million in a suspected drug bust, although no drugs were found, they kept the money anyway because of traces of cocaine found on the bills—despite the fact that it has long been common knowledge that used bills often contain traces of cocaine due to the widespread use of the drug.[59] Due to contamination by counting machines and other factors, approximately four of every five bills in circulation carry trace amounts of cocaine![60]

Not only is the war on drugs failing to solve many of the problems associated with drug abuse, but as we have been seeing, it *creates* a multitude of problems. From the perspective of Eric E. Sterling, president of the Criminal Justice Policy Foundation and former counsel to the U.S. House of Representatives Committee on the Judiciary from 1979 until 1989, we see that "the strategy to reduce supply by arresting participants in the distribution [of illegal drugs] actually has a positive, strengthening effect on the illegal drug market. . . . Drug enforcement weeds out the less effective, less ingenious participants and encourages the more ruthless and the more cunning."[61]

Our Drug War Supports Terrorists

One of the greatest and most widespread of the many problems created by the drug war is the damage it does to everyone by supporting international terrorism. "Prohibition forces drugs into an underground, unregulated market, which creates a highly lucrative source of funding and personnel in the armed and violent actions against civilians and governments around the world," warns the Drug Policy Alliance.[62] If all drugs were legal, prices would drop dramatically, depriving terrorists of a major source of much-needed funding.

Our lawmakers have long known that they are aiding terrorist activity. Former Secretary of State, Secretary of Labor, and Secretary of the Treasury George Shultz warned us way back in 1984 that "money from drug smuggling supports terrorists."[63] We were warned again in 1994 by Interpol's chief drug-enforcement officer, who reported that "drugs have taken over as a chief means of supporting terrorism."[64] Sheldon Richman, writing for the Future of Freedom Foundation, quotes former Republican House Speaker Dennis Hastert as saying, "The illegal drug trade is the financial engine that fuels many terrorist organizations around the world." Richman points out that even former drug czar William Bennett (notwithstanding his intransigent drug-war advocacy) owns up to this fact. Richman quotes Bennett as saying on the *Wall Street Journal* editorial page, "We have learned a great deal about the connection between terrorism and illegal drugs, including the fact that our enemies in Afghanistan have derived considerable sustenance and resources from the drug trade."[65]

Considering the grave threat posed by terrorists, if high-level government officials know that drugs laws are supporting terrorists, then why does the drug war continue? Follow the money. The drug war is a function of an established and powerful system that feeds many families and provides them with security. The system protects itself. By design, those who object to the system can have only a very limited impact. Threaten the integrity of a powerful system, and you can expect to pay a price.

Drug warriors are not just aiding terrorists; they are creating them. According to a report in a conservative Oklahoma newspaper, U.S. drug agents were alleged to have "kidnapped, raped and tortured Bolivians while trying to build a drug case." The story reported, "Twenty-nine Bolivians allege in sworn declarations that the Drug Enforcement Administration and Bolivian army used brutal methods . . . while seeking information." A woman claimed to have been "blindfolded, interrogated, given electric shocks and raped. Others alleged they were beaten with rifle butts. One man claimed agents pulled out one of his toenails."[66] Nor is government-sponsored terrorism limited to the federal level. In Oklahoma, a plot to kidnap and torture a suspected north Texas drug dealer was uncovered when Marietta police Lieutenant Tom Hankins notified the FBI in response to a request by Sheriff Wesley Liddell Jr. to participate in the kidnapping. Liddell confessed to the FBI after he was arrested. According to FBI spokesman Dan Vogel, Liddell told the FBI in a recorded conversation that he and his brother-in-law, a Marietta, Oklahoma, police officer, planned to use "a heated curling iron [as] the instrument of torture because it could be applied to certain parts of the body and would not leave any marks."[67] "Sometimes you got to break the law to help the law," Liddell was heard saying in one recording. In another recording, the sheriff's son-in-law, Roger Ray Hilton, can be heard talking about getting rid of the man they planned to kidnap, saying that "if for some reason something goes wrong and somebody is going to have to kill him, I'd just as soon Junior (Liddell) did it."[68]

Commenting on the local community's attitude—one of rousing support of the pair—an Oklahoma City columnist expressed concern. "The attitude which some of these people have taken is that it doesn't really matter if Liddell and Hilton are guilty. They support the pair, not because they think they are innocent, but because the two were trying to fight the war on drugs."[69] In court, the pair claimed they were not planning to carry out the planned act and were acquitted.

Local attitudes tend to reflect state and national attitudes, which can be summed up as, "Do whatever it takes to win, even if that means ignoring the facts of science, the justice of law, and the will of the people." In what was described as a "desperate and transparent" attempt by Congress to support the federal government's drug policies by prohibiting changes to drug policy, Congress barred the District of Columbia from spending any money to count the votes on Initiative 59, a medical marijuana measure on the November 1998 ballot. "Exit polls showed that the measure was being approved by a vote of 69 to 31 percent,"[70] reports former California Superior Court Judge James P. Gray in *Why Our Drug Laws Have Failed and What We Can Do About It: A Judicial Indictment of the War on Drugs.*

Congress must have been surprised by the response. "All over the country, newspapers wrote editorials denouncing Congress's act, saying such things as, 'It is hard to imagine that in the history of American elections—or of American democracy—there is precedent for stifling the legally expressed will of the people by denying the money necessary to count their ballots.'"[71] Yet Congress was unbowed—which was typical, since the separatist response of dualistic consciousness provides us with an easy way to mentally evade our critics: we simply ignore them. In 2014 the District voted to legalize the limited possession and cultivation of minimal amounts of marijuana by adults 21 and over—though it is still illegal to sell. Once again, leaders in Congress tried to block implementation. Nevertheless, in February 2015 the new law went into effect.

"Medieval and Sadistic"

In war, winning is everything. In war, justice, or the will of the people, has little if any value. You use the laws that benefit you and ignore the ones that do not. The same goes for the facts. And blue ribbon commissions? Likewise—unless they support you, you ignore them. After annual increases in penalties for marijuana possession, and seeing that marijuana use was still increasing among middle-class youth, President Richard Nixon set up the Shafer Commission to study the issue. "In 1972, after reviewing the scientific evidence, [the commission concluded] it was 'of the unanimous opinion that marihuana use is not such a grave problem that individuals who smoke marihuana, and possess it for that purpose, should be subject to criminal prosecution,'" wrote Lynn Zimmer and John P. Morgan in *Marijuana Myths, Marijuana Facts.* Unhappy with the findings, Nixon ignored the report, but "between 1969 and 1977, government-appointed commissions in Canada, England, Australia, and the Netherlands all issued reports that agreed with the Shafer Commission's conclusions. All found that marijuana's dangers had been greatly exaggerated."[72]

As is well known, former U.S. Representative Ron Paul (R-Texas until 2013) has not been afraid to criticize his fellow conservatives for their nonadherence to what should be a bedrock conservative principle: that one cannot be a true defender of liberty while ignoring or opposing the basic individual freedoms, even if they involve activities we disapprove of. Explaining why conservatives should oppose the drug war, Paul points out, "Government intervention in *social* matters [produces] the same unintended consequences, distortions, and inefficiencies as government intervention in *economic* matters [emphasis added]." Paul believes that "although . . . philosophical questions rarely surface in the drug debate, they are critically important. When we fail to adopt a consistent guiding philosophy, we allow emotions rather than principles to frame the debate. . . . In America, the overriding principle should be that human freedom is our greatest priority."[73]

Ron Paul reminds us that the drug war ramped up

> in a decade when conservative, limited-government thinking was otherwise ascendant. . . . President Reagan famously told the nation that government was the problem, not the solution. Reagan conservatives argued that individual initiative and personal responsibility . . . were the keys to a better life for Americans. Yet the war on drugs turned the idea of personal responsibility upside down, placing the blame for personal moral failure on drugs rather than the individuals abusing them. Drugs became a national boogeyman, while individuals were reduced to helpless victims. In this sense the war on drugs mirrored the gun-control movement's [liberal] push to ban firearms, as both attempted to blame inanimate objects for the misdeeds of individuals.[74]

The drug war has contributed to the polarization of America. "The addict belongs in the hospital, not in the prison," wrote Alfred R. Lindesmith, a professor of sociology at Indiana University, in the *Nation*. Referring to Congress's escalation of the use of mandatory minimums, Lindesmith described its legislation as reflecting "conceptions of justice and penology which can only be adequately described as *medieval* and *sadistic.*"[75] A prominent viewpoint from the prohibitionist side—that of former drug czar William Bennett—certainly lends credence to Lindesmith's strong characterizations. Bennett believes that even drug *users* belong in prison. Speaking at W. R. Thomas Middle School in Miami, Bennett encouraged youngsters to turn in their relatives and friends if they used drugs.[76] When asked on a television program why we don't behead drug dealers as they do in Middle Eastern countries, Bennett responded, "Morally, I don't have any problem with that at all."[77] Here Bennett shows us the impersonal, egoic, "remove and destroy the threat" attitude toward problem solving that we often find associated with dualistic complete dominance.

Even if you don't do drugs and face no threat from drug-funded terrorism because you don't travel, or because you live in an isolated area of the country, as an American you still face substantial risks as a result of the drug war. Law enforcement, like every organization on the planet, makes mistakes. For example, they sometimes go to the wrong address in their attempts to root out drugs. Because of that one fact, every day many of us play Russian roulette with our lives and those of our family and pets.

If a clean-living city mayor can be threatened, so can you. Such was the case with the mayor of Berwyn Heights, Maryland. On the basis of a package of marijuana delivered to the mayor's house on July 29, 2008, a SWAT team broke down his front door and shot his two Labrador retrievers. The mayor and his mother-in-law were kept bound for nearly two hours next to the two pets and interrogated while blood from the dogs pooled on the floor. Although authorities initially claimed to have been operating under a "no-knock" warrant, it later came out that the police did not have, nor did they even seek, such a warrant. A Maryland state senator who represented the district said it was just another example of frequent police action in minority communities. But this time, it drew far more attention because it involved a mayor. The mayor believes his dogs were executed the very second the SWAT team entered. And law enforcement's attitude toward the mayor? The sheriff said the dogs' deaths were justified—the officers felt threatened. By focusing on everything but their own damaging activities, they were able, in their minds, to separate themselves from responsibility. The county police chief portrayed the mayor as the victim of a local drug ring.[78]

Although we trust that most members of law enforcement are honorable, we have already seen that some law enforcement officers ignore the law altogether at times and can place people's lives in great peril in the process—as, for example, in the story of the Love County Sheriff and his policeman brother-in-law. Another such example is the case of Rachel Hoffman, a 23-year-old college graduate who occasionally used marijuana. After a Tallahassee, Florida, police raid found some marijuana in her home, she faced five years in prison and a fine. According to Paul Armentano, NORML (National Organization for Reform of Marijuana Laws) deputy director, Hoffman was threatened with jail and told that if she cooperated by helping with a drug operation, the police would not file charges. Untrained and unsupervised, and in flagrant violation of Tallahassee Police Department protocol, she was instructed to meet with two men whom she had never met and purchase a large quantity of cocaine and ecstasy, and a handgun. Since Hoffman was already enrolled in a drug court program from a prior marijuana possession charge, cooperating with Tallahassee police would have been in violation of her probation, and police were required to first gain formal approval from the state prosecutor's office. "Knowing that the office would likely not sign off on their deal . . . police simply decided to move forward with their informal arrangement and not tell anybody." As Armentano put it, "Rachel became the bait; the Tallahassee police force went trolling for sharks." On May 12, 2008, Hoffman was shot and killed by the two men.[79]

We are engaged in a war that creates terrible conflict in the lives of millions of our brothers, sisters, parents, and children, and costs billions of dollars every year, yet as a culture we have never openly and freely discussed it. Because there has never been an open and honest discussion, it is often difficult for people to get the facts, sort out the fundamentals, and find the truth—or even recognize the irony of their words and actions.

The Real Reason Cannabis Was Criminalized
According to most scientific findings, the psychoactive component of cannabis is one of the safest of common drugs, if not *the* safest in many respects. (Unlike most drugs, cannabis has never caused anyone to die from an overdose.) At the very least, considered as a whole, it is no more of a problem than caffeine. Yet federal laws treat cannabis as a *very* dangerous

drug. The objection to cannabis seems to be that people use it to get high, to alter their consciousness—and in the minds of many people, it is a bad thing to alter your consciousness. But what if you could grow cannabis that would *not* make you high? Well, you can. Cannabis has long been used for its strong fibers. In fact, "the first laws addressing any of the currently illicit substances were passed during colonial times, and they *required* the various townships to grow a certain amount of cannabis sativa, or hemp [emphasis added]."[80] Yet laws treat this otherwise commercially valuable plant as a harmful psychoactive drug. The discrepancy between science and American drug policy with respect to hemp is rather strange, don't you think?

James P. Gray reports that prior to the Harrison Narcotic Act of 1914, other than "a couple of state and local statutes . . . there were no illegal drugs in the United States."[81] And no drug war. The fibers of the cannabis plant were widely used to make rope by the U.S. Navy, farmers, and fishermen, for example. "Several drafts of the Declaration of Independence were printed on parchment made from the same natural substance. . . . [Hemp paper] was even used as money from 1631 until the early 1800s. George Washington, Thomas Jefferson, and a large number of other famous planters in the colonial period all grew large crops of hemp."[82] In *Intoxication: Life in Pursuit of Artificial Paradise*, Ronald K. Siegel explains that "the Harrison Act was widely interpreted as national prohibition of . . . opium, morphine, heroin, coca, and cocaine . . . but it was merely a law for the orderly marketing of these drugs in small quantities over-the-counter and in larger quantities on a physician's prescription. Marijuana was not included because of strong lobbying by the pharmaceutical industry."[83]

The next round in drug prohibition was instituted by moralist idealists and was aimed at alcohol. Started in 1920, it was a disastrous war that officially ended on December 5, 1933. During this period, "the United States saw a material increase in death from poisoned liquor, crime, violence, and corruption," writes James P. Gray in *Why Our Drug Laws Have Failed and What We Can Do About It*. "It also saw a higher consumption per capita of stronger beverages like whiskey than of weaker beverages like beer, in accordance with a cardinal rule of prohibition: there is always more money to be made in pushing the more concentrated substances. In many cities there were actually more 'speakeasies' during Alcohol Prohibition than there previously had been saloons."[84]

Next to become a prohibitionist target was cannabis. This time, however, the lead was taken by corporate interests whose goal was not so much to combat drug usage, which was minimal at the time, as to eliminate economic competition from hemp, a strong but soft and versatile fiber. As Jack Herer, a best-selling author and political activist, explains in *Hemp and the Marijuana Conspiracy: The Emperor Wears No Clothes*, "When mechanical hemp fiber stripping machines and machines to conserve hemp's high-cellulose pulp finally became state-of-the-art, available and affordable in the mid-1930's, the enormous timber acreage and business of the Hearst Paper Manufacturing Division, Kimberly Clark (USA), St. Regis—and virtually all other timber, paper and large newspaper holding companies—stood to lose billions of dollars and perhaps go bankrupt."[85]

Indeed, hemp seems to have so many good uses, and so few drawbacks, that one might think it is a God-sent gift. Perhaps that is why, in Neale Donald Walsch's *Conversations with God: An Uncommon Dialogue, Book 2*, God says to Walsch, concerning hemp:

> If it were grown, half the cotton growers, nylon and rayon manu-facturers, and timber products people in the world would go out of business. Hemp happens to be one of the most useful, strongest, toughest, longest-lasting materials on your planet. You cannot pro-duce a better fiber for clothes, a stronger substance for ropes, an easier-to-grow-and-harvest source for pulp. You cut down hundreds of thousands of trees per year to give yourself Sunday papers, so that you can read about the decimation of the world's forests. Hemp could provide you with millions of Sunday papers without cutting down one tree. Indeed, it could substitute for so many resource materials, at one-tenth the cost. And *that is the catch*. Somebody *loses money* if this miraculous plant—which also has extraordinary medicinal properties, incidentally—is allowed to be grown. And *that is why marijuana is illegal in your country.*[86]

The rise of hemp also threatened another powerful corporation. "In 1937 DuPont had just patented processes to make plastics from oil and coal, as well as new sulfate/sulfite processes to make paper from wood pulp which would, according to their own corporate records and historians, account for over 80% of all its railroad car-loadings for the next 50 years." Herer concludes that "if hemp had not been made illegal, 80% of DuPont's business would never have come to be."[87]

By threatening DuPont's business, hemp also threatened DuPont's chief financial backer, Andrew Mellon, who, in his role as secretary of the Treasury, appointed his future nephew-in-law, Harry J. Anslinger, to be head of the newly reorganized Federal Bureau of Narcotics and Dangerous Drugs, the predecessor of the DEA (Drug Enforcement Administration). Jack Herer explains, "Testimony before Congress in 1937 for the purpose of outlawing hemp consisted almost entirely of Hearst's and other sensational and racist newspaper articles read aloud by . . . Anslinger." Anslinger testified that "marijuana is the most violence causing drug in the history of mankind." Preying on racial fears, he testified that about half "of all violent crimes committed in the U.S. were committed by Spaniards, Mexican-Americans, Latin Americans, Filipinos, Negroes, and Greeks, and these crimes could be traced directly to Marijuana." American Medical Association (AMA) doctors, upon learning of the bill two days prior to the vote, protested that Congress was about to outlaw a "benign substance used in scores of illnesses, for 100 years in America, with perfect safety," and that the law had been prepared in secret over a span of two years without the medical profession having been consulted. But it was too late. And when a member of Congress asked, before voting, if anyone had consulted with the AMA on the bill, he was falsely told that the AMA had been consulted and was in complete agreement.[88]

In 1970, Congress provisionally categorized cannabis as a Schedule 1 drug, a drug with a high tendency for abuse and no accepted medical use. Schedule 1 drugs cannot be prescribed. If you can't prescribe it, there can be no legal medical demand for it. If there is no legal demand for it, there is no need for anyone to produce it—*and that seems to be the key*. If there were a legal demand, people would need to farm cannabis for its medicinal purposes. And that would create a serious problem for some powerful individuals. If farmers were allowed to grow cannabis for its medicinal value, what would stop them from growing it for its fiber, or for one of its other commercially valuable properties?

And then there's the CIA's connection with drugs, which the late Michael C. Ruppert, a former Los Angeles narcotics detective, studied for more than 25 years. Ruppert valued the CIA's cut of the illegal drug trade at around $600 billion per year.[89] According to Ruppert, "The CIA has been dealing drugs since before it was the CIA," starting back in World War II when it was the OSS. "The use of the drug trade to secure economic advantage . . . is at least as old as the British East India Company's smuggling of opium from India into China in the late 1600s."[90]

According to Jim Willie CB (editor of the *Hat Trick Letter*, a subscription publication that discusses currencies, the world economy, and other related topics), "The irony is that the US agencies known as the Central Intelligence Agency (CIA) and the Drug Enforcement Agency (DEA) act precisely as drug cartels . . . but under the aegis of the U.S. Government. . . . The DEA has long acted as the private security force for the CIA syndicated operations, turning over seized narcotics to syndicate inventory, and killing competitors. In fact, the inside joke among US Government agencies unsympathetic to the cause is their name of Cocaine Importing Agency. Confirmation is easy," Willie reports. "To me it came from three military contacts and a defense industry consultant. That consultant, formerly an employee at Northrop Grumman, claims that defense contractors earn considerable profit by using private corporate jets for narcotic shipments on a routine regular basis, with no customs inspections."[91] The CIA connection to drug running gained widespread public attention in the mid-1980s after an insider confession that linked CIA drug activity to an airport at Mena, Arkansas.

Once you head down this road, it is difficult to turn back. And any activities that interfere with these profits must be prohibited at all costs, even if it means ignoring science and incarcerating people—which in turn means separating them from their families. This might even include killing disabled war veterans.

Gary Shepherd of Kentucky, a shotgun-carrying 45-year-old disabled war veteran, smoked pot to ease the pain from his war-incurred injuries. When Kentucky police and National Guard troops went to his property to cut down and burn his 55 marijuana plants, Shepherd refused to let them. After a seven-hour standoff, police ordered Shepherd to lower his shotgun. As he complied, he was shot and killed, his four-year-old son standing beside him. Shepherd's wife, with hands up, was shot in the head but miraculously survived. Shepherd never fired. Following the shooting, a member of the assembled force was heard to remark, "We've killed Jesus!" "Jesus" was the police code name for the long-haired Shepherd.[92]

But perhaps there is another sense in which they "killed" Jesus. It has often been said that we "crucify" Jesus when we turn our back on his teachings and example and refuse the lessons that he came here to teach—to love your neighbor as yourself, to treat others as you would have them treat you, to be a peacemaker, to practice unconditional love. Which of these teachings are being held up in the war on drugs as it is being waged today? What would Jesus say and do about all of this?

A Spirit-Based Perspective on Drugs

Since most American antidrug crusaders in the United States are Christian, it might be helpful to see what can we glean from the New Testament that might help us to understand Jesus's attitude toward drugs and drug users. The book of John (John 2:1–11) says that Jesus went to a wedding party where they served wine, and that the wine ran out. It says that the house where the wedding party took place had six stone jars, each capable of holding 20 to 30 gallons (76–114 liters), and Jesus asked that they be filled to the brim with water, which Jesus then turned into wine.[93]

Was there a greater crowd than expected? Was there heavy drinking? On these matters we can't know for sure, but with that much wine, and knowing human nature, we can make a pretty good guess that at least some people drank heavily. We do know without a doubt that the alcohol in wine is a powerful drug and that the amount created was 120 to 180 gallons—and that it was *in addition* to the wine provided by the host. It therefore seems reasonable to assume that Jesus tolerated the liberal use of alcoholic intoxicants.

Would Jesus have been tolerant of other intoxicants? Jesus's comments recorded in the Gospel of Mark (Mark 7:15) suggest a "yes" answer or, at the very least, leave an opening: "Nothing that goes into a man from outside can defile him; no, it is the things that come out of him that defile a man."[94] Might examples of defiling conduct include the actions of legislators, law enforcement, and judges who wage war on otherwise peaceful people for selling and possessing relatively safe intoxicants—as well as our own actions and votes in support of these individuals?

We might expect Jesus to respect the findings of fact-based science. Given his clear acceptance of wine, reason suggests that less powerful and less harmful intoxicants (as we know cannabis and caffeine to be) would also be acceptable for adult use. We might expect the conservative side of Jesus to support conservative use while cautioning us to take care of ourselves. His liberal side would consider the whole of the issue, the conservative view as well as context, such as the situation and environment.

Jesus was a *peacemaker*. It is consistent with everything we know about him to believe that his actions would not be warlike—that he would not act against another's will. Thus, it is difficult to imagine that Jesus would declare war on anyone over his or her choice of intoxicant, or especially on young people, whose natural tendency is to experiment and ignore authority.

Jesus was a *healer*. The compassionate holistic, freedom-serving right brain of Jesus would surely allow people to have cannabis if it was of help to them. The realistic, rational left brain of Jesus would recognize that differences in individuals are sometimes best served with different intoxicants, and governments are not in the best position to make that determination.

Jesus was a *teacher*. Had he thought people needed to do something other than what they were doing, we might expect he would have sought educational means, rather than force, to effect change. In *A Course in Miracles* Jesus is quoted as saying, "You must change your mind, not your behavior, and this *is* a matter of willingness. You do not need guidance except at the mind level. Correction belongs only at the level where change is possible. Change does not mean anything at the symptom level, where it cannot work."[95] Of course, most American cultures are focused at the symptom level.

What about other great teachers? What, for example, do the teachings of the Buddha offer that might help us better deal with the issue of drug use?

Gautama Buddha, according to His Holiness the Dalai Lama, would encourage us to "explore for ourselves ways of training and educating the mind, developing the emotions, becoming aware of ourselves, managing our negative habits, and detoxifying ourselves from our mental toxins."[96] According to Professor Ron Epstein, lecturer for the Global Peace Studies

Program at San Francisco State University, "The Buddha taught that peaceful minds lead to peaceful speech and peaceful actions. If the minds of living beings are at peace, the world will be at peace."[97]

What would most great spiritual leaders do? We don't know exactly what their response would be under every circumstance, but we do know that these individuals typically achieve their lofty status by transcending the fears of their fellow humans, transcending the urge to control their fellow man, and coming to understand that love and freedom go hand in hand. Therefore, we might expect that most great spiritual leaders would be in harmony with what we know of the Buddha and Jesus.

War Causes More Problems Than It Solves

The issue of how to deal with drugs is a very serious one, and we would be foolish to ignore the advice of seasoned veterans who have experienced the front lines of the drug war. One such individual is Edward Ellison, who spent years in Scotland Yard organizing its antidrug squad and fighting drug use. His conclusions are not unique; in fact, Ellison's advice is pretty much the same advice you would get if you asked a number of other individuals, including former U.S. Secretary of State George Shultz, former Attorney General Gustave de Greiff of Colombia, the late author and syndicated columnist William F. Buckley Jr., former New Mexico Governor Gary Johnson, U.S. District Court Judge Robert Sweet (New York), former federal prosecutor and Superior Court Judge James P. Gray (Orange County, California), and—for that matter—Dear Abby.[98] But Ellison's conclusions are those of an insider—one whose passion is born of deep knowledge and personal experience. Ellison says:

> As a former drugs squad chief, I've seen too many youngsters die. I'm determined my children don't get hooked—which is why I want all drugs legalized. Seventeen years of my life was spent in Scotland Yard's anti-drugs squad, four as its head. I saw the misery that drug abuse can cause. I saw first-hand the squalor, the wrecked lives, the deaths. And I saw, and arrested when I could, the people who do so well out of drugs: the dealers, the importers, the organizers. I saw the immense profits they were making out of human misery, the money laundering, the crime syndicates they financed. We have attempted prohibition. All that happened was that courts became clogged with

thousands of cases of small, individual users, and a generation of young people came to think of the police as their enemies. There were no resources left to fight other crime. I say legalize drugs because I want to see less drug abuse, not more. And I say legalize drugs because I want to see the criminals put out of business.[99]

In the fight for freedom, a fight that pits individuals against a massive militarized industrial-congressional complex, individuals have received limited support from philanthropic organizations. Writing for the *Drug Policy Letter*, David C. Condiffe, former executive director of the Drug Policy Foundation, reminds us that "for too long, mainstream philanthropy has been timid and halfhearted in the field of drug policy reform."[100] And we need to act quickly. U.S. Supreme Court Justice William O. Douglas (1898–1980) warned us that "the privacy and dignity of our citizens is being whittled away by sometimes imperceptible steps. Taken individually, each step may be of little consequence. But when viewed as a whole, there begins to emerge a society quite unlike any we have seen—a society in which government may intrude into the secret regions of a person's life."[101] Obviously, this has already happened, but it is not too late to reverse the trend.

Reflecting a perspective that incorporates both foresight and hindsight, James P. Gray suggests that "we will look back in astonishment that we allowed our former policy to persist for so long, much as we look back now at slavery, or Jim Crow laws, or the days when women were prohibited from voting—and we will wish fervently that we had not waited so long to abandon these failed and destructive policies."[102]

CHAPTER 16

Finding Peace, Being Peace

The choice today is no longer between violence and nonviolence. It is either
nonviolence or nonexistence.

—Martin Luther King Jr.

Is the United States a peace-loving nation? Based on an annual
comprehensive survey of the world's nations by the Institute for
Economics and Peace, apparently not. A worldwide team of experts assisted
by the Economist Intelligence Unit, publishes the Global Peace Index,
an annual ranking of the world's nations according to their peacefulness.
Nations are graded based on 23 indicators, which include internal factors
such as transparency and human rights, as well as external factors such as
war and relations with other nations. In the 2016 survey, which looked at
163 countries, the United States was in 103rd place. Iceland was listed as
the most peaceful country, and Syria occupied last place.[1]

Peace, as the Global Peace Index acknowledges, can be internal
to a country as well as external. A stable democracy, governmental
transparency, and a system that applies justice equally and fairly are all
external signs of peace. But peace is also an energy, an aspect of love
latent within each of us. In this chapter, we will look at peace with an
emphasis on inner peace.

In *The Way: Using the Wisdom of Kabbalah for Spiritual Transformation and Fulfillment*, Michael Berg reminds us that peace and

conflict often originate at a personal level, such as in interactions with family and friends. "When sages speak of peace through study, they refer to peace within ourselves. When each of us is at peace with the person we see when we look in the mirror, strife between nations will cease."[2]

Paramahansa Yogananda, the famous Indian yogi and guru who introduced many in the Western world to yoga and meditation through his best-selling book *Autobiography of a Yogi*, taught that "peace in the world starts with peace in individual hearts."[3] In *Inner Peace: How to Be Calmly Active and Actively Calm*, Yogananda explains that "peace emanates from the soul, and is the sacred inner environment in which true happiness unfolds."[4] It is this "sacred inner environment"—which is a reflection of *individual* peace—to which we are usually referring when we speak of peace in this chapter. Outer or external peace, which reflects *collective* peace, is achieved when enough individuals have inner peace. We bring peace to the world by changing ourselves and, once we have peace, by helping others to change themselves.

Religion as an Obstacle to Peace

In our quest for peace, we face a number of obstacles. Not least among these is religion, which ought to be a primary force—perhaps *the* primary force—for peace in the world. "There can be no world peace until the great religions make peace with one another," Nobel Peace Prize winner Mairead Corrigan Maguire says.[5] Our religious beliefs tend to be the most value-laden (and therefore valuable) of our beliefs, and thus they naturally become a prime focus of our cultural attention, our security, and, consequently, our wars—or at least they do when holistic consciousness is marginalized. In the above quotation, Maguire is referring to *external* peace—that is, to cultural peace, a peaceful environment. Irrespective of what the religions of the world do, as individuals, we can always access our *internal* peace.

When we look closely at the relationship between religion and war, a fact of geography quickly becomes apparent. The three monotheistic religions—Judaism, Christianity, and Islam—share common holy ground in the Middle East, and these religions have an extensive history of warfare. The three also share the fact of being managed by dualistic males who have mostly, and in some cases completely, excluded holistic females from leadership roles, including scriptural interpretation. This exclusion of holistic consciousness at the cultural level of religion creates a system of religious governance that is the cultural equivalent of genetic complete dominance: there is a near-total reliance on one of the brain's operating systems and an almost complete blindness to the other.

As we have seen, the dualistic male mind-set tends to be separation-oriented rather than unification-oriented, selfish rather than sharing, competitive rather than cooperative, and prone to the use of force to obtain its goals. Since the upper echelon of religious leadership in these three religions tends to be exclusively male with some exceptions, this means that these religions are led by individuals who, as a whole, are poorly equipped to share, poorly equipped to cooperate, poorly equipped to maintain peace. All of this is only made worse by the fact that their holy lands lie in an area that has a long history of extreme violence—something we might expect, since it is in close proximity to what is thought to be the cradle of civilization.

As early populations grew, and shortages of resources forced people to move away from the place where they were born, irrespective of religion, the strongest and most aggressive would have stayed—genetic complete dominants operating on dualistic consciousness. Dualistic-based values would have dominated on a collective level as well, creating a relatively pure dualistic culture. More peaceful individuals, reluctant to fight over resources or control issues, would have been inclined to leave, preferring the security afforded by colder climes to war. This process would have created a culture of aggression within a broad area, encompassing the Middle East and extending southward into Africa, where humanity is believed to have originated.

The more peaceful you were, the farther you would have had to travel in order to escape the violence. Thus, centuries later, we see peace awards being handed out in cold but relatively peaceful Sweden and Norway, and year after year, Iceland is number one in the Global Peace rankings. And at the bottom? As we might expect, year after year we find countries from the region of the planet where human life and the three great monotheistic religions were birthed.

Because so much of the violence on the world stage radiates outward from the cradle of Western civilization, let's survey that locale for a moment from the perception of an Israeli theoretical physicist (and chair of the Davidson Institute of Science Education), Haim Harari, whose family has lived in the region for almost 200 years. Providing what he calls the views of the "proverbial taxi driver," Harari reminds us that the ongoing Arab-Israeli conflict is far from the only source of strife in this part of the world. In fact, his blunt assessment is that "this entire . . . region [stretching from Morocco to Pakistan] is totally dysfunctional." He cites the war in Sudan, where Arabs slaughter black Christians; the on-and-off violence in Algeria; Iraq's invasion of Kuwait and its war with Iran; the elder Assad of Syria, who killed tens of thousands of his own citizens in one week; and the Taliban in Afghanistan. Harari mentions the Saudi role in 9/11 and other acts of force, often directed toward women who come into conflict with rules severely restricting their rights, noting that the social status of women in the Arab world is "far below what it was in the Western world 150 years ago." And, he points out, the dysfunctionality of this region goes well beyond the issue of women's rights or sectarian struggles. "According to a report prepared by a committee of Arab intellectuals and published under the auspices of the U.N., the number of books translated by the entire Arab world is much smaller than what little Greece alone translates." The region's poverty and general state of cultural decline, he suggests, create a "breeding ground for cruel dictators, terror networks, [and] fanaticism." Harari acknowledges that most Muslims are not part of the violence that we find in this region, but neither do they actively oppose it. Afraid to express their views, they become double victims—victims of their own environment and victims of an outside world that has developed Islamophobia.[6]

Nor is the Jewish state without its divisions and hatreds. Following the reelection of Benjamin Netanyahu in 2015, Doron Cohen, writing in *Maariv*, a Hebrew-language daily newspaper published in Israel, suggests, "The only clear lesson from this election is that the true 'existential threat' facing Israel is not Hamas, or even Iran, but our own internal divisions. Israel is awash in hatreds: 'between the religious and the secular, Right and Left, Sephardim and Ashkenazi, Tel Avivites and settlers, Jews and Arabs.'"[7] This might be the area of the world where violence is most highly concentrated, but this is *a* problem—it is not *the* problem. *The* problem is that violence is everywhere, and it is coming from many sources, including some of our major religions, and it is coming from all levels, including the very highest, as we will see.

Since the association of religion with violence is such a sensitive subject, let us begin by distinguishing between what religion actually is, and the violence that occurs within and between religions. Religion is a faith-based perspective of the spiritual world; violence is the result of an overly aggressive response to something. Religion per se cannot be violent, although someone's expression of it can be violent. In all of the great religions, we find people who are violent and people who are peaceful.

Let us also distinguish between individuals at the higher levels of the religious hierarchy and their followers (some of whom act in leadership roles, creating a leadership gray area). Most religious followers are literally acting on faith, trusting in their leaders to interpret scripture for them and otherwise tell them what God asks of them. Thus, religious leaders and their spiritual devotees are not equals in creating religious wars. The responses of most followers—whether they rise up in anger, have a muted response, or have none—depend on what they are taught. And most often they are taught by dualistic men, whose natural response tends toward violence when they want something that is not forthcoming. Not every Muslim becomes angry when told that someone has drawn a likeness of Muhammad. That response is *taught.*

Religious violence can be relatively subtle, as when Cardinal Ratzinger (later to become Pope Benedict) can be seen on film striking *ABC News* reporter Brian Ross on the hand as a result of a tough question the cardinal apparently disliked. A more energetic exercise of religious violence can be found in a number of largely unnamed but powerful conservative religious leaders in the Middle East. Because our conservative operating system is also our violent operating system, the more conservative and doctrinaire wings of religions are the most contentious and are much more likely to force their values on others. To reiterate Ken Wilber's point in chapter 12, the typical conservative response to solving social tensions is to take its particular values and try to impose them on everyone else.

Religions are not violent; some of the people in them are. The message of religion is not violent; some religious misinterpretations are. Even though religions urge us to live in peace, when people have lost touch with their peace (which is easy to do for left-brain-dominant individuals and cultures), their religious expression can turn violent. And remember that the degree to which a teacher or follower is violent will vary. At the lower end of the scale, violence can be subtle and unnoticed.

Again, while violence is not inherent in any religion, all religions have some violent adherents, just as all societies have some violent citizens. A religious adherent should not take offense when such violence is pointed out. In fact, taking offense in itself can create or exacerbate violence. Since most males—including those who are peaceful—are informed by their aggressive dualistic operating system, most males have a naturally violent operating system guiding them. It is important that dualistically inclined males recognize and manage their dualistic tendencies in a way that maximizes peace.

Ever wonder how someone, under the banner of religion, could be willing to support or carry out some of the violent acts that are perpetrated in the name of religion? Part of the explanation is that dualistic consciousness is impersonal, fearful, and violent. When our consciousness is dualistic, and our surrounding culture is completely dominated by dualistic consciousness, how does the holistic insight that cares about people and transcends violence find its way into our consciousness for consideration? And if it does come in, is it welcome? Do we pay attention to it?

Sunni and Shia Muslims are split over a religious divide that began long ago as a political issue: how to determine a successor to Muhammad. And though many Sunni and Shia live in peace in the Middle East, large numbers of them are engaged in a bloody war over differences in belief.

Another major intra-Muslim war in the Middle East springs from differences in brain dominance. The war on Sufis—a much more holistic-oriented, liberally inclusive, mystical offshoot of Islam—gets little publicity in the Western world, since it lacks the large-scale implications of the inter-sectarian wars, but to those who get caught up in its jaws, it can be just as deadly. This war is actually two wars, as both of the two warring dualistic sects—Sunni and Shia—are independently at war with Sufi Muslims. As with the drug war in America, there is an imbalance of forces—in this case, a holistic, relatively liberal branch of Islam is under attack by two much larger dualistic, conservative branches, with the warring energies flowing mainly in one direction.

Wars between religions have an extended tradition, especially in the Middle East. Of those Muslims who identify as highly conservative, meaning those that closely adhere to dualistic values, most have long been at war with Jews. When we look at the most conservative end of the Jewish continuum, we find a similar warlike attitude toward Muslims, and again, this is a result of the dominance of dualistic consciousness. Unfortunately their battleground is expanding geographically as the world is becoming more closely connected. It now includes London, Paris, Copenhagen, and other major cities where the two cultures clash.

Another war coming from within the ranks of conservative Islam involves freedom of expression, and this war has gone international. Severely limited freedom of expression is a fact of life in many Middle Eastern cultures, especially with regard to women. The aggressive and controlling dualistic consciousness of these leaders extends beyond controlling fellow Muslims and—as with some ultraconservative Christians and Jews—includes the desire to broaden their sphere of influence into the rest of society and eliminate all secularizing influences as well as religious heresies. Hence, attacks are made or threatened against anyone, Muslim or not, who is perceived to denigrate their religion or their God, or even their religious law. We see this in responses such as the "death sentence" imposed by Iran's supreme leader against Salman Rushdie for his *Satanic Verses* in 1989 and never officially removed (in fact, a new bounty was placed on him by several radical Islamic groups in 2016)[8], and the 2015 mass murders of the staff of the French satirical newspaper *Charlie Hebdo* by two brothers associated with an al-Qaeda branch in Yemen. When anyone says or does something that a person under the dominating influence of dualistic consciousness strongly disagrees with, their aggressive dualistic energy comes to the fore and becomes a force for conflict—unless it is consciously or unconsciously restrained as a consequence of experience or education.

Of course, many peaceful Muslims have marched in support of press freedom and peace, but, judging by the Muslim world's reaction to the *Charlie Hebdo* drawings, the numbers that support a violent response are much larger; and now, thanks to the Internet and cell phones, these supporters of violence are globally connected. If we are dualistically directed, we do not have to be taught to respond violently (although teachings can certainly incite or exacerbate our natural tendencies), nor do we need to be told to defend our religion; these come naturally. We need only be taught who the enemy is. A peaceful response to the warring behavior of the dualistic mind can be developed through education.

What are the beliefs that would lead one to commit violence against another's free expression? On the surface, the divide, and resulting fight, behind the *Charlie Hebdo* massacre and numerous other similar incidents is about depicting Muhammad; however, if we look underneath this belief, we find that the situation is more complex. Here, as exemplified by the war on Sufis, a polarization exists between beliefs born of conservative consciousness and beliefs born of liberal consciousness. So, for example, if you are Muslim and do not know how Muhammad might feel about being depicted, and you wish to avoid possible offense, then the conservative response is to prohibit visual representation. Of course, to be liberal in response is to be unconstrained by traditional fears and rules, and so a drawing of Muhammad poses no threat to your beliefs and is not upsetting. For most people, the two different viewpoints present existential conflict.

The Koran does not explicitly forbid images of Muhammad; however, a commonly associated group of teachings, the Hadith, is often followed by Muslims, and some interpretations of them ban depictions. Also, among many branches of Islam (and in some other faiths as well) there is a strong tradition known as *aniconism*, a belief in shunning or avoiding images of divine beings. Many Muslims believe it is blasphemous to make images of Jesus, let alone Muhammad. Since this is a belief that predates the Hadith, we can imagine that it must have helped inspire its teachings. And with the spread of Islam, this ancient belief has often traveled along.

Another war that these religious men find themselves engaged in is one they share with conservative men of other religions—a war on women. Ironically, they are all at war with the embodiment of the Divine Feminine. Again, this war has little to do with religion, and you can see this in the large number of nonreligious men who are involved. The war against women is a consequence of the fears projected by a dominant left brain, and so members of this group inevitably include men in religious roles. Attractive women stir a strong passion in most men, and when men are trying to be pious and religious, the influence of women is more than highly distracting. Having been taught by their religions to transcend such feelings, these men experience their passions as an intense reminder of their spiritual inadequacies, and they do not like how they respond. Dualistically, the easiest way to solve this problem is to cover up the women's heads and bodies, keep them separate, and limit their contribution.

All over the world, advertisements for *The Hunger Games: Mockingjay—Part 2* featured its heroic female star, Jennifer Lawrence—except for multiple locations in Israel, where her image had to be removed. The reason for having a special poster made up, according to the *Hollywood Reporter*, was to accommodate ultra-Orthodox Jews and thus avoid the "endless vandalization" that typically occurred whenever women were displayed on movie posters in certain areas.[9] The visual presence of women had such an effect on the minds and bodies of these men that they refused to allow them to be depicted even on a movie-theater poster!

Considering the overpowering feelings associated with lust and jealousy, we can perhaps understand why so many religious men do what they do. But why are they allowed to discriminate in this way? The answer is the exemptions granted to religion. Religions provide a setting in which dualistic males are able to legitimize certain behaviors by claiming that they are demanded by God. By asserting a behavior to be part of a religion, one can openly treat women as second-class citizens and force them via cultural sanctions to do things like cover themselves in public in front of men. Males would not force *themselves* to wear a burka-like garment while working in a field in the hot sun, or hide their hair every time they went out in public. For the most part, men in certain strict religious traditions are likely to impose limits on their dress or freedoms only in church settings, where they may require of themselves head coverings or the like. The origin of this repressive, misogynistic behavior is not in religion itself, but in dualistic consciousness and the ways it affects our feelings. Because most males are left-brain-dominant, most religions have adopted controlling behaviors at some point in their development. As religions liberalize, women are increasingly freed.

When you have an ancient, dualistic system combined with a culture in which holistic consciousness is marginalized or banned, the usual checks on force and intimidation that occur in more balanced cultures are ineffective or nonexistent. Add to this the fact that these extreme dualistic cultures have full access to modern technologies that create instant worldwide communication—and, mainly as a result of this, access to all the modern means of destructive warfare on large and small scales—and a deadly, dangerous brew is created that can threaten our planetary future. This confluence of circumstances means that the attempts by a few powerful, aggressive, dualistic religious teachers and their followers to impose their beliefs on others, with all the above-mentioned dangers, has turned into a worldwide movement and a new kind of war: a war not so much between superpowers (although they certainly play a role) as between conflicting ideologies and visions that reflect the differences between our holistic and dualistic operating systems. We are today faced with a challenge that the world has never before encountered on a planetary scale; and the challenge comes not only from the religious extremists, but also from leaders in secular societies (such as the United States and some European countries) who *react* to these extremists in ways that are themselves dualistic and therefore tend to exacerbate the conflict.

The solution to ending religious war on the planet, and eventually all war, seems obvious. The world's religions need to remove the glass ceiling and allow qualified holistic women into top leadership positions. They will also need to release them from the anchor of dualistic rules and responses as required by their dualistic systems. Successful systems, whatever their function, must be allowed to adapt to changing conditions. Of course, these changes cannot be forced on a religion or culture, but there are many things we can do to accelerate such changes, as past efforts have demonstrated in both religious and secular contexts.

No religion has the right to demand, let alone force, people in other religions to adhere to its particular beliefs. Until religious followers everywhere insist that their leaders respect our differing beliefs and teach the tolerance and peace of unity, we will lack outer peace. Of course, to the extent that we cultivate inner peace, we can begin to lay the groundwork for a holistic society in which outer peace will become increasingly possible.

Finding Peace through Meditation

How do we calm the agitated head and bring peace to the weary heart? Considering the disruption of peace that occurs whenever conflict is introduced, if we are to have inner peace, we must be able to detach from the dualistic system's propensity for aggression and conflict. This is what the lateral split in our brain does for us. It gives us two mind-sets, two choices, two arenas of consciousness to enter into. One is violent and the other is peaceful.

To achieve peace, Yogananda, like many others, suggests an approach long advocated by wise men and women—meditation. "When . . . human knowing and feeling [is] calmed by meditation, the ordinary agitated ego gives way to the blessed calmness of soul perception."[10] Once one has become filled with peace, he says, this calmness then "pours out freely to one's family, friends, community, nation, and the world. If everyone lived the ideals exemplified in the life of Jesus, having made those qualities a part of their own selves through meditation, a millennium of peace and brotherhood would come on earth."[11] In meditation, we occupy holistic consciousness. Meditation is not always easy to achieve, but even before we become practiced, in our efforts to meditate we may bounce in and out of meditation. It has often been commented that novice meditators may seem to access only the noise of their thoughts, but this itself is a form of recognition beyond what most people achieve in their daily lives, when this noise is largely unconscious. Thus meditation is not only about peace, but about understanding our usual, relatively "disturbed" state; and understanding furthers peace. A meditative state may also be greatly assisted by guided processes, such as those discussed below.

In *Change Your Thoughts—Change Your Life: Living the Wisdom of the Tao*, Wayne W. Dyer, internationally renowned author and speaker in the field of self-development, reminds us of the wisdom traditionally attributed to the Chinese Taoist philosopher Lao-tzu (sixth century BCE), who wrote or inspired the Tao Te Ching. This seminal work of Taoism taught a path to peace that comes from living without force. In Dyer's words, "Force creates a counterforce, and this exchange goes on and on until all-out war is in progress." He quotes from and then expands on the Tao Te Ching, which states, "You must never think of conquering others by force. Whatever strains with force will soon decay. It is not attuned to the

Way." The Tao Te Ching, Dyer says, encourages us to look for alternatives to force when we need to settle a dispute. Moreover, it suggests that if we can find no other option, we need to abandon any reference to ourselves as winners or conquerors. "The Great Way of Tao," Dyer explains, "is that of cooperation, not competition."[12] And, of course, as we know, the way of cooperation and forgiveness is the way of holistic consciousness; the way of competition is the way of dualistic consciousness.

A discussion of peace is useful, but keep in mind that words are instruments through which we seek to express feeling. Thoughts, and the energies they create, can help orient us toward peace, but remember that peace is a *felt* experience. Want peace? Find the *feeling* of peace. Look to your feelings for guidance. Those of us whose dominant operating system is dualistic tend to focus on thoughts, and in the process we often overlook information coming from our feelings. Compared with someone using one of the other three operating systems, those of us who are guided by a dualistic system are relatively separated from our feelings—at least until our feelings overwhelm us or otherwise demand our attention. By changing our external environment and thus escaping some of its irritants, we can often lessen feelings of conflict and achieve a degree of peace. But to have real peace, we have to change internally—which means that some of our personal attitudes and actions must change. The external world may *trigger* conflicts, but our conflicts are already at least latently present even without an outer stimulus.

To move in the direction of peace, imagine the feeling of love, the feeling of peace, and the feeling of freedom as being connected parts of a whole rather than separated out. *Be* love, *be* peace, and *be* freedom; know that your peace is only as strong as the weakest of these three. Now, having established your internal environment, turn outward and imagine a peaceful environment, and be there now without regret of the past or stress over the future. For a moment, let every thought and every action go, and just be and feel peace. When you strip away all your attachments, what you are left with is your core self—your essential self—which is now and always at peace. Even if, a moment later, the conflict of life rushes back in, be grateful for the present moment and recognize that, with practice, a moment can grow into seconds, seconds into minutes, and minutes into hours and days. When you want to reward yourself for some reason, instead of turning outward to your favorite addiction for a feeling of satisfaction, consider turning inward and rewarding yourself with a peaceful moment.

Peace Is a Choice

Peace is mostly a function of our beliefs. It is the beliefs of the terrorist that program him or her to create acts designed to instill terror. It is the beliefs of the peaceful that create peaceful responses. Since we have the freedom to choose our beliefs, ultimately peace becomes a function of the choice of beliefs that we make. But if peace is a choice, if we are gods, and if our lives are ours to control, then why do so many of us have so little peace?

A series of books could be written in answer to this question, but it is fair to say that, generally, the liberal and conservative halves of our individual and cultural self are at war, and as a result, there is a great deal of personal and cultural confusion and fighting going on. In this dynamic context, challenging problems come up; impatience overcomes us; and to create the circumstances we think we need in order to succeed, we resort to the ubiquitous cultural solution—force. This creates an energy of conflict and blurs (if not obscures) the internal harmony that is our guide to peace and the freedom it gives. Force, we quickly learn, gives us leverage. Even the threat of force often produces results.

When we do manage to find our way to peace—when we at last still the voice within that is constantly demanding an attachment to certain things and relationships (a list that for many of us seems to be never-ending)—we inevitably find that our peace is difficult to maintain.

To maintain our peace, we must transcend the needy desires of the dualistic hemisphere's egoic persona and be comfortably in our holistic hemisphere. If we believe that we must have a new car or a certain item of clothing to be happy, we have created a situation in which our beliefs (in other words, our attachments to certain ideas) determine whether or not we can be happy and at peace. We feel a temporary sense of peace when we acquire and attach to the things we believe we need, yet it is a feeling that quickly dissipates once the new distraction is no longer new and no longer distracts. Material indulgences can never truly bring us peace, but not having them can get in the way of our peace if we believe they are essential to our happiness. It is a system that must be fed.

Introduce other people and losses (accidental or otherwise) into this equation and the situation becomes explosive. Someone damages a valued possession or terminates a relationship, and suddenly our attachment is damaged. Typically, we immediately abandon whatever internal peace we had. *We feel emotionally harmed.* We become upset. Yet we have not been forced to feel harmed. People can't dictate how we feel; it's impossible. Feeling is an internal mental and spiritual response that only we are capable of controlling.

Notice that the overall damage is neither stabilized nor decreased by our typical response; rather, it is *increased.* Notice that *we* increase it. But this is how we've been taught to respond: someone hurts something of ours that we value (or apparently "hurts" us), and we respond by becoming upset, which is to say, by hurting ourselves. And more often than not, we pass our hurt onto others.

So how do we detach? In his book *Waking Up in Time: Finding Inner Peace in Times of Accelerating Change*, Peter Russell offers some clarification. Describing peace as "an intrinsic quality of life itself, not something that can be created or destroyed," Russell acknowledges that it can, however, be made elusive through attachment. Peace comes when we "let go of the belief that what goes on around [us] determines whether or not [we are] content."[13]

As we have said, the creative, energetic link between the physical reality of things and the spiritual reality of feelings is *mind.* Once we arrive at a state of consciousness that allows us to understand that physical reality is a creation of spiritual reality, we have an opportunity to disconnect from the drama. Knowing that only spiritual feeling is of real value, and that physical things and ideas are just tools and toys of spirit, we can simply take an adult attitude and avoid emotional fights over our tools and toys. If we feel it necessary to defend our territory (and it might sometimes be), we can still defend it, but then we can do so with an elevated attitude and with more positive physical and spiritual feelings—an attitude more like that of being in a spirited contest with a tough, respected competitor. In essence, the emotional connection between things and feelings exists in potential—and through our intent, we can either actualize the connection or not. This is part of our creative choice. Beliefs, mobilized by intent and directed by attention, direct energy.

Observe that when we experience a negative response to some damaging incident, our feelings correspond with our *beliefs* regarding the damage, not with the damage itself. We can *believe* that we have been hurt by someone's actions, and consequently *feel* hurt, even though, as it later turns out, there was a misunderstanding and no hurtful actions were taken. And even if there is intent to harm, it is still up to us to determine how we want to feel. For example, do we want to feel like a victim? Do we want to overcome this hurt by taking revenge? Or do we choose the emotional release of forgiveness?

To escape the traditional response—the habitual choice to be emotionally (internally) hurt by external events—it helps to acknowledge that being mentally and spiritually hurt is often a choice, a learned behavior. In many cases, the choice to be hurt has become so habitual with lifelong repetition that it is no longer viewed as a choice. Add to that the fact that often the people around us are responding in the same habitual way, and it can seem as if we don't have a choice, even when we do.

Once we decide to change our habitual response to damaging encounters, we must choose a replacement response. We must choose how to react to damage. At this point—having made the choice to respond peacefully—the follow-up step is to *practice* it. Because habitual dualistic patterns resist change, practicing a peaceful response can be challenging.

The reality is that other people are able to manipulate our internal environment only when we let them—when we cooperate with them. We can learn to avoid stepping *out* of our peace, and learn to step back *into* it. This is not easy for most people to do, but people have been doing it for centuries, so it is not beyond our reach.

Begin by respecting your innate sense of what is right.

In airline-flight safety briefings we are told to secure our own oxygen mask before we attempt to help others. A similar approach applies in preparing for peace. Our primary creative responsibility as peacemakers must begin with our own peace; we must monitor the mental atmosphere that we are creating internally. Basically, we are seeking an atmosphere of self-respect. Our innate sense of what is right (in Christian theology this is the spirit of truth), not our beliefs, should be the ultimate arbiter of the direction of our path and the choices we make. When we find we've attained peaceful self-respect, we are on course.

That which we create as individuals also contributes to our collective creation, so each choice we make has two responses. One of our most powerful individual and collective acts of creation is our vote. Because we are isolated from many of the people our vote will impact, it is easy to allow our violent tendencies and our fears to hold sway when in the voting booth. We want to remember to be responsible, informed, peaceful voters, not ballot-box bullies.

To find peace, seek harmony.
To create a greater experience of peace, cultivate harmony within yourself. As a start, find a way to bring unity to the two operating systems so that they can take part in the same dance of life, rather than living in a struggle with one another. Let them fall in love with one another, and send your light of peace out into the universe. Our two perspectives and responses may appear to be opposites, one bad and the other good, but to "side" with one of them only increases our sense of polarization and reduces our effectiveness, as individuals and as a society. We especially encounter this separatist attitude in social conservatives due to the strong drive for survival that comes with being guided by dualistic consciousness. We see this in the vigor with which they attack holistic ideas and perceptions, especially liberal ideology.

The fast track to spiritual harmony and its healing effects shows up when we find ways to *appreciate* those who see reality from a point of view that is the opposite of our own dominant perspective—those we often view as the enemy. *Appreciation* is an extraordinarily potent spiritual energy. If you identify with conservatives and feel threatened by liberals, learning to appreciate their responses will result in being able to grow and be more creative in your own responses. If we identify with liberals and are uncomfortable with conservatives, learning to appreciate the conserving viewpoint will make conservatives seem less of a threat and will help us expand the scope of our holistic thinking and actions. None of this means that we must like or embrace opposing ideas—or even the sometimes ignorant people who espouse them; it simply means that they are no longer perceived as a threat.

To enhance our inner peace, we should harmonize our *ideas* and bring them to a state of peace with one another. Harmony is what we are after, and it is perhaps best achieved by identifying and facing the conflict, and then resolving it by working through it. We often see disharmony in others and view it as hypocrisy and ignorance, but fail to notice our own disharmony in dealing with facts—a situation that is ironic since it is much more valuable to see one's own inconsistencies than to see those of others. Once we recognize that we have two or more ideas that are in conflict, we can then attempt to resolve their conflict through the use of harmonizing elements such as honesty, facts, and forgiveness.

Searching for errors within our belief system is not necessarily a difficult process, but it can be a long one. Basically, we request of our mind or our higher self that it show us the conflicts that are impediments to our mental and/or spiritual development. Having to make a request is a self-protective measure: if we have been consciously hiding our conflict, we must consciously choose to retrieve it. We must then open up to the presence of any conflict that might show up, and be willing to engage it. If a response to our request is not immediate—and this is typical—we must then have the presence of mind and patience to wait for the experience that will trigger our recognition of the conflict. This can take days, weeks, or even longer.

Perhaps you were taught the belief that *God is the essence of love and mercy*. But this seems to conflict with another belief of many—that *God sends people to everlasting hell*. If you notice that something isn't right about this or another combination of ideas, you might want to find out why. How do you do this? Explore your own conflict in the same way that you might explore conflicting information coming from your child or partner. If your mind suggests that sending someone to hell forever doesn't seem loving or merciful, pay attention to that. In the process of resolving conflicts like this, we often learn lessons. (You might learn that there are religions that don't believe in hell and progressive groups within Christianity that think this belief is nothing more than an ancient scare tactic inserted into scripture to get people to church with the good intent to save their soul.) You might never resolve this example, but if you seek to uncover conflicts in your belief system, you will be shown your own examples, and they will have attainable resolutions.

The process of achieving harmony through the process of resolving conflict can take many forms. It might involve reconciling opposing points of view by recognizing common features and strengths on both sides. Or it might be much more complex, involving whole new ways of seeing things (for example, learning how to perceive and think holistically, or learning how to recognize arbitrary cultural pressures). Or the issues themselves might be of such complexity that we need to learn the art of critical observation. We also need to recognize that, to the extent that we use critical observation, we often use it as a weapon to attack ideas we don't like and fail to apply this valuable process to our own ideas. Becoming intelligently critical of our own ideas and being willing to change them is a fundamental benchmark for attaining truth.

To acquire internal peace, it is necessary to *be* peace. Being peaceful is a function of having peaceful ideas. The removal of conflict from our ideas moves us toward harmony. This is not a balancing operation; rather, our job is to find and remove any conflict between our two operating systems so that each accepts the other as one would accept a beloved teammate. It means that ideological territory is defended firmly, though not angrily. Our dominant side will remain dominant, but with a greater respect for and appreciation of the intelligence coming from the recessive side.

If our dominant perspective is dualistic, we must make peace with holistic perspectives and processes, the beliefs they create and support, and the people who are guided by them, even those perceived as extremists. It is important to acknowledge their value; they can help show us the context of our ideas, help us to refine them, and help us to detect and consequently remove errors. The result is that our ideas will become clearer, stronger, more true, and thus more effective. If our dominant perspective is holistic, we will become more effective if we make peace with dualistic perspectives, processes, and beliefs (such as we find in rationality and hierarchies). Understanding the ways the dualistic perspective can help us will bring us clarity, even if dualistic beliefs are born out of conflict and out of details that seem unimportant from a holistic perspective.

Expand your perspective.

To enhance our peace, we can expand the scope of our perspective. When we expand our perspective, we are able to see more of our context and thus enlarge our body of information. This in turn expands our perception. With our perception sufficiently expanded, big problems appear smaller and more manageable, and our fears and conflicts start to melt away—as we can see from this *Urantia Book* excerpt:

> In the mind's eye conjure up a picture of one of your primitive ancestors of cave-dwelling times—a short, misshapen, filthy, snarling hulk of a man standing, legs spread, club upraised, breathing hate and animosity as he looks fiercely just ahead. Such a picture hardly depicts the divine dignity of man. But allow us to enlarge the picture. In front of this animated human crouches a saber-toothed tiger. Behind him, a woman and two children. Immediately you recognize that such a picture stands for the beginnings of much that is fine and noble in the human race, but the man is the same in both pictures. Only in the second sketch you are favored with a widened horizon. You therein discern the motivation of this evolving mortal. His attitude becomes praiseworthy because you understand him. If you could only fathom the motives of your associates, how much better you would understand them. If you could only know your fellows, you would eventually fall in love with them.[14]

With true love comes true peace.

Traditional Paths to Peace

Although a strongly separative, dualistic consciousness has dominated the male outlook throughout history, and is reflected in much of the history of religions, including the founding scriptures, all traditional religions have at their core a strong holistic message of peace and unity. Ironically, this message can be found most explicitly and radically in the teachings of Jesus himself—I say "ironically" because throughout its long history the Christian tradition has often been led by men that were anything but peaceful or unified. The teachings of the Buddha (Siddhartha Gautama), although different in emphasis, lead to similarly radical conclusions (such as the belief that we are gods, and therefore we have everything and are therefore naturally service-oriented, rather than self-oriented). Below is a small but instructive sampling of such radical traditional teachings.

Christianity on Peace

The Jewish/Christian Old Testament reflects a collective culture dominated by males whose lives and beliefs were largely restricted to what they
saw from their separative, competitive, dualistic consciousness. Because
dualistic consciousness separates holons, the God we see dualistically is
separate from man.

The New Testament presents us with a more holistic perspective
of our world. In Mark 9:38–41, for example, we see the disciple John
and others encountering a man who is healing in the name of Jesus,
someone with whom they are unfamiliar. Seeing the man as separate
from them, the disciples try to force him to stop. Their response reflects
a typical protective attitude of disliking someone who infringes on one's
territory. Unable to mentally bridge the gap between Jesus's work and
the man trying to do good in Jesus's name, they view the man as being
a competitor who is undermining Jesus's ministry. The response of Jesus
when told of the incident is one of inclusion—a holistic response: Leave
him alone. Allow the man the freedom to follow his heart. Let him help
us (reflecting the holistic system's inclusiveness). "He that is not against
us is for us," he says (referencing a dualistic perspective, but informed by
a broad, holistic view).

When Jesus comes upon a woman caught in adultery and about to be
stoned according to Old Testament law (John 8:1–11), he responds in a
similar way. He comes to the woman's rescue with his inclusive response.
In effect, he is saying that whatever choices she has made, she is still one
of us. She is an individual and deserving of our love and her freedom.
Be forgiving (holistic). Don't judge (dualistic). In trying to maintain the
peace, Jesus embodies the holistic liberal stance, which embraces but
transcends the dualistic conservative stance.

Buddhism on Peace

People tend to view Buddhism as a religion, but according to Robert
Thurman, professor of Indo-Tibetan Buddhist studies at Columbia University, "The Buddha founded an educational movement rather than a
religion. His vision was to bring out our own wisdom rather than to assert
the truth. . . . In that sense, the Buddha was a scientist—a noetic scientist.
He understood that the most important factor in the quality of life for
a human being is how the person's mind is managed." The Buddha

therefore focused on human beings, on the transformation of human consciousness, rather than on God.[15]

Ron Epstein, research professor at the Institute for World Religions in Berkeley, California, explains, "Buddhists believe that the minds of all living beings are totally interconnected and interrelated, whether they are consciously aware of it or not." Like a combined radio station and radio, mind constantly transmits and receives. "Even the most insignificant thoughts in our minds have some effect on all other beings. . . . Each thought in the mind of each and every one of us brings the world either a little closer to the brink of global disaster or helps to move the world a little farther away from the brink," says Epstein.[16] "Buddhism teaches that whether we have global peace or global war is up to us at every moment. . . . Peace or war is our decision. The fundamental goal of Buddhism is peace. . . . The Buddha taught that peaceful minds lead to peaceful speech and peaceful actions."[17]

Control of Our Thoughts and Creations

Consider the perspective of a collective known as the Hathors, a group of ascended beings who claim to have energetically worked with Tibetan lamas in the formative period of Tibetan Buddhism, as well as with the ancient Egyptians and others.[18] (Hathor likenesses—now associated with the goddess Hator—are prominently located in several ancient Egyptian temples.) Masters of love and sound (vibration), the Hathors currently work through a number of individuals. One who has written a book about his experiences is the scientist, sound healer, shaman, psychotherapist, and musician Tom Kenyon. In *The Hathor Material*, the Hathor collective advises, "Nothing can be done without the power of God because the power of One is what sustains, creates and continues all realms. Yet one has free will to do certain types of actions within whatever level one has achieved or entered. Ultimately it is God that does it all. However, within each realm where beings have choice, they experience the results of their creation, whether it be positive or negative. One must experience the results of one's own creation."[19]

Our interactions with life energies have consequences—physical, mental, and spiritual. Thoughts, words, and deeds move energy toward peace or toward war. In *Peace Is Every Step: The Path of Mindfulness in Everyday Life*, Thich Nhat Hanh advises us of the importance of being mindful of the *quality* of the energy flows to which we attach ourselves. That naturally includes the energies we attach ourselves to for the purposes of entertainment—they are not always helpful, which is why we need to be mindful. "Our senses are our windows to the world," he says, "and sometimes the wind blows through our openings and disturbs everything within us. Some of us leave our windows open all of the time, allowing the sights and sounds of the world to invade us. . . . Do you ever find yourself watching an awful TV program, unable to turn it off?" he asks. "Why do you torture yourself in this way? . . . Watching a bad TV program, we become the TV program." To expose ourselves like this is "leaving our fate in the hands of others who may not be acting responsibly. We must be aware of which programs do harm to our nervous systems, minds, and hearts, and which programs benefit us." And, he adds, "I am not talking only about television"; we are in fact surrounded by many lures, and we must constantly be mindful of protecting our peace.[20]

In spite of religion's role of bringing peace to the planet, we find a great deal of violence in our religions; and, as we have seen, those who practice violence are almost always found near the conservative end of the cultural continuum since it is the conserving side of the brain that defends and attacks. But progressives, too, sometimes fight for things they value. After all, they have a conservative operating system on call, and it is fully equipped to help them fight. However, when holistic consciousness (whether that of liberals or conservatives) is trying to institute change, and even when holistic individuals are trying to force it, their attention tends to be on things like injustice, poverty, ignorance, and similar issues.

This, then, is where we can start to refocus. We can turn our collective attention on the conservative men at the top echelons of the various religions and to top assemblies of leaders, and we can demand that they show respect for one another, and that they unite with leaders of other sects and religions to end their wars with one another. We have the choice of refusing to contribute to their power unless they quickly bring peace to the planet's religions, and until their message of peace to their followers is unified and relentless.

Of course, Muslims aren't inclined to listen to Christians, and certainly not to Jews. Nor would we expect most Christians or Jews to take religious advice from each other, or even from many of their own — let alone from Muslims, Hindus, or Buddhists. In banding together in faith, we form a strong emotional bond, and from its position of "strength" we feel free to ignore our critics — and, if we are dualistically oriented, to go to war with them. Human behavior is also such that when we take advice, it is usually from within our tribe and from chosen leaders that reflect our views. All of this keeps us divided and self-contained. But unity cannot be imposed from without — and the only way each individual, and each religion, and each culture and nation, can end violence is to go to its origin. Every religion and culture and nation can achieve unity and peace only by stopping violence within its own ranks. And the final responsibility and power for nipping violence in the bud and achieving peace rests in the heart and mind of each individual.

As a final reminder of how our holistic operating system functions, and its role in achieving inner and outer peace, we return to the invaluable insights of Jill Bolte Taylor, the brain scientist who — as a result of a massive hemorrhagic stroke in her left brain hemisphere — was able to observe firsthand (with all her scientific curiosity intact) the workings and experiences of the right hemisphere unmediated by the left. She describes that experience as "nirvana," and in the following words, she unequivocally states that such an experience of peace and joy is available to all of us.

> We have the power to choose, moment by moment, who and how we want to be in the world. Right here, right now, I can step into the consciousness of my right hemisphere, where we are — I am — the life-force power of the universe . . . at one with all that is. Or, I can choose to step into the consciousness of my left hemisphere, where I become a single individual, a solid — separate from the flow, separate

from you. . . . Which would you choose? Which *do* you choose—and when? I believe that the more time we spend choosing to run the deep inner-peace circuitry of our right hemisphere, the more peace we will project into the world, and the more peaceful our planet will be.[21]

May we all find, be, and transmit this peace.

Acknowledgments

I am profoundly appreciative of the many individuals and influences that have guided and inspired me since the inception of this very personal project some 25 years ago.

First and foremost, I would like to acknowledge my appreciation for the work of the many brain researchers, neuroscientists, psychiatrists, psychologists, and physicists involved in helping me to develop a greater understanding of the functioning of the brain. They are too many to name, but a few stand out in my experience, including Michael Gazzaniga, Joseph B. Hellige, Ned Herrmann, Iain McGilchrist, Robert Ornstein, Lawrence "Scotty" Schkade, and Roger Wolcott Sperry. I must single out the work of Carl Jung for providing the initial impetus for awakening my interest in psychology and the brain.

From the philosophical community, Ken Wilber stands out as a major influence as a result of his discoveries about the structure of wholeness.

Special thanks also to Fritjof Capra, Steven Danford, Tom Kenyon and Judi Sion, Drunvalo Melchizedek, David Muir, and Neale Donald Walsch for their enriching educational contributions.

When involved in such a multidisciplinary project, communicating the fullest context in a clear fashion is critical, and the additional perspectives of my editors have made all the difference. In fact, they have given *me* new perspectives that helped expand and clarify the text. My chief editor, Larry Boggs, helped bridge the worlds of science, philosophy, spirituality, and everyday life, and contributed enormously to the beauty, organization, and clarity of this book. Elianne Obadia, the first editor to work on the book, provided valuable insights that helped me to develop its overall structure, thus greatly facilitating its successful completion. Elissa Rabellino expertly served to give the book its final polish and ferret out hidden glitches.

I would also like to express my deep appreciation to my multitalented publisher, Byron Belitsos, for his valuable editorial feedback and philosophical contributions, for his role in the book's artistic design, for providing essential logistical support, and for enabling this book to be published in the first place.

I am grateful to my late friend David "Buddha" Ashbaucher for his seminal influence on this book. It was through him that I first became aware of the existence of modern spiritual texts (which I refer to as "modern revelation"). In combination with the findings of modern physics, modern revelation helped me to better outline a broad conceptual matrix into which the operation of the brain fits.

Finally, I would like to thank my parents, Miles and Nellie Olson, who surely were a pair of angels sent to provide me with the financial, educational, and spiritual resources required in order to survive the many years of difficult, lonely work that led up to the production of this book.

Selected Bibliography

Adi Da. *Not-Two Is Peace: The Ordinary People's Way of Global Cooperative Order*, 3rd ed. Middletown, CA: Dawn Horse, 2009.

The Arbinger Institute. *The Anatomy of Peace: Resolving the Heart of Conflict.* San Francisco: Berrett-Koehler Publishers, 2006.

Beck, Don Edward, and Christopher C. Cowan. *Spiral Dynamics: Mastering Values, Leadership, and Change.* Malden, MA: Blackwell, 1996.

Bentov, Itzhak. *A Brief Tour of Higher Consciousness: A Cosmic Book on the Mechanics of Creation.* Rochester, VT: Destiny Books, 2000.

———. *Stalking the Wild Pendulum: On the Mechanics of Consciousness.* Rochester, VT: Destiny Books, 1988.

Berg, Michael. *The Way: Using the Wisdom of Kabbalah for Spiritual Transformation and Fulfillment.* Hoboken, NJ: John Wiley & Sons, 2001.

Blanton, Brad. *Radical Honesty: How to Transform Your Life by Telling the Truth.* New York: Dell, 1996.

Bonner, William, and Addison Wiggin. *Empire of Debt: The Rise of an Epic Financial Crisis.* Hoboken, NJ: John Wiley & Sons, 2006.

Braden, Gregg. *Beyond Zero Point: The Journey to Compassion.* DVD. Arvada, CO: Gaiam/ConsciousWave, 2001.

Buchanan, Patrick J. *Where the Right Went Wrong: How Neoconservatives Subverted the Reagan Revolution and Hijacked the Bush Presidency.* New York: Thomas Dunne, 2004.

Buckminster Fuller Institute. "Challenge" webpage includes online video (2015) on the Fuller Challenge, with annually updated "call for proposals." http://bfi.org/challenge (accessed March 19, 2016).

Capra, Fritjof. *The Hidden Connections: Integrating the Biological, Cognitive, and Social Dimensions of Life into a Science of Sustainability.* New York: Doubleday, 2002.

———. *The Tao of Physics: An Exploration of the Parallels between Modern Physics and Eastern Mysticism*, 4th ed. Boston: Shambhala, 2000.

———. *Uncommon Wisdom: Conversations with Remarkable People.* New York: Simon & Schuster, 1988.

Carter, Rita. *Mapping the Mind.* Berkeley: University of California Press, 1998.

Chopra, Deepak. *Peace Is the Way: Bringing War and Violence to an End.* New York: Harmony Books, 2005.

Collins, Owen, ed. *Speeches That Changed the World.* Louisville, KY: Westminister John Knox, 1999.

A Course in Miracles—Text, 2nd ed. Glen Ellen, CA: Foundation for Inner Peace, 1992.

A Course in Miracles—Workbook for Students, 2nd ed. Glen Ellen, CA: Foundation for Inner Peace, 1992.

Court, Jamie. *Corporateering: How Corporate Power Steals Your Personal Freedom and What You Can Do About It.* New York: Tarcher/Putnam, 2003.

Dalai Lama, foreword to *Peace Is Every Step: The Path of Mindfulness in Everyday Life*, by Thich Nhat Hanh. Edited by Arnold Kotler. New York: Bantam, 1992.

Diamond, Lisa M. "Female Bisexuality from Adolescence to Adulthood: Results from a 10-year Longitudinal Study." *Developmental Psychology* 44 (1), 2008, 5–14.

Dobbs, Lou. *Exporting America: Why Corporate Greed Is Shipping American Jobs Overseas.* New York: Warner Business Books, 2004.

Dossey, Larry. *The Extraordinary Healing Power of Ordinary Things: Fourteen Natural Steps to Health and Happiness.* New York: Three Rivers Press, 2006.

Dyer, Wayne W. *Change Your Thoughts—Change Your Life: Living the Wisdom of the Tao.* Carlsbad, CA: Hay House, 2007.

Ehrenfeld, Rachel. *Narco Terrorism: How Governments Around the World Have Used the Drug Trade to Finance and Further Terrorist Activities.* New York: Basic Books, 1990.

Eight Translation New Testament. Wheaton, IL: Tyndale House, 1974.

Friedman, Milton, and Thomas S. Szasz. *Friedman & Szasz on Liberty and Drugs: Essays on the Free Market and Prohibition.* Edited by Arnold S. Trebach and Kevin B. Zeese. Washington, DC: Drug Policy Foundation Press, 1992.

Gazzaniga, Michael S. *Tales From Both Sides of the Brain: A Life in Neuroscience.* New York: Ecco, 2015.

———. *Who's in Charge? Free Will and the Science of the Brain.* New York: Ecco, 2011.

Girshick, Lori B. *Transgender Voices: Beyond Men and Women.* Lebanon, NH: University Press of New England, 2008.

Glick, Stanley, ed. *Cerebral Lateralization in Nonhuman Species.* E-book: Orlando, FL: Academic Press, 1985.

Gray, James P. *Why Our Drug Laws Have Failed and What We Can Do About It: A Judicial Indictment of the War on Drugs.* Philadelphia: Temple University Press, 2001.

Gray, Martin. *Sacred Earth: Places of Peace and Power.* New York: Sterling Publishing, 2007.

Grinspoon, Lester, and James B. Bakalar. *Marihuana: The Forbidden Medicine.* New Haven, CT: Yale University Press, 1993.

Harman, Willis. *Global Mind Change: The Promise of the 21st Century,* 2nd ed. San Francisco: Berrett-Koehler Publishers, 1998.

Haskell, Brent. *Journey Beyond Words: A Companion to the Workbook of the Course.* Marina del Rey, CA: DeVorss & Co., 1994.

———. *The Other Voice: A Companion to the Text of the Course, Chapters 1–15.* Marina del Rey, CA: DeVorss & Company, 1997.

Hellige, Joseph B. *Hemispheric Asymmetry: What's Right and What's Left.* Cambridge, MA: Harvard University Press, 2001.

Herer, Jack. *Hemp & The Marijuana Conspiracy: The Emperor Wears No Clothes.* First fully revised edition. Edited by Chris Conrad, Lynn Osburn, and Judy Osburn. Van Nuys, CA: Hemp Publishing, 1992. (Further updates continued until Herer's death in 2010, when the most recent edition was published under the main title *The Emperor Wears No Clothes.*)

Herrmann, Ned. *The Whole Brain Business Book: Unlocking the Power of Whole Brain Thinking in Organizations and Individuals.* New York: McGraw-Hill, 1996.

Horowitz, Norman H. "Roger Wolcott Sperry," Nobelprize.org. http://www.nobel prize.org/nobel_prizes/medicine/laureates/1981/sperry-articlehtml?print=1#. VR3mNEuaL1o (accessed March 16, 2016).

Howard, Pierce J. *The Owner's Manual for the Brain: Everyday Applications from Mind-Brain Research,* 3rd ed. Austin, TX: Bard Press, 2006.

Huffington, Arianna. *Pigs at the Trough: How Corporate Greed and Political Corruption Are Undermining America.* New York: Crown, 2003.

Jamison, Kay Redfield. *Exuberance: The Passion for Life.* New York: Alfred A. Knopf, 2004.

Johnston, David Cay. *Perfectly Legal: The Covert Campaign to Rig Our Tax System to Benefit the Super Rich—and Cheat Everybody Else.* New York: Portfolio, 2003.

Keirsey, David. *Please Understand Me II: Temperament, Character, Intelligence.* Del Mar, CA: Prometheus Nemesis, 1998.

Kelly, Marjorie. *The Divine Right of Capital: Dethroning the Corporate Aristocracy.* San Francisco: Berrett-Koehler Publishers, 2003.

Kenyon, Tom. *Brain States.* Naples, FL: United States Publishing, 1994.

Kenyon, Tom, and Virginia Essene. *The Hathor Material: Messages from an Ascended Civilization.* Santa Clara, CA: Spiritual Education Endeavors, 1996.

King, Godfré Ray. *The "I AM" Discourses by the Ascended Master Saint Germain.* Schaumburg, IL: Saint Germain Press, 1940.

Krugman, Paul. *The Great Unraveling: Losing Our Way in the New Century.* New York: W. W. Norton, 2003.

Lawlor, Robert. *Sacred Geometry: Philosophy and Practice.* London: Thames & Hudson, 1982.

LeVay, Simon. *Gay, Straight, and the Reason Why.* New York: Oxford University Press, 2011.

Lipton, Bruce H. *The Biology of Belief: Unleashing the Power of Consciousness, Matter & Miracles.* Santa Rosa, CA: Mountain of Love/Elite, 2005.

MacLean, Paul D. *The Triune Brain in Evolution: Role in Paleocerebral Functions.* New York: Plenum Press, 1990.

Maguire, Mairead Corrigan. "Gandhi and the Ancient Wisdom of Nonviolence." In *Peace Is the Way.* Edited by Walter Wink. Maryknoll, NY: Orbis Books, 2000.

Martineau, John. *A Little Book of Coincidence in the Solar System.* New York: Walker Publishing, 2001.

Masters, Sheriff Bill, ed. *The New Prohibition: Voices of Dissent Challenge the Drug War.* St. Louis, MO: Accurate Press, 2004.

McGilchrist, Iain. *The Master and His Emissary: The Divided Brain and the Making of the Western World.* New Haven, CT: Yale University Press, 2010.

McTaggart, Lynne. *The Intention Experiment: Using Your Thoughts to Change Your Life and the World.* New York: Free Press, 2007.

Melchizedek, Drunvalo. *The Ancient Secret of the Flower of Life.* 2 vols. Flagstaff, AZ: Light Technology Publishing, 1998.

———. *Living in the Heart: How to Enter into the Sacred Space within the Heart.* Flagstaff, AZ: Light Technology Publishing, 2003.

———. *2012: The Prophecies from the Heart.* DVD. Santa Monica, CA: Arthouse, 2009.

Metzner, Ralph. *The Unfolding Self: Varieties of Transformative Experience.* Novato, CA: Origin Press, 1998.

Nace, Ted. *Gangs of America: The Rise of Corporate Power and the Disabling of Democracy.* San Francisco: Berrett-Koehler Publishers, 2003.

Newberg, Andrew, and Mark Robert Waldman. *Why We Believe What We Believe: Uncovering Our Biological Need for Meaning, Spirituality, and Truth.* New York: Free Press, 2006.

The New English Bible with the Apocrypha, The New Testament. 2nd ed. New York: Oxford University Press, 1971.

Nithyananda. *You Are God: Discourse on Bhagavad Gita, Chapter 2.* Bangalore: Nithyananda Foundation, 2006.

Ohiyesa. "Native American Tradition: The Ways of the Spirit." In *One: Essential Writings on Nonduality.* Edited by Jerry Katz. Boulder, CO: Sentient Publications, 2007.

Ornstein, Robert. *The Right Mind: Making Sense of the Hemispheres.* New York: Harcourt Brace, 1997.

Ornstein, Robert, and Paul Ehrlich. *New World New Mind: Moving Toward Conscious Evolution.* New York: Doubleday, 1989.

Pert, Candace B. *Molecules of Emotion: Why You Feel the Way You Feel.* New York: Scribner, 2003.

Peterson, Peter G. *Running on Empty: How the Democratic and Republican Parties Are Bankrupting Our Future and What Americans Can Do About It.* New York: Farrar, Straus & Giroux, 2004.

Phillips, Kevin. *Wealth and Democracy: A Political History of the American Rich.* New York: Broadway Books, 2002.

Pink, Daniel H. *A Whole New Mind: Why Right-Brainers Will Rule the Future.* New York: Riverhead Books, 2006.

Ratey, John J. *A User's Guide to the Brain: Perception, Attention, and the Four Theaters of the Brain.* New York: Vintage, 2002.

Renard, Gary R. *The Disappearance of the Universe: Straight Talk About Illusions, Past Lives, Religion, Sex, Politics, and the Miracles of Forgiveness.* Carlsbad, CA: Hay House, 2004.

Ruppert, Michael C. *Crossing the Rubicon: The Decline of the American Empire at the End of the Age of Oil.* Gabriola Island, BC, Canada: New Society, 2004.

Russell, Peter. *Waking Up in Time: Finding Inner Peace in Times of Accelerating Change.* Novato, CA: Origin Press, 1998.

Schiffer, Fredric. *Of Two Minds: The Revolutionary Science of Dual-Brain Psychology.* New York: Free Press, 1998.

Schlitz, Marilyn Mandala; Vieten, Cassandra; and Amorok, Tina. *Living Deeply: The Art & Science of Transformation in Everyday Life.* Oakland, CA: New Harbinger, 2007.

Schneider, Andrew, and David McCumber. *An Air That Kills: How the Asbestos Poisoning of Libby, Montana, Uncovered a National Scandal.* New York: G. P. Putnam's Sons, 2004.

Schweickart, David. *After Capitalism.* Lanham, MD: Rowan & Littlefield, 2002.

Shultz, Jim. *The Democracy Owners' Manual: A Practical Guide to Changing the World*. New Brunswick: Rutgers University Press, 2002.

Siegel, Ronald K. *Intoxication: Life in Pursuit of Artificial Paradise*. New York: Pocket Books, 1990.

Springer, Sally P., and Georg Deutsch. *Left Brain, Right Brain: Perspectives from Cognitive Neuroscience*, 5th ed. New York: W. H. Freeman/Worth, 1998.

Sullum, Jacob. *Saying Yes: In Defense of Drug Use*. New York: Tarcher/Putnam, 2003.

Taylor, Jill Bolte. "My stroke of insight" (TED talk—video and transcript). TED. http://www.ted.com/talks/jill_bolte_taylor_s_powerful_stroke_of_insight.html (accessed March 16, 2016).

Taylor, Jill Bolte. *My Stroke of Insight: A Brain Scientist's Personal Journey*. New York: Viking Penguin, 2006.

Thich Nhat Hanh. *Living Buddha, Living Christ*. New York: Riverhead Books, 1995.

———. *Peace Is Every Step: The Path of Mindfulness in Everyday Life*. Edited by Arnold Kotler. New York: Bantam, 1992.

Thomson, Lenore. *Personality Type: An Owner's Manual*. Boston: Shambhala, 1998.

Three Initiates. *The Kybalion, by Three Initiates: The Hermetic Philosophy*. Charleston, SC: Forgotten Books, 2008.

Thurman, Robert. "Living Deeply: The Fate of the Earth." Foreword to *Living Deeply: The Art & Science of Transformation in Everyday Life*, by Marilyn Mandala Schlitz, Cassandra Vieten, and Tina Amorok. Oakland, CA: New Harbinger, 2007.

Tolle, Eckhart. *A New Earth: Awakening to Your Life's Purpose*. New York: Plume, 2006.

———. *The Power of Now: A Guide to Spiritual Enlightenment*. Novato, CA: New World Library, 1999.

The Urantia Book. Chicago: Urantia Foundation, 1955.

Vos Savant, Marilyn. *The Power of Logical Thinking: Easy Lessons in the Art of Reasoning . . . and Hard Facts About Its Absence in Our Lives*. New York: St. Martin's Press, 1996.

Walsch, Neale Donald. *The New Revelations: A Conversation with God*. New York: Atria Books, 2002.

———. *Tomorrow's God: Our Greatest Spiritual Challenge*. New York: Atria Books, 2004.

Wilber, Ken. *The Collected Works of Ken Wilber*. Vol. 7, *A Brief History of Everything*. Boston: Shambhala, 2000.

Wink, Walter, ed. *Peace Is the Way: Writings on Nonviolence from the Fellowship of Reconciliation.* Maryknoll, NY: Orbis Books, 2000.

Yogananda, Paramahansa. *Inner Peace: How to Be Calmly Active and Actively Calm.* San Rafael, CA: Self-Realization Fellowship, 1999.

———. *The Second Coming of Christ: The Resurrection of the Christ Within You.* 2 vols. Los Angeles: Self-Realization Fellowship, 2004.

Zimmer, Lynn, and John P. Morgan. *Marijuana Myths, Marijuana Facts: A Review of the Scientific Evidence.* New York: Lindesmith Center, 1997.

Notes

Introduction

1. Iain McGilchrist, *The Master and His Emissary: The Divided Brain and the Making of the Western World* (New Haven, CT, & London: Yale University Press, 2010), 5.

2. Stanley Glick, ed., *Cerebral Lateralization in Nonhuman Species* (e-book: Orlando: Academic Press, 1985), 2–6.

3. Joseph B. Hellige, *Hemispheric Asymmetry: What's Right and What's Left* (Cambridge & London: Harvard University Press, 2001), 65.

Chapter 1

1. Einstein is quoted in an interview by G. S. Viereck, October 26, 1929. Reprinted in *Glimpses of the Great* (New York: The Macaulay Company, 1930).

2. Norman H. Horowitz, "Roger Wolcott Sperry" biography, Nobelprize.org, http://www.nobelprize.org/nobel_prizes/medicine/laureates/1981/sperry-article.html?print=1#.VR3mNEuaL1o (accessed February 15, 2016).

3. See Michael S. Gazzaniga, *Tales From Both Sides of the Brain: A Life in Neuroscience* (New York: HarperCollins, 2015), 16, 42.

4. See, for example, William James, *The Varieties of Religious Experience* (1902), a classic that is still in print.

5. McGilchrist, *The Master and His Emissary*, 142.

6. See, for example, McGilchrist, 81.

7. McGilchrist, 9. In this quotation he references works by Sherrington (1906) and Kinsbourne (1988).

Chapter 2

1. See Jill Bolte Taylor, *My Stroke of Insight: A Brain Scientist's Personal Journey* (New York: Viking Penguin, 2006).

2. Jill Bolte Taylor, "My Stroke of Insight," TED talk, February 2008. Video and transcript. http://www.ted.com/talks/jill_bolte_taylor_s_powerful_stroke_of_insight (accessed March 14, 2016).

3. See Robert Ornstein, *The Right Mind: Making Sense of the Hemispheres* (New York: Harcourt Brace, 1997), 157.

4. See McGilchrist, *The Master and His Emissary*, 40. Also see M.I. Posner and M. Raichle, *Images of Mind* (New York: Scientific American Library, 1994).

5. See, for example, K. K. Voeller, "Right-hemisphere deficit syndrome in children," *American Journal of Psychiatry*, 1986, 143(8), 1004–09; A.R. Luria, *The Working Brain* (London: Allen Lane, 1973); and D. van Lancker, "Personal relevance and the human right hemisphere," *Brain and Cognition*, 1991, 17(1), 64–92.

6. See F. Lhermitte, F. Chedru, and F. Chain, "À propos d'un cas d'agnosie visuelle," *Revue Neurologique*, 1973, 128(5), 301–22.

7. See McGilchrist, 55, for a discussion of the various studies referred to in this paragraph.

8. Ibid., 58–59. Cites Voeller, 86, et al.

9. If your perspective is conservative, you might think this is backwards. After all, liberals are famous for imposing controls over corporate activities, and these activities are often the center of conservative attention. However, it is the liberals' conservative hemisphere that is, in effect, encouraging them to impose control. Concerning a broad range of personal freedoms, liberals are clearly less controlling than conservatives, and more pro-freedom, something that is evident in the laws they champion. The control-oriented nature of the dualistic OS is evident in the body of suppressive laws advocated by conservatives—laws governing such areas as drugs, voting rights, immigration, protection against racial discrimination, and women's and gay rights, to name a few. Notice that all of these laws are a response to fear—they are the product of an operating system that is energized by fear. Conservatives, like liberals, want freedom, but it is their holistic right brain that wants it. Their dualistic hemisphere wants to control anything that might pose a threat.

10. McGilchrist, 171.

11. Ibid., 40.

Chapter 3
1. McGilchrist, *The Master and His Emissary*, 234.

2. See Ornstein, *The Right Mind*, 157.

3. See McGilchrist, 40.

4. See, for example, Lhermitte's aforementioned 1973 study.

5. McGilchrist, 209.

6. McGilchrist, 61; B. Kolb, B. and B. Milner, "Performance of complex arm and facial movements after focal brain lesions," *Neuropsychologia*, 1981, 19(4), 491–503; T. Indersmitten and R. C. Gur, "Emotion processing in chimeric faces: hemispheric asymmetries in expression and recognition of emotions," *Journal of Neuroscience*, 2003, 23(9), 3820–25.

7. See my comments about freedom and control in note 9 of chapter 2.

8. Kay Redfield Jamison, *Exuberance: The Passion for Life* (New York: Alfred A. Knopf, 2004), 256–62.

9. McGilchrist, 137.

10. McGilchrist, 40 and 352–53.

Chapter 4

1. Simon LeVay, *Gay, Straight, and the Reason Why: The Science of Sexual Orientation* (New York: Oxford University Press, 2011), 271.

2. Ibid., 277.

Chapter 5

1. See Harvard University, "Gay Men Prefer Masculine-Faced Men, Study Suggests," *Science Daily*, October 30, 2009. http://www.sciencedaily.com/releases/2009/10/091030125044.htm. (Accessed June 13, 2012.)

2. Lori B. Girshick, *Transgender Voices: Beyond Women and Men* (Lebanon, NH: University Press of New England, 2008), 206.

3. Ibid.

4. Anouk Vleugels, "Research: Bisexuality Is Natural for Women," *United Academics*, October 21, 2011, http://www.united-academics.org/magazine/2272/bisexuality-is-natural-for-women/ (accessed March 9, 2016). Quotes a Boise State University study of principally heterosexual women that found 60 percent of study's respondents admitted being attracted to other women; article states that some previous research had shown 20 percent of women being attracted to other women. See also Elizabeth M. Morgan and Elizabeth Morgan Thompson (2011), "Processes of Sexual Orientation Questioning among Heterosexual Women," *Journal of Sex Research*, 48 (1), 16–28.

5. The findings of this study, involving 79 women with starting ages of 18–25, monitored over 10 years, were summarized in a *NovaNewsNet* article, "Bisexuality in Women Is Real—Study" by Aaron Burnett, January 29, 2008, http://older. kingsjournalism.com/nnn/nova_news_3588_13818.html (accessed March 9, 2016). For the full study, see Lisa M. Diamond (2008), "Female Bisexuality from Adolescence to Adulthood: Results from a 10-year Longitudinal Study," *Developmental Psychology*, 44 (1), 5–14, psycnet.apa.org/journals/dev/44/1/5/ (accessed March 9, 2016).

6. Vleugels, "Research: Bisexuality Is Natural for Women," *United Academics*, http://www.united-academics.org/magazine/2272/bisexuality-is-natural-for-women/ (accessed March 9, 2016).

7. Pierce J. Howard, *The Owner's Manual for the Brain: Everyday Applications from Mind-Brain Research*, 3rd edition (Austin, TX: Bard Press, 2006), 275.

8. Andy Goghlan, "Gay Brains Structured Like Those of the Opposite Sex," *NewScientist*, June 16, 2008, http://www.newscientist.com/article/dn14146-gay-brains-structured-like-those-of-the-opposite-sex.html (accessed March 9, 2016). Summarizes and quotes from study conducted by Ivanka Savic at the Karolinska Institute in Stockholm, Sweden, published in *Proceedings of the National Academy of Sciences* (DOI: 10.1973/pnas.0801566105).

9. Ibid.

10. Quoted from National Geographic News summary of the same Karolinska Institute study, titled "Gay Men, Straight Women Have Similar Brains," June 16, 2008, http://news.nationalgeographic.com/news/2008/06/080616-gay-brain.html (accessed March 9, 2016).

11. McMaster University study, "Genetics Has a Role in Determining Sexual Orientation in Men, Further Evidence," *ScienceDaily*, November 8, 2007, http://www.sciencedaily.com/releases/2007/11/071107170741.htm (accessed March 9, 2016). Italics in last quotation added for emphasis.

12. York University study, "Gay Men's Bilateral Brains Better at Remembering Faces, Study Finds," *ScienceDaily*, June 22, 2010, http://www.sciencedaily.com/releases/2010/06/100622074612.htm (accessed March 9, 2016).

Chapter 6

1. Ken Wilber, *The Collected Works of Ken Wilber*, vol. 7: *A Brief History of Everything* (Boston: Shambhala, 2000), 70.

2. *A Course in Miracles—Text*, 2nd ed. (Glen Ellen, CA: Foundation for Inner Peace, 1992), 155.

3. Bruce H. Lipton, *The Biology of Belief: Unleashing the Power of Consciousness, Matter, and Miracles* (Santa Rosa, CA: Mountain of Love/Elite, 2005), 27.

4. See, for example, *What the Bleep!? Down the Rabbit Hole*, Quantum ed. (5-DVD boxed set): Disk 1, Scene 11. (Beverly Hills, CA: Twentieth Century Fox Home Entertainment, 2006.)

5. Bruce H. Lipton, "The Biology of Perception, the Psychology of Change, Retreat" (lecture and conversation), Breckenridge, CO, August 2007, http://www. spirit2000.com/docs/2007brochure.pdf (accessed March 2, 2016).

6. *A Course in Miracles: Workbook for Students*, 2nd ed. (Glen Ellen, CA: Foundation for Inner Peace, 1992), 257–58.

7. Wilber, 77.

Chapter 7

1. This and much of the following discussion of sacred geometry and spheres can be found in the Drunvalo Melchizedek DVD, *2012: The Prophecies from the Heart* (Santa Monica, CA: Arthouse, 2009).

2. Robert Lawlor, *Sacred Geometry: Philosophy and Practice* (London: Thames & Hudson, 1982), 10.

3. Martin Gray, *Sacred Earth: Places of Peace and Power* (New York: Sterling Publishing, 2007), 8, 9.

4. Drunvalo Melchizedek, *The Ancient Secret of the Flower of Life*, vol. 1 (Flagstaff, AZ: Light Technology Publishing, 2000), 1, 29.

Chapter 8

1. Ned Herrmann, *The Whole Brain Business Book: Unlocking the Power of Whole Brain Thinking in Organizations and Individuals* (New York: McGraw-Hill, 1996), 12–16.

2. Lawrence Schkade, e-mail message to author, May 24, 2007.

3. Rita Carter, *Mapping the Mind* (Berkeley: University of California Press, 1998), 39.

Chapter 9

1. Fritjof Capra, *The Tao of Physics: An Exploration of the Parallels between Modern Physics and Eastern Mysticism*, 3rd ed. (Boston: Shambhala, 1991), 27.

2. Three Initiates, *The Kybalion, by Three Initiates: The Hermetic Philosophy* (Charleston, SC: Forgotten Books, 2008), 75.

3. Lipton, *The Biology of Belief*, 80.

4. Ornstein, *The Right Mind*, 17, 18.

5. Herrmann, *The Whole Brain Business Book*, 16–17.

6. Gregg Braden, *Beyond Zero Point: The Journey to Compassion*, DVD (Arvada, CO: Gaiam/ConsciousWave, 2001).

7. *The Urantia Book* (Chicago: Urantia Foundation, 1955), 1583, 2047.

8. Ibid., 43.

9. Three Initiates, *The Kybalion*, 77.

Chapter 10

1. Andrew Newberg and Mark Robert Waldman, *Why We Believe What We Believe: Uncovering Our Biological Need for Meaning, Spirituality, and Truth* (New York: Free Press, 2006), 94.

2. Ibid., 67.

3. Ohiyesa, "Native American Tradition: The Ways of the Spirit," in *One: Essential Writings on Nonduality*, ed. Jerry Katz (Boulder, CO: Sentient Publications, 2007), 84.

4. Michael S. Gazzaniga, *Tales from Both Sides of the Brain: A Life in Neuroscience* (Ecco, New York, 2015), 151.

5. McGilchrist, *The Master and His Emissary*, 330–31, 353.

6. *Analysis* is listed under the Acquisition Disposition head in chapter 3 to highlight the acquisitional aspect of it, but it is more often associated with the cognitive process, as it is here. Acquisition is a disposition of mind (spirit through mind acquires), so all of the characteristics listed under Acquisition Disposition fit under both cognitive and spiritual categories. Acquisition serves cognition, which serves spirit.

7. Ornstein, *The Right Mind*, 157.

8. Ibid., 152.

9. Ibid., 153–54.

10. Right-brain-dominant males exhibit this pattern of seeking multiple partners as well, but keep in mind that they also have a left brain with its characteristic frequent change of focus. Even when the left brain is subservient to the right, it still can be extraordinarily powerful, especially when combined with male sex hormones. In fact, it is probably accurate to say that the effect of hormones simply overpowers brain perspective in many males.

11. Mark Mazzetti, "Spy Agencies Say Iraq War Worsens Terrorism Threat," *New York Times*, September 24, 2006, http://www.nytimes.com/2006/09/24/world/middleeast/24terror.html (accessed February 29, 2016).

12. Gary R. Renard, *The Disappearance of the Universe: Straight Talk About Illusions, Past Lives, Religion, Sex, Politics, and the Miracles of Forgiveness* (Carlsbad, CA: Hay House, 2004), 113.

13. *A Course in Miracles—Text*, 367.

14. Ibid., 205.

Chapter 11

1. Itzhak Bentov, *Stalking the Wild Pendulum: On the Mechanics of Consciousness* (Rochester, VT: Destiny Books, 1988), 117.

2. Melchizedek, *The Ancient Secret of the Flower of Life*, vol. 2, 375.

3. John Hasnas, "The One Kind of Diversity Colleges Avoid," *Wall Street Journal*, March 31, 2016, http://www.wsj.com/articles/the-one-kind-of-diversity-colleges-avoid-1459464676 (accessed April 21, 2016).

4. Justin Wm. Moyer, "Washington State University class bans 'offensive' terms like male, female, tranny, illegal alien," *Washington Post*, September 2, 2015, https://www.washingtonpost.com/news/morning-mix/wp/2015/09/02/washington-state-university-class-bans-offensive-terms-such-as-illegal-alien-and-tranny/ (accessed April 30, 2016).

5. Carter, *Mapping the Mind*, 71.

Chapter 12

1. Quoted in *Time* magazine, June 8, 2015, 29.

2. Terry M. Clark, "A manifesto—I must be a conservative," Coffee with Clark, *Edmond Life & Leisure*, August 19, 2004.

3. Andrew Rice, "When liberals win conservative awards," *Oklahoma Gazette* (Commentary section), December 8, 2004.

4. Wilber, *The Collected Works of Ken Wilber*, vol. 7, 37.

5. Ibid., 7.

6. Ibid., 38.

7. Peter G. Peterson, *Running on Empty: How the Democratic and Republican Parties Are Bankrupting Our Future and What Americans Can Do About It* (New York: Farrar, Straus & Giroux, 2004), 146.

8. "Democratic Sen. Zell Miller Delivers Keynote at Republican Convention," *ABC News*, September 1, 2004, http://a.abcnews.com/Politics/Vote2004/story?id=123470&page=1 (accessed March 3, 2016).

9. This is obviously a highly idealistic appraisal of a party that often fails to achieve its goals. We all know that many Democrats are self-serving—and this is especially true of the leadership—but as a whole, reflecting their dominant brain perspective, right-brain-dominant Democrats tend to be biased toward the collective, which includes service to others.

Chapter 14

1. William Bonner and Addison Wiggin, *Empire of Debt: The Rise of an Epic Financial Crisis* (Hoboken, NJ: John Wiley & Sons, 2006), 14.

2. Kevin Phillips, *Wealth and Democracy: A Political History of the American Rich* (New York: Broadway Books, 2002), xviii.

3. Robert Ornstein and Paul Ehrlich, *New World New Mind: Moving Toward Conscious Evolution* (New York: Doubleday, 1989), 59, 151.

4. Jamie Court, *Corporateering: How Corporate Power Steals Your Personal Freedom and What You Can Do About It* (New York: Tarcher/Putnam, 2003), 44.

5. Paul Krugman, *The Great Unraveling: Losing Our Way in the New Century* (New York: W. W. Norton, 2003), 122.

6. Phillips, *Wealth and Democracy*, 418.

7. "With One Word, Bernanke Reveals Who Actually Runs the Country," Washington's Blog, March 4, 2009, http://georgewashington2.blogspot.com/2009/03/with-one-word-bernanke-reveals-who.html (accessed March 4, 2016).

8. David Sirota, "Big Money vs. Grassroots: The Fight for the Heart of the Democratic Party," *Washington Spectator*, September 1, 2006, 1–3.

9. David Cay Johnston, *Perfectly Legal: The Covert Campaign to Rig Our Tax System to Benefit the Super Rich—and Cheat Everybody Else* (New York: Portfolio, 2003), 10.

10. Ibid., 2.

11. Phillips, *Wealth and Democracy*, 326.

12. Ibid., 413–14.

13. Patrick J. Buchanan, *Where the Right Went Wrong: How Neoconservatives Subverted the Reagan Revolution and Hijacked the Bush Presidency* (New York: Thomas Dunne, 2004), 210.

14. *NOW with Bill Moyers*, "Big Media," January, 30, 2004—Media Regulation Timeline chart, http://www.pbs.org/now/politics/mediatimeline.html (accessed November 19, 2015).

15. Court, *Corporateering*, 200.

16. Ibid., 199.

17. NOW *with Bill Moyers*, transcript of December 17, 2004, broadcast, http://www.pbs.org/now/transcript/transcript351_full.html (accessed November 19, 2015).

18. Ibid.

19. Ibid.

20. NOW *with Bill Moyers*, transcript of January 30, 2004 broadcast, http://www.pbs.org/now/printable/transcript305_full_print.html (accessed November 19, 2015).

21. Buchanan, *Where the Right Went Wrong*, 7–8.

22. Ibid., 211–13.

23. Ted Nace, *Gangs of America: The Rise of Corporate Power and the Disabling of Democracy* (San Francisco: Berrett-Koehler Publishers, 2003), 1.

24. See Don Edward Beck and Christopher C. Cowan, *Spiral Dynamics: Mastering Values, Leadership, and Change* (Malden, MA: Blackwell Publishers, 1996).

25. Lou Dobbs, *Exporting America: Why Corporate Greed Is Shipping American Jobs Overseas* (New York: Warner Business Books, 2004), 1.

26. Marjorie Kelly, *The Divine Right of Capital: Dethroning the Corporate Aristocracy* (San Francisco: Berrett-Koehler Publishers, 2003), 5.

27. Ibid., 3.

28. Ibid., 8–9.

29. Court, *Corporateering*, 4.

30. NOW *with Bill Moyers*, transcript of February 18, 2005, broadcast, http://www.pbs.org/now/transcript/transcriptNOW107_full.html (accessed November 19, 2015).

31. John C. Bogle, "What We Must Do to Restore Owners Capitalism," Bogle Financial Markets Research Center, October 1, 2003, http://johncbogle.com/speeches/JCB_WIB1003.pdf (accessed November 19, 2015).

32. Kelly, *The Divine Right of Capital*, xiii–xiv.

33. Nace, *Gangs of America*, 222.

34. Ibid., 241–42.

35. Ibid., 206.

36. After a letter-writing campaign, Texaco made a "good will" payment that partially covered the loss of income. BNSF initially offered $500 but following Internet publicity, paid $2,000 in damages after I signed an agreement in which BNSF denied any responsibility.

37. Court, *Corporateering*, 41–42.

38. Thom Hartmann, "Now Corporations Claim the 'Right to Lie,'" January 1, 2003, http://www.thomhartmann.com/2003/01/01/now-corporations-claim-the-right-to-lie/ (accessed November 19, 2015).

39. Andrew Schneider and David McCumber, *An Air That Kills: How the Asbestos Poisoning of Libby, Montana, Uncovered a National Scandal* (New York: G. P. Putnam's Sons, 2004), 23, 92–93, 166–67, 180, 383, 166, 195. May 8, 2009 update: A federal jury acquitted the company, along with three former executives, of all charges. Defense lawyers argued that "the asbestos danger in Libby was no secret to the federal government." Update from http://www.bloomberg.com/apps/news?pid=20601087&sid=a2KONaswwu1Y&refer=home (accessed November 19, 2015).

40. "Bechtel vs. Bolivia," the Democracy Center, http://www.thebellforum.com/showthread.php?t=12944 (accessed November 19, 2015).

41. "Spain, the Lawless Sea," *Frontline*, http://www.pbs.org/frontlineworld/stories/spain/thestory.html (accessed November 19, 2015).

42. "Thousands of Prestige oil spill volunteers suffer health problems," *Olive Press*, June 21, 2007, http://theolivepress.es/2007/06/21/thousands-of-prestige-oil-spill-volunteers-suffer-health-problems/ (accessed November 19, 2015).

43. "Prestige Oil Spill," Wikipedia article, https://en.wikipedia.org/wiki/Prestige_oil_spill (accessed November 19, 2015).

44. Peter Russell, *Waking Up in Time: Finding Inner Peace in Times of Accelerating Change* (Novato, CA: Origin Press, 1998), 65.

45. Buchanan, *Where the Right Went Wrong*, 15.

46. *NOW with Bill Moyers*, transcript of December 5, 2003, broadcast, http:/www.pbs.org/now/transcript/transcript245_full.html (accessed November 19, 2015).

47. Rumsfeld "adversary" speech, Sept 10, 2001, http://www.c-span.org/video/?c4497613/rumsfeld-dept-def (accessed November 19, 2015).

48. Scot J. Paltrow, Reuters, Special Report: The Pentagon's doctored ledgers conceal epic waste, filed November 18, 2013, http://www.reuters.com/article/2013/11/18/us-usa-pentagon-waste-specialreport-idUSBRE9AH0LQ20131118 (accessed November 19, 2015).

49. Franklin C. Spinney, "The Defense Reform Trap," *CounterPunch*, June 27, 2008, http://www.counterpunch.org/2008/06/27/the-defense-reform-trap/ (accessed November 19, 2015).

50. Buckminster Fuller Institute, *The Buckminster Fuller Challenge* (film), https://vimeo.com/1163719 (accessed November 19, 2015).

Chapter 15

1. Walsch, *The New Revelations*, 166.

2. Ralph Metzner, *The Unfolding Self: Varieties of Transformative Experience* (Novato, CA: Origin Press, 1998), 130–31.

3. *A Course in Miracles—Text*, 155.

4. Ibid., 138.

5. Ed Godfrey, "Drug Sentencing Questioned," *Daily Oklahoman*, December 7, 1992, http://www.newsok.com.

6. Paul Armentano (NORML Deputy Director), "Alternet: 'The Five Worst States to Get Busted With Pot,'" May 16, 2011, http://blog.norml.org/2011/05/16/alternet-the-five-worst-states-to-get-busted-with-pot/ (accessed February 17, 2016).

7. Ronald K. Siegel, *Intoxication: Life in Pursuit of Artificial Paradise* (New York: Pocket Books, 1990), viii.

8. Russell, *Waking Up in Time*, 70.

9. Ibid.

10. Lester Grinspoon and James B. Bakalar, *Marihuana: The Forbidden Medicine* (New Haven, CT: Yale University Press, 1993), ix–x, 3.

11. Jack Herer, *Hemp and the Marijuana Conspiracy: The Emperor Wears No Clothes*, ed. Chris Conrad, Lynn Osburn, and Judy Osburn (Van Nuys, CA: Hemp Publishing, 1992), 33.

12. "Deglamorising Cannabis," editorial, *Lancet* 346, no. 8985 (November 11, 1995).

13. "How Experts Rate Problem Substances," *New York Times*, August 2, 1994.

14. Bill Bonner, "A Looney Tunes United States," *Daily Reckoning*, July 24, 2008, http://news.goldseek.com/DailyReckoning/1216926000.php. A letter based on a story sent to author by the woman in the story, July 24, 2008. (Accessed March 2, 2016.)

15. Lynn Zimmer and John P. Morgan, *Marijuana Myths, Marijuana Facts: A Review of the Scientific Evidence* (New York: Lindesmith Center, 1997), 33.

16. Ibid., 37. For more on this subject, see Douglas A. McVay, ed., *Drug War Facts*, online edition, http://www.drugwarfacts.org/gatewayt.htm (accessed March 2, 2016).

17. *A Course in Miracles—Text*, 440.

18. Anna Kuchment, "Make That a Double," *Newsweek*, July 30, 2007, 48.

19. Merideth A. Addicott, Lucie L. Yang, Ann M. Peiffer, et al. "The Effect of Daily Caffeine Use on Cerebral Blood Flow: How Much Caffeine Can We Tolerate?" *Human Brain Mapping* 30, issue 10 (October 2009), 3102–14, http://www.ncbi.nlm.nih.gov/pmc/articles/PMC2748160/ (accessed March 11, 2016).

20. Jacob Sullum, *Saying Yes: In Defense of Drug Use* (New York: Tarcher/Putnam, 2003), 13.

21. Ibid., 27.

22. Ibid., 15. Sullum cites Jonathan Shedler and Jack Block, "Adolescent Drug Use and Psychological Health," *American Psychologist* 45, no. 5 (May 1990), 612–30.

23. Ibid., 15.

24. Ronald K. Siegel, *Intoxication: Life in Pursuit of Artificial Paradise* (New York: Pocket Books, 1990), ix–x.

25. Radley Balko, "Overkill: The Rise of Paramilitary Police Raids in America," White Paper (Executive Summary), July 17, 2006, Cato Institute, http://www.cato.org/pub_display.php?pub_id=6476 (accessed March 12, 2016).

26. Radley Balko, "Senseless Overkill," FoxNews.com, March 12, 2008, http://www.foxnews.com/story/0,2933,336850,00.html (accessed March 12, 2016).

27. "Law Enforcement: Goose Creek Agrees to Pay Up, Change Ways in Settlement of Notorious High School Drug Raid Case," StoptheDrugWar.org, July 14, 2006, http://stopthedrugwar.org/chronicle/444/goose-creek-drug-raid-settlement.shtml (accessed March 12, 2016).

28. Rhonda Cook, "Documents Reveal: Cops Planted Pot on 92-Year Old Woman They Killed in Botched Drug Raid," *Atlanta Journal-Constitution*, http://www.alternet.org/story/51151/documents_reveal%3A_cops_planted_pot_on_92-year_old_woman_they_killed_in_botched_drug_raid (accessed March 11, 2016).

29. Radley Balko, "Kathryn Johnston: A Year Later," Reason.com, November 23, 2007, http://reason.com/archives/2007/11/23/kathryn-johnston-a-year-later (accessed March 12, 2016).

30. Dave Kopel and Mike Krause, "License to Kill: The (drug) war on civilians in Peru," *National Review Online*, August 16, 2001, http://www.davekopel.org/NRO/2001/License-to-Kill.htm (accessed March 2, 2016).

31. Ibid.

32. Ibid.

33. Fatema Gunja, "The Social Costs of a Moral Agenda," in *The New Prohibition: Voices of Dissent Challenge the Drug War*, ed. Sheriff Bill Masters (St. Louis: Accurate Press, 2004), 103.

34. "Marijuana Arrests for Year 2006—829,625 Tops Record High . . . Nearly 6 Percent Increase Over 2005," NORML, September 24, 2007, http://norml.org/news/2007/09/24/marijuana-arrests-for-year-2006-829625-tops-record-high-nearly-6-percent-increase-over-2005 (accessed March 2, 2016).

35. Russ Belville, NORML Stash, "872,721 marijuana arrests in 2007, up 5.2% from 2006," NORML Blog, September 15, 2008, http://blog.norml.org/2008/09/15/872721-marijuana-arrests-in-2007-up-52-from-2006/ (accessed March 2, 2016).

36. Stephen W. Dillon, "It's Not Your Parents' Prohibition," welcome address to 37th annual NORML conference, October 17–18, 2008, NORML Blog, November 10, 2008, http://blog.norml.org/2008/11/10/opening-remarks-at-norml-2008-norml-board-chair-stephen-dillon-esq/ (accessed March 2, 2016).

37. Walter Cronkite, "Mandated Injustice," *Alva Review-Courier*, August 8, 2004.

38. John L. Kane, "Policy Is Not a Synonym for Justice," in *The New Prohibition: Voices of Dissent Challenge the Drug War*, ed. Sheriff Bill Masters (St. Louis: Accurate Press, 2004), 49.

39. Ibid.

40. Marc Kaufman, "Worried Pain Doctors Decry Prosecutions," *Washington Post*, December 29, 2003, http://pqasb.pqarchiver.com/washingtonpost/doc/409619821.html?FMT=ABS&FMTS=ABS:FT&date=Dec+29%2C+2003&author=Kaufman%2C+Marc&pub=The+Washington+Post&edition=&startpage=A.01&desc=Worried+Pain+Doctors+Decry+Prosecutions (accessed March 2, 2016).

41. Zimmer and Morgan, *Marijuana Myths, Marijuana Facts*, 155. Zimmer and Morgan cite A. DiChira and J. F. Galliher, "Dissonance and Contradictions in the Origins of Marihuana Decriminalization," *Law and Society Review* 28, no. 1 (1994), 52.

42. "Albert Knew . . . ," http://deoxy.org/prohib2.htm (accessed March 2, 2016).

43. Milton Friedman and Thomas S. Szasz, *Friedman & Szasz on Liberty and Drugs: Essays on the Free Market and Prohibition*, ed. Arnold S. Trebach and Kevin B. Zeese (Washington, DC: Drug Policy Foundation Press, 1992), 70.

44. Jesse Ventura, foreword to *The New Prohibition: Voices of Dissent Challenge the Drug War*, ed. Sheriff Bill Masters (St. Louis, MO: Accurate Press, 2004), vii–viii.

45. Radley Balko, "Tracy Ingle: Another Drug War Outrage," Reason.com (Hit & Run blog), May 7, 2008, http://www.reason.com/blog/show/126284.html (accessed March 2, 2016).

46. Associated Press (U.S.), "Jury Convicts After No-Knock Police Search," April 15, 2009, http://www.november.org/thewall/cases/ingle-t/ingle-t.html (accessed March 2, 2016).

47. "Oklahoma Re-Imprisons Paraplegic Jimmy Montgomery on Pot Charge: Family Fears for His Life," NORML Special Bulletin, April 6, 1995; Rob Stewart, "Outrage in Oklahoma: The Jim Montgomery Story," Newsbriefs, *Drug Policy Letter* 26 (Spring 1995), 17. Though this story sometimes reads like fiction, please note that I know this gentleman and can personally verify that this is all true.

48. Peter Gorman, "The Strange and Tragic Case of Jimmy Montgomery", http://petergormanarchive.com/THE_STRANGE_AND_TRAGIC_CASE_OF_JIMMY_MONTGOMERY.html (accessed March 2, 2016); "Jimmy Montgomery Back in Prison," http://www.drcnet.org/rapid/1995/4-14-1.html (accessed March 2, 2016).

49. "Profiles of Injustice," Families Against Mandatory Minimums Foundation, http://famm.org/ProfilesofInjustice/StateProfiles/SheilaDevereuxOklahoma.aspx? (accessed February 13, 2010).

50. Tim Talley, Associated Press, "High female incarceration rate bemoaned by state lawmakers," *Tulsa World*, September 3, 2009, http://www.tulsaworld.com/archives/high-female-incarceration-rate-bemoaned-by-state-lawmakers/article_b9176361-40dd-5377-a307-418a906708b4.html (accessed March 2, 2016).

51. Christopher Hartney, "U.S. Rates of Incarceration: A Global Perspective" (Fact Sheet), National Council on Crime and Delinquency, November 2006, http://www.nccdglobal.org/sites/default/files/publication_pdf/factsheet-us-incarceration.pdf (accessed March 2, 2016).

52. David Crary, Associated Press, "Drug-Free School Zone Laws Questioned," March 23, 2006, http://www.justicestrategies.net/?q=node/85 (accessed March 2, 2016).

53. Roger McKenzie, "Bar proprietor, bartender arrested on drug charges," *Alva Review-Courier*, February 22, 2007.

54. Alain L. Sanders, Anne Constable, and James Willwerth, "Lifting the Lid on Garbage," *Time*, May 30, 1988, http://www.time.com/time/magazine/article/0,9171,967509,00.html (accessed March 2, 2016).

55. Roger McKenzie, "Garbage leads to arrest of two Alva men on drug charges," *Alva Review-Courier*, January 20, 2008.

56. "Suspected Marijuana User Gunned Down in Home," NORML's *Active Resistance* 3, no.1 (Spring 1995), 1.

57. Pete Guither and Hypatia (guest post), "Using the Drug 'War' to Expand Government Power," April 7, 2006, Unclaimed Territory—by Glenn Greenwald (blog), http://glenngreenwald.blogspot.com/2006/04/using-drug-war-to-expand-government.html (accessed March 2, 2016).

58. "Official ATF swag inscribed: 'Always Think Forfeiture,'" June 10, 2008, http://majikthise.typepad.com/majikthise_/2008/06/official-atf-sw.html (accessed March 2, 2016).

59. Clark Duffe, "Good police work that went awry," At Random, *Oklahoma Gazette*, August 30, 1989.

60. Barbara Mikkelson, "Drug Money," February 19, 2007, Snopes.com, http://www.snopes.com/business/money/cocaine.asp (accessed March 2, 2016).

61. Eric E. Sterling, "A Businessperson's Guide to the Drug Problem," in *The New Prohibition: Voices of Dissent Challenge the Drug War*, ed. Sheriff Bill Masters (St. Louis: Accurate Press, 2004), 72.

62. "Terrorism," Drug Policy Alliance, July 19, 2004, http://www.drugpolicy.org/global/terrorism/ (accessed February 9, 2010).

63. Ehrenfeld, *Narco Terrorism*, xxi–xxii.

64. "The Links Between Drug Prohibition and Terrorism," Canadian Foundation for Drug Policy, http://www.cfdp.ca/terror.htm (accessed March 10, 2016).

65. Sheldon Richman, "The Drug War and Terrorism," *Freedom Daily* (Future of Freedom Foundation), January 2002, https://fff.org/explore-freedom/article/the-drug-war-and-terrorism/ (accessed March 10, 2016).

66. Associated Press, "Drug Agents Accused of Torture," *Daily Oklahoman*, October 26, 1992.

67. Wayne Singleterry, "Lawmen Charged in Plot to Kidnap Suspect," *Daily Oklahoman*, May 19, 1989.

68. Don Mecoy, "Love County Sheriff, Police Officer Bound Over for Trial," *Daily Oklahoman*, May 31, 1989.

69. Clark Duffe, "Some Marietta folk going too far," At Random, *Oklahoma Gazette*, June 7, 1989.

70. James P. Gray, *Why Our Drug Laws Have Failed and What We Can Do About It: A Judicial Indictment of the War on Drugs* (Philadelphia: Temple University Press, 2001), 146. Gray cites Peter Slevin and Caryle Murphy, "Results of D.C. Marijuana Vote Kept Secret Pending Court Action," *Washington Post*, November 4, 1998.

71. Gray, *Why Our Drug Laws Have Failed*, 146. Gray cites editorial, "Marijuana Madness," *Des Moines Register*, November 9, 1998, 6A.

72. Zimmer and Morgan, *Marijuana Myths, Marijuana Facts*, 151.

73. Ron Paul, "A View of the Drug War from Capitol Hill," in *The New Prohibition: Voices of Dissent Challenge the Drug War*, ed. Sheriff Bill Masters (St. Louis, MO: Accurate Press, 2004), 53, 52.

74. Ibid., 54.

75. Alfred Ray Lindesmith, "Traffic in Dope: Medical Problem," *The Nation*, April 21, 1956, 339; "Dope: Congress Encourages the Traffic," *The Nation*, March 16, 1957, 228.

76. News Makers, *Daily Oklahoman*, May 19, 1989.

77. "Bennett's Bold Suggestion," editorial, *Daily Oklahoman*, June 19, 1989.

78. Brett Zongker, Associated Press, "Police Clear Name of Md. Mayor after Drug Raid," August 8, 2008, http://www.foxnews.com/story/2008/08/08/police-clear-name-maryland-mayor-after-drug-raid.html (accessed March 10, 2016); "Police Botch Raid on Maryland Mayor's Home," *Marijuana Policy Report* 14, no. 3 (Fall 2008), 10.

79. Paul Armentano, "The Killing of Rachel Hoffman and the Tragedy That Is Pot Prohibition," July 29, 2008, *AlterNet*, http://www.alternet.org/drugreporter/93082/the_killing_of_rachel_hoffman_and_the_tragedy_that_is_pot_prohibition/ (accessed March 10, 2016).

80. Gray, *Why Our Drug Laws Have Failed*, 20. Gray cites Chris Conrad, *Hemp: Lifeline to the Future* (Los Angeles: Creative Xpressions Publications, 1993), 23–27.

81. Ibid., 214.

82. Ibid., 20.

83. Siegel, *Intoxication*, 270.

84. Gray, *Why Our Drug Laws Have Failed*, 23.

85. Herer, *Hemp and the Marijuana Conspiracy*, 22.

86. Walsch, *Conversations with God, Book 2*, 137.

87. Herer, *Hemp and the Marijuana Conspiracy*, 22.

88. Ibid., 26–27.

89. Michael C. Ruppert, *Crossing the Rubicon: The Decline of the American Empire at the End of the Age of Oil* (Gabriola Island, B.C., Canada: New Society, 2004), 58.

90. Ibid., 62–68.

91. Jim Willie CB, "Gold and Currency Report," *Hat Trick Letter*, no. 58, January 15, 2009, http://www.goldenjackass.com (accessed March 10, 2016).

92. "Drug War Murders," August 1993, NORML handout; November 21, 1993, conversation with Shepherd's wife.

93. *Living Bible, Revised Standard Version, Today's English Version, New International Version, Jerusalem Bible*, and *New English Bible*, among others. *Phillips* reports 20-gallon jars. The *King James* translation describes the capacity in firkins.

94. Mark 7:15, *The New English Bible with the Apocrypha, The New Testament*, 2nd ed. (New York: Oxford University Press, 1971), 52.

95. *A Course in Miracles—Text*, 29.

96. Robert Thurman, "Living Deeply: The Fate of the Earth," in Marilyn Mandala Schlitz, Cassandra Vieten, and Tina Amorok, *Living Deeply: The Art & Science of Transformation in Everyday Life* (Oakland, CA: New Harbinger, 2007), viii.

97. Ron Epstein, "Buddhist Ideas for Attaining World Peace," introduction, Lectures for the Global Peace Studies Program, San Francisco State University, November 7 and 8, 1988, http://online.sfsu.edu/~rone/Buddhism/BUDDHIST%20IDEAS%20FOR%20ATTAINING%20WORLD%20PEACE.htm (accessed March 10, 2016).

98. Gray, *Why Our Drug Laws Have Failed*, 214.

99. Ibid., 213.

100. David C. Condiffe, "DPF Supports Sentencing Report—Where Were Others?" *Drug Policy Letter* 28 (Spring 1996), 13.

101. *Osborne v. United States*, 385 U.S. 343 (1066), http://www.supreme.justia.com/us/385/323/case.html.

102. Gray, *Why Our Drug Laws Have Failed*, 5.

Chapter 16

1. Global Peace Index, 2016, http://reliefweb.int/sites/reliefweb.int/files/resources/GPI%202016%20Report_2.pdf (accessed July 26, 2016).

2. Michael Berg, *The Way: Using the Wisdom of Kabbalah for Spiritual Transformation and Fulfillment* (Hoboken, NJ: John Wiley & Sons, 2001), 202.

3. Yogananda, *The Second Coming of Christ*, 55.

4. Paramahansa Yogananda, *Inner Peace: How to Be Calmly Active and Actively Calm* (San Rafael, CA: Self-Realization Fellowship, 1999), 3.

5. Mairead Corrigan Maguire, "Gandhi and the Ancient Wisdom of Non-violence," *Peace Is the Way*, Walter Wink, ed. (Maryknoll, NY: Orbis Books, 2000), 161.

6. Haim Harari, "A View from the Eye of the Storm," http://southerncrossreview.org/35/harari.htm (accessed January 27, 2016).

7. Quoted in "Was Netanyahu's win a victory for security or fear?" *The Week*, March 27, 2015, 15.

8. Samuel Osborn, "Salman Rushdie: Iranian state media renew fatwa on Satanic Verses author with $600,000 bounty," *Independent*, February 21, 2016, http://www.independent.co.uk/news/people/salman-rushdie-iranian-state-media-renew-fatwa-on-satanic-verses-author-with-600000-bounty-a6887141.html (accessed March 17, 2016).

9. Etan Viessing, "Jennifer Lawrence Removed From 'Hunger Games: Mockingjay 2' Poster in Israel," http://www.hollywoodreporter.com/news/jennifer lawrence-removed-hunger-games-842418 (accessed January 27, 2016).

10. Yogananda, *The Second Coming of Christ*, 440.

11. Ibid., 56.

12. Wayne W. Dyer, *Change Your Thoughts—Change Your Life: Living the Wisdom of the Tao* (Carlsbad, CA: Hay House, 2007), 144–46.

13. Russell, *Waking Up in Time*, 91.

14. *The Urantia Book*, 1098.

15. Robert Thurman, "Living Deeply: The Fate of the Earth," foreword, in Schlitz et al., *Living Deeply*, viii.

16. Ron Epstein, "Buddhist Ideas for Attaining World Peace," Lectures for the Global Peace Studies Program, San Francisco State University (1988), http://online.sfsu.edu/~rone/Buddhism/BUDDHIST%20IDEAS%20FOR%20ATTAINING%20WORLD%20PEACE.htm (accessed January 27, 2016).

17. Ibid.

18. Tom Kenyon and Virginia Essene, *The Hathor Material: Messages from an Ascended Civilization* (Santa Clara, CA: Spiritual Education Endeavors, 1996), 1–2.

19. Ibid., 90.

20. Thich Nhat Hanh, *Peace Is Every Step: The Path of Mindfulness in Everyday Life*, ed. Arnold Kotler (New York: Bantam, 1992), 13–14.

21. Jill Bolte Taylor, "My stroke of insight," TED talk, http://www.ted.com/talks/jill_bolte_taylor_s_powerful_stroke_of_insight.html (accessed January 27, 2016).

Index

Numerals in 'bold' denotes images.

About the Author

James Olson is an independent philosopher who has engaged in a lifetime of study of psychology, art, religion, politics, philosophy, and neuroscience. He has attended Oklahoma State University, the University of Vienna, Oklahoma University, the University of Missouri, and the Kansas City Art Institute. Following the unifying guidelines of integral philosophy, and drawing on his broad education, Olson has made it his mission to help bring the planet's masculine (dualistic left-brain) and feminine (holistic right-brain) energies into greater harmony through his advocacy of whole-brain thinking and his pioneering analysis of the social impact of our civilization's left-brain bias.

Olson's previous book, **The Whole Brain Path to Peace** (Origin Press, 2011) won eight national awards including *Foreword Review* Book of the Year in Philosophy; the Nautilus Award (Silver in Social Change), Independent Publisher Award (Bronze in Psychology), and the International Book Award (winner in Philosophy and Self-Help).